The Insistent Self

Bahá'í
Publications
Australia

The Insistent Self

How to Nurture our Spirit

Lesley Shams

The Insistent Self
How to Nurture our Spirit

Copyright © 2015 by the National Spiritual Assembly of the Bahá'ís of Australia Incorporated

All Rights Reserved

Published by Bahá'í Publications Australia

ISBN: 978-1-925320-01-5

Distributed by:
Bahá'í Distribution Services
P.O. Box 300
Bundoora Vic 3083
Australia

Email: bds@bahai.org.au
www.bahaibooks.com

Cover design and book layout: Massoud Tahzib

Table of Contents

	Page
Introduction	1
Chapter 1: The Insistent Self	23
Chapter 2: Turning to God	65
Chapter 3: Meditation	103
Chapter 4: Observing the Fast	133
Chapter 5: Detachment, Self-Surrender and Selflessness	157
Chapter 6: Trials for our Perfection	193
Chapter 7: Ignite a Candle of Love	221
Chapter 8: Becoming a Channel	267

Introduction

In this introduction I want to explain a little about myself and my journey which led me to write this book. I also want to give you some information about the Bahá'í Faith since the Writings in the book are mainly from this source.

Quite early in life, I was fascinated with exploration of the self. I remember in high school getting a few other students to draw a house, a tree and a person (having read about this "test") and analyzing the drawings to determine their unique personality characteristics and their sense of self. I suppose it was not a surprise to them that I decided to study psychology at university. I finished a B.A. in psychology and worked at a Child Guidance Clinic for 5 years, before deciding to pursue a teaching career.

As a teacher, I really wanted students to know that they were special, that they could become the best they could be. I had high expectations for them and they strived to meet them and felt proud of their accomplishments. I also incorporated work on building character and virtues. I collected a booklet of activities to build self-esteem and continued to use such activities throughout my teaching career. Over the years I taught students with learning difficulties, autism, mental handicaps, giftedness and emotional and behavioral issues. I always felt that those students – those on the margins of society – needed more encouragement and love to see their own worth since they were always in a position to compare themselves with others and feel that they came up short.

This mattered a great deal to me because I myself experienced a difficult childhood and I began my healing journey later in life. I discovered the 12-step programs and attended ACOA (Adult Children of Alcoholics) meetings regularly and read their literature. I attended counseling sessions focusing on the inner child. I read John Bradshaw's books on "The Family" and "Healing the Shame Within" (family of origin work). I read some of Melody Beattie's work on co-dependency and recognized some of the patterns within me. I belonged to a Bahá'ís in Recovery program. I have explored Chi Gong and other meditation styles and listened to relaxation tapes and I say prayers and seek Bahá'u'lláh's guidance on a daily basis.

Growing up, I felt that I was defective and that there was something wrong with me compared to everyone else. Everyone else was okay. I could see that people had faults and shortcomings but I felt that they were okay; they could work on some issues if they chose to but generally they were fine. I was different. Of course, that is not true and I don't believe it now. Many others who grow up in "dysfunctional" homes feel the same way. In our home (as in many others) we didn't talk about problems or talk and express feelings openly, but we were expected to be strong, good, perfect, happy and look good to those around us. It was important not to be selfish so I felt guilty having needs and wants. And I couldn't trust anybody. I was the invisible, shy, quiet child. Every child in a dysfunctional family takes on a role; mine was only one of the possibilities. I didn't demand anything. I was a people- pleaser. I didn't really know who I was and I learned to depend on others and look to them for guidance as to what I should think, feel and do. So much for a sense of self!

So how does this all relate to the book? First of all, it seemed important to share a little of my journey with my audience, that I owed you this openness and honesty and that it provided important background to my reflections in the book. I have to admit that I am quite reluctant to share my story because any troubles I can recount are nothing in the face of the tragedies faced by so many people in the world and some face incredible hardships every day of their lives. But I think it is important to understand other kinds of suffering so that we can have compassion and serve each other more lovingly.

How did I get from my journey to this book? I remember reading a message from the Universal House of Justice (the supreme body that guides the Bahá'ís of the world) and coming across the phrase "the insistent self". It really stood out for me. I had probably read it before but I wasn't "ready" for it. I found the source in 'Abdu'l-Bahá's Writings and its definition – "the evil promptings of the human heart" and I became curious to learn more and to work with it. The spark was lit! Then I did some training offered by the Bahá'í community for working with junior youth. I was struck by one of the sections of the book indicating the need to encourage and build confidence in junior youth because our materialistic society can crush them and make it difficult for them to cope in life. But building this self-confidence can have the effect of bolstering their egos. So we have to figure out how to support them without waking the insistent self. And I realized from this study that we all have to struggle and strive to become spiritual beings, to overcome our lower natures and that it is possible that we may not realize to what extent we need to strive to allow spiritual teachings to infuse our lives so that we are not as negatively influenced by a materialistic culture which emphasizes the insistent self. It occurred to me that those of us following a spiritual path may feel we are protected from the test of our egos because we have God in our lives and pray and follow His guidance, or at least we can become complacent and feel we have a handle on it, when in fact we need to be ever-vigilant. I've learned perhaps through turning to God more openly and being fully immersed in His Words while studying to write this book that there are powerful tools to help us within the Bahá'í Writings. We are all little children trying to cope as adults while being blocked by our pasts. But we need to give everything up to God. We've been chosen by God with all our defects. It is our spiritual journey, our journey to Him that will make of us the spiritual beings that can change the world. And knowing that we have animal natures, that they are always with us and will always present themselves has made me more relaxed with myself, not constantly striving to be perfect. I can be aware of it taking over and I can laugh about it, let it pass and attempt to take the higher road. My hope is that you, too, will be able to use the tools in this book to assist you on your spiritual journey.

All the material in the book is taken from the Bahá'í Writings and Bahá'í authors with the exception of a few supplementary resources. Since readers may not be familiar with the Teachings of the Bahá'í Faith, I am including some information here. For more information, please refer to other books on the Bahá'í Faith and internet resources. I would recommend these sites: www.bahai.org or http://ca.bahai.org. You can also contact your local Bahá'í community for information and for an opportunity to participate in study and service activities, devotional gatherings, classes for children and junior youth groups.

The Bahá'í Faith is the newest of the world religions. Bahá'ís are those who follow the teachings of Bahá'u'lláh, Whom they believe to be a Manifestation, a Messenger, a Prophet, a Teacher from God. Bahá'u'lláh taught us that the God we all worship is the same God, though we may use different names – Allah, Jehovah, the Creator, our Higher Power. We cannot know God because He is far above our ability to understand His Essence. The only way that we can attempt to perceive a glimmering of His Greatness and to feel His Love for us is through His Messengers. Bahá'ís also believe that over the course of 1000's of years, from time to time and in different parts of the world, a small number of these Enlightened Ones have appeared. Their mission has been to guide humanity spiritually and in its social affairs. Bahá'ís believe that Bahá'u'lláh was the most recent of these teachers. The Bahá'í Faith does not attempt to undermine any religion. Instead, it recognizes the missions of the great religions of the world as stages in the evolution of the spiritual life of humankind. When each one is carefully examined and stripped of the rituals that its followers have implemented, it becomes clear that they have brought the same spiritual teachings of love and goodwill to all humanity, changing hearts and bringing new life to the world. Therefore all the faiths in the world become one integrated religion, each succeeding the last like links in a chain. The only differences between them are the social teachings, teachings that differ because God's Messengers come into the world at different times and their teachings serve the needs of the age in which they live. Each one is like a Divine Physician prescribing medicine that is needed for people at that period in time. Krishna, Buddha, Zoroaster, Abraham, Moses, Jesus and Muhammad are Manifestations through whom God has revealed successively the purpose of religion. These Men changed the course of history. Each at different times re-shaped the life of our planet. Abraham spoke of One God and His heirs became a great nation. Krishna's Teachings civilized India and countries close by. Moses rescued His people from bondage and founded a great civilization. Buddha changed the Asian peoples. Zoroaster tamed an ignorant people. Jesus altered the course of the Western world. Muhammad changed a savage people who worshipped idols, uplifting and unifying them in the knowledge of the one true God to become the Arabian nation. Each of these great Men praised the Messenger Who came before Him and taught that another would come in the future. There have been Messengers from the beginning of man's creation and there will always be because we need them. We are God's creatures and He wants us to reach our potential and to live as spiritual beings.

This is the Covenant between God and man, that He will never leave His servants alone, but will return to guide them to live their lives as noble creatures. He sends a Special Soul to renew the Teachings when mankind has drifted away from Them. It is a promise by God that can only be fulfilled by man under certain conditions. Man must love God and demonstrate pure, selfless dedication and obedience to Him. The Covenant with Abraham gave the glad tidings that through His offspring all the nations of the earth would be blessed. The Covenant with Moses included the Ten Commandments. The Covenant with Christ was delineated in the Sermon on the Mount and people became united into a brotherhood. Every Manifestation makes a Covenant with His followers that they should obey the next Manifestation, the One Who is to come after Him. Man must wait for the next Manifestation.

The historical account of all world religions is the same: one of the inhabitants of a backward and wayward people claims that he possesses a superior knowledge, a knowledge from God; He espouses the necessity for reforms and brings new laws; He encourages them to leave their ways behind and to accept and live the spiritual truths that he voices; by following His ways they will be blessed and achieve true happiness but if they ignore Him they will be discontented and miserable. All the Messengers are distinguished by their devotion, nobility, self-sacrifice and the extent of their influence to shape the history of millions of people. If we read about Their lives, we cannot help but admire and love Them. And as we read, we will discover a pattern. We will see that all of Them gave everything for Their beliefs, for the Teachings they espoused. And each Messenger has brought two gifts to humankind: His example and His Teachings. He is a human being but He is also different because He lives and loves through God's Will. God is the Sun and He is a Ray of the Sun. That is why Jesus, a humble carpenter, could influence the Western world, and Moses, a stutterer, gave laws that human beings follow even to this day all around the world and Muhammad, a merchant and camel driver, changed nations through His Teachings. These Educators came to teach us the purpose of our lives and how we should live our lives.

How do we distinguish these Messengers from other great men who also taught us, good men, courageous men, men who changed the direction of people's lives, philosophers who contributed so much to our understanding of ourselves and the universe? In a Messenger of God we see total consistency. They are men of deeds, not words. Each demonstrated assurance and confidence in pursuing a Path, albeit a dangerous Path laid out by God, and no contradictions can be seen in Their actions. They knew exactly what They were destined to bring to mankind and nothing diverted Them from Their purpose. They demonstrated a quality of goodness stemming from Their love of God, a genuine compassion and endless love for all with no self-interest.

And so religion has been renewed once more at a time when people have become disillusioned with the world and the possibility that religion can provide salvation. At the same time, others demonstrate a religious fanaticism that is a distortion of the Teachings of God, preaching a doctrine that leaves chaos and destruction in its wake. It is a difficult time to be alive. We are so far removed from the morality and timeless values of our forefathers, of the ability to forget ourselves and to serve those who cross our path, sacrificing our own needs and desires for the common good. This book brings us back to those spiritual values that we all admire when we hear stories of heroism, sacrifice, goodwill and generosity. God has not left us alone to figure out our lives in the 21st century, in a world where greed and corruption are allowed to run rampant, where the concepts of truthfulness and honesty are tainted in our everyday dealings with one another, where self-preservation is the primary motive in the workplace and where our materialistic culture threatens to destroy any vestiges of humanity. We search for happiness but cannot attain it because we need to transcend this material existence and attain the life of the spirit. And we can only attain our spiritual destiny and enjoy a fulfilled life through the Teachings of God.

The chief principle and pivotal point of Bahá'u'lláh's Teachings is the unity of the human race. Through science and technology, we can travel to any corner of the globe in a day and communicate with each other instantly. Nations depend on each other's cooperation and the need for understanding and assistance among all nations has generally become accepted. It is therefore possible for mankind to conceive of the idea of uniting the planet. The purpose of the Bahá'í Faith is to erase every trace of enmity and hatred from men's hearts and unite the entire world as one family. The Bahá'í Writings provide the outline of institutions necessary for the establishment of a peaceful, orderly society. These include a world federation or commonwealth, an international auxiliary language, a world economy, a mechanism for world intercommunication and a universal system of currency, weights and measures. And Bahá'u'lláh has given us important Teachings for our time. One of these is the independent investigation of truth. We must search out the truth for ourselves and not follow blindly the ways of others or customs of the past. Science and religion must go hand in hand. Religion that does not agree with science is superstition and can lead to fanaticism. Religion depends on reason, not blind faith. Universal education, another Bahá'í Teaching, assists us to find the truth and to use our power of reasoning. It also provides the framework for all to have equal opportunities to advance so that men and women can advance equally and women throughout the world take their rightful place beside men in working for the peace and prosperity of humankind. Bahá'u'lláh advocates the elimination of the extremes of wealth and poverty and the abandonment of all forms of prejudice. The Bahá'í Writings provide guidance that helps an individual develop the spiritual and intellectual qualities lying at the core of his nature and therefore contribute to an ever-advancing civilization. In addition to prayer to assist us to become spiritual beings, work done in the spirit of service is also considered worship for Bahá'ís and service to humanity is the most worthy endeavor. When difficulties arise in life, as they will, Bahá'ís are asked to accept these trials, putting their whole trust in God and recognizing that God is helping them to become stronger and conquer their attachment to self.

Although the Bahá'í Faith is only about 150 years old, in that short time it has spread to every corner of the planet. There are now Bahá'ís from every cultural and religious background in the world, all working towards the goals of a united humanity and world peace. But all conflicts and travail in the world today will become ameliorated only as man, becoming spiritual in his nature and desires, is motivated to act in more just, unselfish and loving ways. It is important for man to know himself - a wisdom which dates back to classic Greece. What is man's nature? Bahá'u'lláh taught that he is a spiritual being, far above the kingdom of animals, although he can act worse than the beasts of the field. It is the spiritual nature of man that is explored in this book. I recognize that religion is a highly contentious subject and one which arouses every kind of emotion and passion from abhorrence to self-righteousness. But religion is meant to be a unifying force, one that promotes love and agreement among men, not a source of conflict. God's Teachings are meant to refine man's character so that he lives in honor and happiness. If religion becomes the source of contention, Bahá'u'lláh taught that it is better to do without it. Although this book focuses on ideas that are taken from religious teachings, particularly those espoused by the Bahá'í Faith, it is in essence concerned with the spirit of man and is written for all individuals who recognize the need to nurture their higher, spiritual selves and are seeking for tools to assist them in this process.

Let us examine the lives of the miraculous Individuals who brought the Teachings of God to the world of today. The first Person on the scene was a young man from Shiraz in Iran (then called Persia) who became known as the Báb or the Gate. As a young child the Báb was not like most children. He did not care to play like other children but enjoyed chanting his prayers. He had a pure sweet character, a serenity and tender-heartedness. He was meek, courteous and mild-mannered. He astounded all with his wisdom and remarkable knowledge, his ability to grasp subjects beyond his years and to solve adult problems, while remaining entirely humble and modest. His teacher recognized this innate knowledge and confessed that he had nothing to teach the young boy. When He grew up, He worked as a merchant and His truthfulness and sense of justice earned great respect. At one time a man bought something on His behalf and paid too much. The Báb told him to return the item and get a refund, stating that he would not tolerate cheating nor encourage an individual to be dishonest. On another occasion, the Báb paid more than market value to a person selling an item on His behalf. When questioned, the Báb explained that He Himself could have sold the item at the higher price so this man should not be deprived. While the Báb was working as a merchant, some awakened souls had been teaching their disciples that a Promised One from God was to appear and urged the disciples to go out and search for Him. Eighteen disciples found The Báb by attaining His presence or recognized His Revelation through prayer, visions or dreams. The Báb sent them out to spread the new Teachings of justice, mercy, love and forgiveness.

The Báb arose to proclaim a new world religion at a time when Persia had sunk to the lowest level of moral corruption and depravity. The whole society was encompassed by fear, deceit and bribery. For example, a Minister could not obtain a post unless he offered gifts to the King. The people grovelled in obedience and were hypocritical. Religion had become so fanatical that even religious leaders would consider themselves defiled if they touched a Bible or brushed against a Christian or a dog belonging to a Jew. And it was this clergy that ruled the masses. People were cruel and barbaric. Women were considered to be without a soul and often possessions had more value.

The authorities quickly stifled the voice of the Báb and attempted to restrict His freedom. But despite efforts to end His influence, the number of His followers rapidly increased. His Message, carried by His disciples to the towns and villages, was spreading. Some religious leaders embraced the Teachings. And the Prime Minister and other ecclesiastical leaders became incensed. The Báb was banished to the fortress of Mah-Ku in the mountains of Adhirbayjan, a place cold and forbidding. In spite of His high station and noble character, the Báb was still a human being, perhaps more sensitive, more capable of grief than we are. His dreams of meeting the Shah and important secular and religious leaders to announce His Faith had been squelched. His opportunity to teach His countrymen and to lead them to a new life was halted. He must have known what His path would be, that of persecution and finally death, just like Jesus before Him. Hoping to curb His influence and quell the spread of His teachings, the Prime Minister did not realize that no human hand can put out the flame of the Religion of God. The Báb won the respect and admiration of the officials in charge of the fortress. The people in the area became so enamored of The Báb that they went to the fortress before going to work to look upon His face and ask for His daily blessings. They even came to Him to settle their disputes. While in Mah-Ku, The Báb revealed the most important of His books, the Persian Bayan. In this book, He established the laws of His Dispensation, announced the coming of another Revelation greater than His Own and urged His followers to seek and find the New Messenger. Meanwhile, the Persian clergy and rulers rose up against the Bábis (the followers of The Báb) and many were martyred. But nothing could stop the Word of God from spreading. The Báb was banished once more to another fortress near Chihriq. Finally the authorities decided that they must end the Báb's life. He was dispatched to Tabriz, where He had previously been arrested. On that occasion He had been interrogated in front of the Prince and religious dignitaries. He had replied to allegations with such authority, resolve and dignity that the group assembled there had become silent and filled with shame. Once He had finished speaking in a bold and adamant manner, He had then left, bringing the meeting to a close. This time there would be no interrogation. The Báb was bound and placed against the wall along with a youth who had insisted upon being killed with his Lord and a firing squad of 750 soldiers killed Him.

What a short time The Báb had to teach a new way of life to a corrupt, vengeful populace! For all His efforts to bring the Healing Message of God to the inhabitants of Persia, to impress upon them the need for a renewal of religion, to provide them with guidance for their happiness and progress, He had been rewarded with vicious hatred and persecution. He and most of His disciples, leaders of the Cause, had sacrificed their lives courageously rather than deny their beliefs, as did twenty thousand of His followers. There was a smaller band of His followers now, lost and crushed and bereft of guidance. The bright new Faith might have been extinguished but through God's will. A few young misguided Bábis made a foolish and futile attempt to shoot the Shah. A young nobleman was one of the prisoners blamed for the event and thrown into a dungeon, so foul, damp and dark that it was known as the Black Hole. Every Prophet of God has experienced a specific moment of Revelation in order to achieve awareness of His station. Jesus experienced the dove descending upon Him; Zoroaster and Muhammad were visited by the Angel Gabriel. And the Maid of Heaven came to our young nobleman. From that time, He became known as Bahá'u'lláh, the Glory of God. This world religion was to be founded by two Teachers, the one following the other in quick succession.

Bahá'u'lláh was born into a rich family and His father was a nobleman, a favored Minister of the Crown. It is said that even as an infant, Bahá'u'lláh seemed to radiate and display remarkable power. He never cried or became restless. From childhood, He was extremely kind and generous. He loved nature and spent much time outdoors. As a child Bahá'u'lláh did not have or did not need any formal schooling because he had innate knowledge like The Báb. Many recognized his great intelligence and spiritual capacity and by the time he was 14, He could master any argument, but with courtesy and patience. People would bring their problems to Bahá'u'lláh. In large gatherings He would discuss matters with the leading clergy and explain complicated religious questions. He had a loving nature and quiet modesty. He was always thinking of others and sympathized with the poor and suffering. When His father died, He was asked to follow in his footsteps and assume a position in the court. But He refused because He had no interest in titles and honors. He took little part in state or social ceremonies, considering such affairs meaningless. He only wanted to defend the oppressed and be a refuge for the poor and needy. When He married, His home became a shelter and refuge for all. He and His wife gave abundantly and and no one was turned away. They became known for their service to others, He as the Father of the Poor and she as the Mother of Consolation.

After the Báb had declared His Mission, He had sent one of His disciples with a scroll containing some of His Writings to find the Man who should be its recipient. That Man was Bahá'u'lláh, Who knew immediately, upon reading Them, that the Báb's Teachings were the truth and He arose to spread them. The two Prophets exchanged messages but never met. It must have been a great comfort to the Báb when He languished in the fortresses of Mah-Ku and Chihriq and His band of followers faced severe persecution and martyrdom for their Faith, to know that Bahá'u'lláh was with the Bábis, consoling them and inspiring and directing them to spread the Message of the Báb. The Báb alone knew the station of Bahá'u'lláh, but His followers also knew how well-esteemed Bahá'u'lláh was in the eyes of the Báb and perhaps had inklings about Bahá'u'lláh as the Promised One.

When Bahá'u'lláh was released from the dungeon, He was exiled to Baghdad. But after enduring four months in that pestilential dungeon, with a fifty kilo chain around His neck and an attempt on His life through poisoned food, Bahá'u'lláh was ill and exhausted. And He and His family were forced to set out for their new home in the middle of winter with inadequate clothing and little food. Many of the Bábis had found their way to Baghdad before Bahá'u'lláh but they were lost and confused and behaving in a manner not worthy of the Báb and His Teachings. Bahá'u'lláh revived their spirits and guided them back to the right path. Bahá'u'lláh had a brother who was ambitious and he became inflamed with jealousy when he saw the respect and love given to Bahá'u'lláh by the Bábis and the admiration of the officials of the city when he, himself, considered himself the new leader of the Bábis. He determined, with an associate more courageous than he, to sow seeds of doubt among the Bábis about Bahá'u'lláh's intentions so that these precious souls would become fearful and suspicious. Bahá'u'lláh determined to leave Baghdad on his own so that He would not be the Subject of any conflict or hurt. He chose to life in the wilderness for two years alone but in communion with God, leading a simple life with little food and one change of clothing. Gradually He came to be known and loved by the local people. News of the learned man from the cave spread to Baghdad and the believers sent a messenger to beg Him to come back.

When Bahá'u'lláh returned, He once again set about to revive the community, lost without Him and under the precarious leadership of His brother who was not capable of setting an example in keeping with The Báb's Teachings. For seven years Bahá'u'lláh opened his home to all and individuals who met Him were transformed by the power of His wise words, generosity, gentleness and all-encompassing love. News of this Wondrous Soul reached places beyond Baghdad. Officials and religious leaders became His admirers, as did the poor whom He visited regularly to bestow on them His understanding and compassion as well as material comfort. He manifested a goodness surpassing saintliness.

As news of His fame spread, officials of the Persian and Ottoman governments and the clergy initially tried to defame Bahá'u'lláh, then implemented more drastic measures. The consul-general hired someone to shoot Bahá'u'lláh but when this man came face to face with Him he could not carry out the deed. Twice he tried unsuccessfully. Finally, Bahá'u'lláh was asked to leave for Constantinople (now called Istanbul). The Bábi community was overtaken with grief and needed Bahá'u'lláh's reassurances and calming manner to accept that most of them would have to stay behind while He went into exile once more. But He wrote a Tablet for each of the believers in the city: man, woman and child. Prior to setting out for Constantinople, Bahá'u'lláh spent twelve days in a beautiful garden waiting for preparations to be made for the long journey ahead. It was there that He declared His station to the believers.

Bahá'u'lláh and His family only stayed in Constantinople for four months before they were banished to Adrianople, considered the Siberia of the Ottoman Empire. It was a twelve-day journey to Adrianople again in the middle of winter and for the first six months in their new home, the little band lived in a dwelling suitable only as a summer house before being moved to more comfortable quarters.

Bahá'u'lláh won over many of the notables and people in this prison city by His loving-kindness, dignity and courage. As His influence grew once more, His brother became more inflamed with jealousy and he became bolder in his efforts to prevent the Bábis from accepting Bahá'u'lláh's station. His machinations gave the enemies of the Faith more ammunition to attack the Bábis. He attempted to poison Bahá'u'lláh, Who became severely ill for a month and was left with a trembling hand. Another attempt was made when the water in a well used by His family and other believers was poisoned, but it only made them a little sick. A bribe was given to Bahá'u'lláh's barber to kill Him, but the barber told Bahá'u'lláh about the plot. How sorrowful Bahá'u'lláh must have been by the deception of His own brother added to the hardships of exile. But this was a new era for Bahá'u'lláh's followers who now identified with His Station and referred to themselves as Bahá'ís. Bahá'u'lláh began to send Tablets to the kings and rulers of the world and the ecclesiastical leaders, proclaiming the Bahá'í Faith and His Station as the Manifestation of God for this age. The challenges contained in these Tablets and His positive effect upon the people of Adrianople led to the decision to take immediate drastic action to finally annihilate this Faith by sending Him to Akka, now part of Israel, a place of stench and filth where criminals were banished. Bahá'u'lláh later referred to it as the Most Great Prison.

When the group of Bahá'ís arrived in Akka, the order of the Sultan was read publicly in the mosque indicating that they were the vilest of prisoners condemned to life imprisonment and that the inhabitants of Akka were forbidden to associate with them. They were to be kept in strict confinement and it was hoped that the harsh conditions of the barracks where they were lodged would lead to their extermination. For two years Bahá'u'lláh and His company remained in the Most Great Prison. All except two of them got sick and three of them died. The deceased were not given a proper burial. Constant wailing and ravings of other prisoners, lack of adequate food, cruel guards, crowded conditions and the stagnant air were all guaranteed to weaken this brave company but their love for Bahá'u'lláh and His teachings kept them strong and oblivious to the discomfort.

Bahá'u'lláh and His family and followers were fortunate to leave the military barracks which had served as a prison and settle in a house but they were still prisoners, confined to their residence. However, in time, the people of Akka, having been hostile and unfriendly to this little band, began to recognize that they were innocent and the conditions of imprisonment were eased. 'Abdu'l-Bahá, Bahá'u'lláh's son, was largely responsible for this change because He gained the respect and admiration of the inhabitants of Akka. He had recognized His Father's Station while still a child; He had seen the state of His Father in the Black Hole; He and His family had lost their home and worldly possessions when their Father was arrested and had to subsist on a handful of flour instead of bread; He had been pelted with stones when He left their new humble abode on errands because He was considered to be the child of heretics. At the age of 11, when Bahá'u'lláh had retired to the wilderness, He had taken on the responsibility of His family and the Bábi community. He had experienced all the deprivation and calamities that His Father had experienced in being exiled from place to place. As He grew into manhood, He came to be regarded as the embodiment of all the virtues that Bahá'ís long to attain. He was gentle and courteous. He was generous and brave. He combined great wisdom with touching humility. And His love for God and mankind knew no bounds. He spent every day of His life serving others and bringing joy into their lives. The poor and the sick were His special care and the orphans looked upon Him as a father. His friends loved Him to the point of adoration and His enemies could find no blemish in His beautiful character. His life was an example of human perfection.

While still a youth, 'Abdu'l-Bahá had begun to serve as Bahá'u'lláh's secretary. He was Bahá'u'lláh's closest companion and a joy to His Father. He tried to anticipate all his Father's needs, performing all the business chores and tedious daily tasks and negotiating with officials on Bahá'u'lláh's behalf. Many who had thronged to their home in Baghdad were quite satisfied to meet 'Abdu'l-Bahá and bring their questions to Him, although He was still so young. As time went on, Bahá'u'lláh Himself would encourage the followers to take their problems to 'Abdu'l-Bahá. Bahá'u'lláh could then concentrate on writing and laying out the tenets of His Faith.

Eventually Bahá'u'lláh was able to leave the confines of the city and to enjoy the countryside. The people of Akka and the neighbouring regions now treated Him with reverence and respect, despite His formal designation as a prisoner. Even officials came to ask for His advice and guidance. 'Abdu'l-Bahá purchased a house for Him and He also enjoyed a beautiful garden reminiscent of the Garden of Ridvan where He had first declared His mission. Bahá'u'lláh's remaining years were spent in relative comfort. His Teachings began to spread to the West. When He died, He was buried beside His home. This shrine is a place of pilgrimage for the Bahá'ís of the world.

While in His beautiful home, Bahá'u'lláh revealed volumes of guidance, including the *Kitab-i-Aqdas*, the Book of Laws, considered the Most Holy Book. Bahá'u'lláh wrote many books by His own hand or in dictation to a secretary, whose transcription He personally corrected or approved. He wrote more volumes than those set down by the companions of Jesus, Muhammad and the other Holy Messengers. He dictated so rapidly that the secretary had to use a type of shorthand to get it all down on paper. Bahá'u'lláh's words were the outpourings of the Divine Will of God.

Bahá'u'lláh possessed such unimaginable majesty, authority, all-embracing knowledge and power, that many who came into His presence were unable to speak to Him or even gaze on His face. But He always assisted them to come forth and, even if they were unable to express one word, He would read their heart's desire and act accordingly with infinite love and compassion. In the manner of a kindly father, He brought up His children in a considerate and gentle fashion, counselling each according to his level of understanding and capacity. By addressing each person in this way, He deprived no one of His bounty.

Bahá'u'lláh set the example to the world of how mankind could live and progress. But His story did not end with His death. He left 'Abdu'l-Bahá as His heir to guide the Bahá'ís. In a formal Will and Testament, He appointed 'Abdu'l-Bahá as the Head of His Faith with the task of interpreting His Writings and being the Exemplar of His Teachings. He conferred divine authority beyond our ability to comprehend upon

'Abdu'l-Bahá so that the Bahá'ís would receive continued guidance. Bahá'u'lláh knew that 'Abdu'l-Bahá had the qualities necessary for such a task. He reflected the virtues of His Father. His dedication was unquestionable. 'Abdu'l-Bahá lived only for His Father and the Faith. He was noble and admired by all who knew Him. 'Abdu'l-Bahá would be able to implement the plans laid down by Bahá'u'lláh. He would lay the foundation of the Bahá'í Administrative Order and inspire the believers to eventually carry the Teachings to every corner of the planet. There is nothing in any previous Covenant that confers the undisputed authority that Bahá'u'lláh's Will conferred upon 'Abdu'l-Bahá, making certain that no one else was empowered to interpret the Bahá'í Faith or to manage its affairs. This clear appointment of 'Abdu'l-Bahá as the Center of the Covenant after Bahá'u'lláh's passing was to the Bahá'ís their strongest remaining channel and connection with holy and divine truth. Although they had lost Bahá'u'lláh, they still had the continuity of His purpose and plan in 'Abdu'l-Bahá. 'Abdu'l-Bahá was infallible because Bahá'u'lláh, the Manifestation of God, had decreed that He be so. He was human, but divinely inspired and divinely motivated.

It was clear that from the time 'Abdu'l-Bahá was a small child He was different from other children. He was born on the night that the Báb declared His Mission. As stated previously, He had recognized His Father's station while very young and had begged for the privilege of laying down His life for Bahá'u'lláh's sake. 'Abdu'l-Bahá often worked tirelessly and it seemed that there was no limit to the demands on His strength and time. He penned volumes of documents, Tablets, prayers and letters to the Bahá'ís; he also wrote many interpretations and supplemented the Writings of His Father. His selfless devotion to the Cause of His Father was an inspiration to the Bahá'ís. Through His vast correspondence, He kept in constant touch with the Bahá'ís everywhere, answering their questions, guiding their activities, encouraging them in their work and uplifting their spirits. He Himself had endured persecution for many long years. But through it all, He had remained calm and happy. His joy of life and his sense of humour never left Him. When people wondered what kept Him so happy under the most trying conditions in prison, He stated that the only prison is the prison of self.

'Abdu'l-Bahá did not allow anyone to believe or act as if He, 'Abdu'l-Bahá, were a Manifestation of God. His responsibility was to fulfill Bahá'u'lláh's Will and Testament and to continue Bahá'u'lláh's work but He was not to begin anything not already willed by God and His Manifestation.

In the time period when 'Abdu'l-Bahá was living in Akka and Bahá'u'lláh in the countryside, 'Abdu'l-Bahá continually amazed His family and visiting Bahá'ís. He had an astonishing wisdom and intuitive understanding, healing powers and the noblest of virtues. His character was perfect since He of course was the Perfect Exemplar of His Father's Teachings. He astonished everyone with His never-ending goodness and constant concern for the welfare of each and all. He often forgot to sleep or eat out of anxiety for others and put their needs before His own, making sure that everyone had food and a place to sleep. Every Friday He fed the poor, treated the sick or arranged for their treatment, provided clothes for the needy, reassured the distressed, guided those gone astray, helped the widows and assisted the orphans.

In 1908 an uprising led to the release of all the political and religious prisoners of the Turkish Empire and 'Abdu'l-Bahá was free. He set about to complete two tasks of great importance. The first was to entomb the remains of the Báb in Haifa on Mount Carmel, following the wishes of Bahá'u'lláh Who had visited Haifa and picked out the site. The Báb's body had been hidden for almost 60 years, moved from one place of confinement to another at the direction of Bahá'u'lláh, until it could be interred in its final resting-place. His second wish was to visit places in Europe and North America. Already the Bahá'ís in the West were pleading with Him to visit. But He was not a young man, being almost 70 years of age and His health had suffered with the strains of imprisonment. But in 1910, after completing His first task, He arose to the challenge with sublime courage, confidence and resolution and prepared for the long journey. He set out in 1911 and visited London and Paris. From there, He sailed for the U.S. and Canada, arriving in New York in April, 1912 and remaining in North America for eight months, before visiting a few cities in Europe and then returning home. In all of His talks with the Bahá'ís, He emphasized that they should demonstrate sincere love to all and that they should serve strangers as they would their own dear friends. They were to help and comfort the poor. They were to forget themselves and concentrate all their attention on assisting the sorrowful and downtrodden. 'Abdu'l-Bahá greeted everyone He met by asking them, "Are you happy?" and He brought laughter and joy to all. He gave public addresses to various religious audiences, scientists, university students, women's clubs and the poor, relating Bahá'í Teachings to the specific interests and capacities of His audiences. He addressed them with words of cheer and indiscriminating love. From the highest government officials, scientists and philosophers, to the most humble workmen and poorest tramps, 'Abdu'l-Bahá uplifted and inspired them with new hope. It was astounding to many that he could understand other people's problems and had such a vast knowledge of world affairs when He had lived a life of exile and imprisonment. From dawn to dusk He was busy, meeting individuals, conducting interviews and delivering speeches when he was not travelling to the next city. It is astounding to consider the schedule He maintained for such a long period of time, despite His age and broken health. And He did not forget to hand out alms to His beloved ones – the poor and downtrodden. He was also generous to the children, whom He adored and held lovingly in His arms, and to the maids in the hotels. He even gave away a pair of His trousers to a poor soul in need! Millions of people heard about Him and His Message through dozens of articles in the press.

When 'Abdu'l-Bahá returned to the Holy Land, World War I broke out. 'Abdu'l-Bahá had anticipated famine there and the Bahá'ís had therefore grown and stored as much food as they could to share with those in need. 'Abdu'l-Bahá was knighted by the British government for His services during the war but He, of course, did not use the title or permit others to use it. He was, after all, 'Abdu'l-Bahá, the Servant of Bahá'u'lláh. This was His one desire and it summed up His life. Up until the last day of His life, He served mankind, giving out alms, visiting the sick and providing medicine, advice and comfort. He was as much at ease with beggars as with noblemen and gave them all His loving understanding and tenderness. He was interested in all and understood their needs implicitly. He was indeed the Healer of diseased bodies, broken hearts and ravaged minds. He put aside all thoughts of self and gave totally of Himself with remarkable energy, devotion and self-sacrifice.

'Abdu'l-Bahá died in 1921 and His funeral was attended by crowds of people from all walks of life. Representatives of the Muslim, Christian and Jewish Faiths gave eulogies, mourning the loss of such a tender Soul. 'Abdu'l-Bahá wrote a Will and Testament, naming His grandson, Shoghi Effendi, Successor and Guardian of the Bahá'í Faith. When Shoghi Effendi was merely a young boy, 'Abdu'l-Bahá had seen the potential in him and had intimated that he would do great things in the future. The Will and Testament provided the details of an administration that Shoghi Effendi was empowered to develop. And Shoghi Effendi, as Guardian, would ensure the continuity of the Bahá'í Faith without any divisions.

Shoghi Effendi was descended from Bahá'u'lláh on his mother's side and from the Báb on his father's side. He grew up in 'Abdu'l-Bahá's home in Akka. He went away to school but when he came home in the summers, he spent as much time as possible with 'Abdu'l-Bahá, Whom he idolized. Wherever 'Abdu'l-Bahá went, Shoghi Effendi went with him and He accompanied 'Abdu'l-Bahá to official functions. He longed to serve 'Abdu'l-Bahá and dedicated himself to this work. After finishing his studies in Beirut, he was 'Abdu'l-Bahá's translator for two years.

He went to Oxford University in England to study English, to be better prepared to serve his Grandfather as secretary and translator of some of the Bahá'í Writings into English. He in fact became a scholar in the English language, writing with eloquence, depth, clarity and precise vocabulary unfamiliar to many native speakers. When 'Abdu'l-Bahá died, He was 24 years old and still at Oxford. At first, shattered by the death of his Beloved and the knowledge that he was now the Guardian, He fled to Europe to pray, meditate and prepare to take on the mantle of the Guardianship. He returned, ready to take on his responsibilities as leader of the Bahá'í Faith and acted with determination to carry out 'Abdu'l-Bahá's wishes. His early letters to the Bahá'ís asked them to inform him of their needs, plans and activities so that he could contribute to their success through prayer and brotherly assistance. He persuaded the Bahá'ís not to lose time but to set out to accomplish the tasks set by Bahá'u'lláh and 'Abdu'l-Bahá.

Shoghi Effendi began to identify himself as the Head of an independent religion in his country. 'Abdu'l-Baháhad been widely loved and held in great esteem and He was considered to be a Holy Man, exemplifying a spiritual life. He had proclaimed the Faith as an independent religion on His travels but locally He was unable to break customs binding Him so long to the Muslim community and He attended the mosque regularly, like His Father before Him. But Shoghi Effendi had studied in England. He was young, western in his training and habits and he was able to ensure that the Faith was considered a world religion. In fact, through his efforts the State recognized that Israel was indeed the World Centre of the Bahá'í Faith and it was given the same status as that of other religions. And, in turn, Shoghi Effendi assisted the authorities when funds were needed for charitable work. He gave to an earthquake fund and between 1941 and 1952, which were times of great hardship for many people in Palestine, he gave to the poor of all denominations. Following 'Abdu'l-Bahá's wishes, Shoghi Effendi undertook the building of an arcade and dome on the shrine of the Báb in Haifa and he expanded and designed the gardens surrounding the shrine. He acquired land for more gardens, supervising all the business transactions needed for their acquisition. He continued to develop the gardens throughout his life, personally mapping them out and overseeing their progress.

And now Shoghi Effendi could take up the mantle of translator for his beloved Grandfather and Great-Grandfather. He sent to all continents his translations of Bahá'u'lláh and 'Abdu'l-Bahá's original words and other writings with an exquisite mastery and command of language. He was extremely cautious concerning the original Writings of Bahá'u'lláh, the Báb and 'Abdu'l-Bahá to protect Them from being misconstrued. All of his work ensured that the Bahá'ís would be unified in their understanding of the Writings of the Faith. He wrote a stupendous review and history of the first 100 years of the Bahá'í Faith in English and one in Persian and Arabic. He translated five weighty books of the Faith into English. He was also Interpreter of the Bahá'í Writings. He wrote thousands of letters to individuals and to Bahá'í communities all over the world with explanations and clarification of the Bahá'í Writings. He had an individual, intensely personal relationship with each community and expressed a tenderness and kindness in his letters and cables. He maintained courteous relationships with many individuals and lengthy correspondence with royalty, statesmen, university professors and educators.

In 'Abdu'l-Bahá's time, there had been few local assemblies and no national assemblies. The principles governing the Administrative Order established in the Will were defined by Shoghi Effendi during the first year of his ministry in a flood of letters to all believers. There are no priests or clergy in the Bahá'í Faith. In every community where 9 or more Bahá'ís reside, a local Spiritual Assembly is elected to oversee the affairs of the Bahá'í community. The Assembly is not responsible to the electors; it consults continually with the community but is responsible to the Teachings. Shoghi Effendi ensured that the Bahá'ís understood the meaning of authority within the context of the administration. Bahá'í authority in the administration is not given in order to enhance an individual's prestige. Instead, it is measured by humility, self-sacrifice and service. Individuals must consult in their meetings frankly and lovingly in an atmosphere of love, respect, prayerfulness, courtesy and dignity so that rules and regulations do not override the spiritual nature of meetings. Shoghi Effendi spent 16 years laying a firm foundation and erecting a pattern for all Bahá'í administrative institutions. He helped to build strong national institutions and created the International Bahá'í Council, the precursor of the Universal House of Justice, the supreme institution directing the Bahá'ís all over the world in their endeavors.

Shoghi Effendi married a Canadian Bahá'í in 1937. 'Abdu'l-Bahá had stayed in her parents' home in Montreal on his visit to North America and He had been quite fond of the little girl. Ruhiyyih Khanum, as she came to be known, described Shoghi Effendi as trusting and confiding in nature and exceedingly kind and considerate. He was very methodical, thorough, with a sense of perfection and attention to detail, demonstrated in his drawing of maps delineating the spread of the Bahá'í Faith around the world and His plans for the worldwide Bahá'í community. He had a profound humility and was so self-effacing that he would brush aside any adulation and praise and turn any kind words showered upon him by the believers towards the Báb, Bahá'u'lláh and 'Abdu'l-Bahá. He did not want photographs to be taken of himself and he did not give any away, instead encouraging the Bahá'ís to put 'Abdu'l-Bahá's photograph in their rooms. He did not allow anyone to have his discarded clothes or personal possessions and he did not want his birthday celebrated. He has been described by those who knew him all his life as being very dynamic, always busy, restless and intense with incredible powers of concentration and accomplishment. He was shrewd and economical and a determined bargainer, making it possible to save the Bahá'í Faith large sums of money and then go on to engage in new enterprises by using the money saved. But he was also generous in his contributions to the needy and to the Bahá'ís in all their endeavours to pursue the aims of the Faith. He assisted financially with the translation and publication of Bahá'í literature. (The Bahá'í Faith is supported exclusively by voluntary contributions made by the Bahá'ís.) Shoghi Effendi was never intimidated by the magnitude of the tasks he underwent. But he was overburdened with his unremitting work. For 36 years he toiled, finding time to devote to the minute details as well as encompassing the whole planet with his plans, instructions, guidance and leadership. He singlehandedly ensured the establishment of the Faith throughout the world and laid the foundations of the Administrative Order. At the end of his ministry, as a result of his efforts, Bahá'í literature had been translated into 230 languages and 251 territories of the planet knew about the Bahá'í Faith. Until the end of his days he continued to inspire the Bahá'ís with words equal to a number of volumes. His undaunting energy and endless workday most likely precipitated his death at the age of 60. He is buried in London, England where he had been at the time of his death. All through his life he had attempted to unite the East and the West and even in death he continued to do so.

At his passing, it was determined that Shoghi Effendi had not written a Will; there was no heir or Bahá'í relative spiritually or morally able to fit the requirements laid down by 'Abdu'l-Bahá for a successor to the Guardian. But there were Hands of the Cause of God, a unique institution originally brought into being by Bahá'u'lláh in His Own Lifetime, to aid in the development of the Faith. In 'Abdu'l-Bahá's Will and Testament, provisions were made for Shoghi Effendi to appoint Hands of the Cause to assist him with the enormous amount of work entrusted to him. The Hands are learned individuals who act as advisors. Hands of the Cause representing all the continents of the world came together to determine their next steps. Nine Hands were chosen to serve at the World Centre and work for the protection and promotion of the Faith, maintaining correspondence with the other 15 Hands in the world, who assisted national Assemblies with administrative concerns and in following firmly the instructions and policies of Shoghi Effendi. The Universal House of Justice was elected in 1963.

According to the provisions of 'Abdu'l-Bahá's Will and Testament, the Universal House of Justice is universally elected by national Assemblies in the world. It legislates on matters not expressly recorded in the Writings. It guides, organizes and unifies the affairs of the Bahá'ís throughout the world. It gives spiritual guidance to the worldwide Bahá'í community and directs its administrative activities. The Universal House of Justice is elected every 5 years in a free, democratic election by secret ballot. The nine members come from different countries and backgrounds, but work as one soul, one heart and one purpose for the unification of the world, according to the Teachings of Bahá'u'lláh. The Universal House of Justice is considered to be an infallible source under the care and protection of Bahá'u'lláh and His unerring guidance and inspiration.

And so concludes my summary of the Bahá'í Faith. But I could describe the Bahá'í Faith to you with one word that encapsulates its essence. And that word is "love". All of Its Teachings depend on and are outgrowths of love, Its Twin Manifestations were the epitome of love, Its Perfect Example demonstrated love in all His words and deeds, The Guardian permeated love in his dedication and tireless energy in encouraging his followers and pursuing the work of the Faith and the administrative bodies of the Faith act on their mandate of love for humanity.

And it is about selflessness. Both the Báb and Bahá'u'lláh demonstrated purity and selflessness in their lives, dedicating themselves to the fulfillment of their Mission, regardless of the afflictions and persecutions they had to endure. 'Abdu'l-Bahá , the Example of how to live our lives, gave everything – His material possessions, His energy and enthusiasm, His loving-kindness, His generosity and His heart to everyone whose path He crossed. And the precious Guardian, upon receiving notification of the role he was destined to play in guiding the Faith, left home to pray to lose all traces of self and to become a selfless being committed to the work of the Faith.

And it is this love and selflessness that we are called upon to emulate. We express our love for God in prayer and, discarding our preoccupation with self and our meagre lives, we turn in love and compassion to our fellow men. We learn to become more selfless as we turn our hearts and minds to the divine and to free our love from any preconceived ideas, prejudices, or sensitivity to the adverse reactions we may receive. We continue to serve, at the same time fighting our own battles as our selfish nature creeps in and threatens to spoil all our best intentions. It is my dearest wish that those from all backgrounds, those who attempt to live a spiritual life and those who are just starting out on a search for spirituality, will find some gems within the pages of this book to nourish their spiritual beings.

Note: For convenience, I will use "he" to refer to either "he" or "she" (a man or woman) in the text of this book, and "man" or "mankind" to refer to either gender, as does the Bahá'í Holy Writings, many of which were translated from a language in which the same word refers to either "he" or "she". Also, quotations from the Bahá'í Writings were typed exactly as they were found in the books, so there are discrepancies at times in spellings, for example, the use of British English and American English. Quotations from the Bahá'í Writings are typed in bold to differentiate them from other text.

Chapter 1
The Insistent Self

Chapter 1
The Insistent Self

This chapter will explore the "insistent self", the veils and barriers that impede our spiritual growth and the effects of materialism. It will emphasize the purpose of our being and the necessity for constant striving to stay on a spiritual course. Most of the sources for this discussion are from the Bahá'í Writings or from Bahá'í authors reflecting on the Teachings of Bahá'u'lláh.

The first thing we need to do is to establish what is meant by the "insistent self". As I mentioned in the introduction, the term insistent self was coined by 'Abdu'l-Bahá, the son of Bahá'u'lláh, Founder of the Bahá'í Faith and Manifestation of God. He said:

'Abdu'l-Bahá tells us *"O ye loved ones of God! In this, the Bahá'í dispensation, God's Cause is spirit unalloyed. His Cause belongeth not to the material world. It cometh neither for strife nor war, for acts of mischief or of shame; it is neither for quarrelling with other Faiths, nor for conflicts with the nations. Its only army is the love of God, its only joy the clear wine of His knowledge, its only battle the expounding of the Truth; its one crusade is against the insistent self, the evil promptings of the human heart. Its victory is to submit and yield, and to be selfless in its everlasting glory. In brief, it is spirit upon spirit."* [1]

So the "insistent self" is the evil promptings of the human heart. It is the dark side of our nature as opposed to being selfless and "spirit upon spirit".

"'Abdu'l-Bahá was once asked,'What is Satan?' He replied in three words: 'The insistent self.'" [2] It is interesting to me that 'Abdu'l-Bahá uses the adjective "insistent" to refer to this self. A dictionary definition of "insistent" gives us the synonyms demanding, unyielding, persistent, emphatic, persevering and unrelenting. These words give us a clear picture of this side of our nature and emphasizes the need to work diligently to address our nobler side of self. In the quotation, 'Abdu'l-Bahá suggests that there are two meanings of self – one is self-love and self-absorption, the other is selflessness.

Shoghi Effendi, the Guardian of the Bahá'í Faith, who became the interpreter of the Bahá'í Writings and the Head of the Bahá'í Faith at 'Abdu'l-Bahá's passing, clarifies the two meanings of self: "... *self has really two meanings, or is used in two senses, in the Bahá'í writings;*

one is self, the identity of the individual created by God. This is the self mentioned in such passages as 'he hath known himself etc.' The other self is the ego, the dark, animalistic heritage each one of us has, the lower nature that can develop into a monster of selfishness, brutality, lust and so on. It is this self we must struggle against, or this side of our natures, in order to strengthen and free the spirit within us and help it to attain perfection." [3]

"When a reporter of the New York Globe visited 'Abdu'l-Bahá in Haifa, 'Abdu'l-Bahá gave him this message, 'Tell my followers that they have no enemies to fear, no foes to hate. Man's only enemy is himself'. [4] Here 'Abdu'l-Bahá was definitely referring to ***"the ego, the dark animalistic heritage"*** [5] in us.

The Bahá'í Writings differentiate between our two selves: our animal, material or lower nature and our spiritual, divine or higher nature. I feel that it is important to understand the two natures within us and the strength of our natural way (the animal side), or as 'Abdu'l-Bahá clearly designated it, our insistent self, to realize just how important it is to strive to become spiritual beings and to subdue our lower natures. And 'Abdu'l-Bahá explains this:

"In man there are two natures; his spiritual or higher nature and his material or lower nature. In one he approaches God, in the other he lives for the world alone. Signs of both these natures are to be found in man. In his material aspects he expresses untruth, cruelty and injustice; all these are the outcomes of his lower nature. The attributes of his divine nature are shown forth in love, mercy, kindness, truth and justice, one and all being expressions of his higher nature. Every good habit, every noble quality belongs to man's spiritual nature, whereas all his imperfections and sinful actions are born of his material nature." [6]

Bahá'u'lláh denounced self and passion as *"the worst of all human characteristics"* [7] in this Tablet addressed to Ali Pasha, the Grand Vizir of Turkey who was responsible for His exile to Akka:

"The lowliest and most abject of all things holdeth sway over thee, and that is none other than self and passion, which have ever been reprehensible." [8]

And He exhorted us:

*"O MY SERVANT!
Free thyself from the fetters of this world, and loose thy soul from the prison of self. Seize thy chance, for it will come to thee no more."* [9]

"O My servants! Could ye apprehend with what wonders of My munificence and bounty I have willed to entrust your souls, ye would, of a truth, rid yourselves of attachment to all created things, and would gain a true knowledge of your own selves -- a knowledge which is the same as the comprehension of Mine own Being. Ye would find yourselves independent of all else but Me, and would perceive, with your inner and outer eye, and as manifest as the revelation of My effulgent Name, the seas of My loving-kindness and bounty moving within you. Suffer not your idle fancies, your evil passions, your insincerity and blindness of heart to dim the luster, or stain the sanctity, of so lofty a station. Ye are even as the bird which soareth, with the full force of its mighty wings and with complete and joyous confidence, through the immensity of the heavens, until, impelled to satisfy its hunger, it turneth longingly to the water and clay of the earth below it, and, having been entrapped in the mesh of its desire, findeth itself impotent to resume its flight to the realms whence it came. Powerless to shake off the burden weighing on its sullied wings, that bird, hitherto an inmate of the heavens, is now forced to seek a dwelling-place upon the dust. Wherefore, O My servants, defile not your wings with the clay of waywardness and vain desires, and suffer them not to be stained with the dust of envy and hate, that ye may not be hindered from soaring in the heavens of My divine knowledge. [10]

Adib Taherzadeh, a Bahá'í writer and historian, provides an explanation of the previous quotation by Bahá'u'lláh. (Mr. Taherzadeh served on National Spiritual Assemblies in Britain and as a member of the Universal House of Justice for twelve years. Prolific in his writings, he is probably best known for his four volumes about the life of Bahá'u'lláh and Bahá'u'lláh's Writings. In these volumes he provided explanations of the Bahá'í Writings using English translations as well as those in their original language. References to his explanations constitute a large portion of the material in this book.) Mr. Taherzadeh explains that the two forces in opposition in man are similar to gravity pulling a bird down and its wings raising it up.[11] If a man shuns religious teachings, his soul will be in the dark and will not have the power needed to rise up from the "fetters" of the mortal world. The animal side will be victorious and the soul will become a slave to self and passion. But as we have been discussing, because our animal natures are strong, it is in our nature to be selfish, to follow our instincts and meet our basic needs and once they are met to strive for security and, if desired, power and wealth. It is in our nature to be attached to material things, to self and passion.

John Ebenezer Esslemont was an accomplished medical doctor and linguist. Several chapters of his book, *Bahá'u'lláh and the New Era* were reviewed by 'Abdu'l-Bahá. In his discussion about the nonexistence of evil, he points out that evil is *"but the absence or lesser degree of good – the undeveloped state,"* states that *"if [a man] is selfish, the evil is not in his love of self – all love, even self-love is good, is divine. The evil is that he has such a poor, inadequate, misguided love of self and such a lack of love for others and for God. He looks upon himself as only a superior sort of animal, and foolishly pampers his lower nature as he might pamper a pet dog- with worse results in his case than in that of the dog."* [12]

Bahá'u'lláh warns us:

". . . Watch over yourselves, for the Evil One is lying in wait, ready to entrap you. Gird yourselves against his wicked devices, and led by the light of the All-Seeing God, make your escape from the darkness that surroundeth you. . . . The Evil One is he that hindereth the rise and obstructeth the spiritual progress of the children of men. [13]

So this writer concludes that we must make efforts to overcome our lower nature. And, once we have decided, because of our love for God and His spiritual teachings that we want to be spiritual beings, within us there is the constant battle to keep the material side in check. The development of our spiritual nature is not controlled by nature. The soul aspires to spirituality but we need to put forth great effort to acquire it and to use our free will. And it takes courage.

Bahá'u'lláh encourages us:

"O MY SERVANT!
Thou art even as a finely tempered sword concealed in the darkness of its sheath and its value hidden from the artificer's knowledge. Wherefore come forth from the sheath of self and desire that thy worth may be made resplendent and manifest unto all the world. [14]

And from Gautama Buddha:

"Though one should conquer a 1000 times a 1000 men in battle, he who conquers his own self is the greatest of all conquerors." [15]

'Abdu'l-Bahá tells us that there is no point to life if we are to be like the animals:

" . . . What result is forthcoming from material rest, tranquillity, luxury and attachment to this corporeal world? It is evident that the man who pursues these things will in the end become afflicted with regret and loss.

Consequently, one must close his eyes wholly to these thoughts, long for eternal life, the sublimity of the world of humanity, the celestial developments, the Holy Spirit, the promotion of the Word of God, the guidance of the inhabitants of the globe, The Promulgation of Universal Peace *and the proclamation of the oneness of the world of humanity! This is the work! Otherwise like unto other animals and birds one must occupy himself with the requirements of this physical life, the satisfaction of which is the highest aspiration of the animal kingdom, and one must stalk across the earth like unto the quadrupeds.*

Consider ye! No matter how much man gains wealth, riches and opulence in this world, he will not become as independent as a cow. For these fattened cows roam freely over the vast tableland. All the prairie and meadows are theirs for grazing, and all the springs and rivers are theirs for drinking! No matter how much they graze, the fields will not be exhausted! It is evident that they have earned these material bounties with the utmost facility.

Still more ideal than this life is the life of the bird. A bird, on the summit of a mountain, on the high, waving branches, has built for itself a nest more beautiful than the palaces of the kings! The air is in the utmost purity, the water cool and clear as crystal, the panorama charming and enchanting. In such glorious surroundings, he expends his numbered days. All the harvests of the plain are his possessions, having earned all this wealth without the least labor. Hence, no matter how much man may advance in this world, he shall not attain to the station of this bird! Thus it becomes evident that in the matters of this world, however much man may strive and work to the point of death, he will be unable to earn the abundance, the freedom and the independent life of a small bird. This proves and establishes the fact that man is not created for the life of this ephemeral world – nay, rather, is he created for the acquirement of infinite perfections, for the attainment to the sublimity of the world of humanity, to be drawn nigh unto the divine threshold, and to sit on the throne of everlasting sovereignty!" [16]

And it is only by the grace of God that we are able to realize our spiritual existence because throughout the ages he has sent Teachers to assist us to reach our potential:

"The holy Manifestations of God come into the world to dispel the darkness of the animal or physical nature of man, to purify him from his imperfections in order that his heavenly and spiritual nature may become quickened, his divine qualities awakened, his perfections visible,

his potential powers revealed and all the virtues of the world of humanity latent within him may come to life. These holy Manifestations of God are the educators and trainers of the world of existence, the teachers of the world of humanity. They liberate man from the darkness of the world of nature, deliver him from despair, error, ignorance, imperfections and all evil qualities. They clothe him in the garment of perfections and exalted virtues. Men are ignorant; the Manifestations of God make them wise. They are animalistic; the Manifestations make them human. They are savage and cruel; the Manifestations lead them into kingdoms of light and love. They are unjust; the Manifestations cause them to become just. Man is selfish; they sever him from self and desire. Man is haughty; they make him meek, humble and friendly. He is earthly; they make him heavenly. Men are material; the Manifestations transform them into semblance divine. They are immature children; the Manifestations develop them into maturity. Man is poor; they endow him with wealth. Man is base, treacherous and mean; the Manifestations of God uplift him into dignity, nobility and loftiness. These holy Manifestations liberate the world of humanity from the imperfections which beset it and cause men to appear in the beauty of heavenly perfections. Were it not for the coming of these holy Manifestations of God all mankind would be found on the plane of the animal. They would remain darkened and ignorant like those who have been denied schooling and who never had a teacher or trainer. Undoubtedly such unfortunates will continue in their condition of need and deprivation." [17]

It seems to me that we have some extremely good reasons not to indulge in self-interest, not to worship ourselves and promote our own material interests, not to seek diligently our own benefit, not to be captives of the world of nature but to be *"freed from the bondage of satanic suggestions"* [18]

First of all and most importantly, according to the Bahá'í Writings, man is not created for the material world. He is created for an eternal life and he therefore needs to be prepared for it.

"…in this world he must prepare himself for the life beyond. That which he needs in the world of the Kingdom must be obtained here." [19]

'Abdu'l-Bahá tells us what is needed:

"By what means can man acquire these things? How shall he obtain these merciful gifts and powers? First, through the knowledge of God. Second, through the love of God. Third, through faith. Fourth, through philanthropic deeds. Fifth, through self-sacrifice. Sixth, through severance from this world. Seventh, through sanctity and holiness.

Unless he acquires these forces and attains to these requirements he will surely be deprived of the life that is eternal.[20]

The Bahá'í Teachings espouse that man is not created for living like the animals; he is created to be noble and virtuous. And out of gratitude for His love and blessings and bringing His Teachings to the world, we want to please Him and follow His laws. We are asked to "fight" our animal nature, our material side, purely for the sake of God:

"Burn away wholly for the sake of the Well-Beloved, the veil of self with the flame of the undying Fire and with faces, joyous and beaming with light, associate with your neighbor." [21]

"I supplicate God to make His beloved ones . . . glow with the fire of Sinai . . . meek and lowly for the sake of God among His beloved, denying self and passion, grasping the robe of piety, so that they may be lamps of guidance in those regions." [22]

'Abdu'l-Bahá tells us that we can only be truly happy if we are following a spiritual path:

"Man is, in reality, a spiritual being, and only when he lives in the spirit is he truly happy." [23]

"True happiness depends on spiritual good and having the heart ever open to receive the Divine Bounty." [24]

"Happiness consists of two kinds; physical and spiritual. The physical happiness is limited; its utmost duration is one day, one month, one year. It hath no result. Spiritual happiness is eternal and unfathomable. This kind of happiness appeareth in one's soul with the love of God and suffereth one to attain to the virtues and perfections of the world of humanity. Therefore, endeavor as much as thou art able in order to illuminate the lamp of thy heart by the light of love." [25]

And here's another reason to shun the world of nature, according to the Bahá'í Teachings:

"O maid-servant of God!

Thy letter was understood. Thou hast asked, very humbly, for certain things and all were worthy to be coveted. Thou desirest forgiveness of sins; didst ask for great unity and peace; sought nearness to the

Threshold of God; hoped to be detached from thine own will, seeking the will of God; prayed for rescue from self-love (or selfishness); hoped for progress in the station of knowledge; desired to serve God; and prayed that thy honorable husband and thy children may be set aglow with the fire of the love of God and may manifest light on their brows through the radiance of the knowledge of God. All these wishes are well worthy of asking. Especially the rescue from self-love. This is a strange trait and the means of the destruction of many important souls in the world. If man be imbued with all good qualities but be selfish, all the other virtues will fade or pass away and eventually he will grow worse." [26]

This seems to me to be a particularly strong statement by 'Abdu'l-Bahá. The woman who wrote to Him asked for many things that 'Abdu'l-Bahá considered to be worthy but most important to Him was being rescued from the love of self, so important in man that any other qualities will disappear if he is selfish and he will not grow spiritually.

And again He says:

"If he is alloyed with the slightest trace of passion, desire, ostentation or self-interest, it is certain that the results of all efforts will prove fruitless, and he will become deprived and hopeless." [27]

O army of God! Whensoever ye behold a person whose entire attention is directed toward the Cause of God; whose only aim is this, to make the Word of God to take effect; who, day and night, with pure intent, is rendering service to the Cause; from whose behavior not the slightest trace of egotism or private motives is discerned – who, rather, wandereth distracted in the wilderness of the Love of God, and drinketh only from the cup of the knowledge of God, and is utterly engrossed in spreading the sweet savours of God, and is enamoured of the holy verses of the Kingdom of God – know ye for a certainty that this individual will be supported and reinforced by heaven; that like unto the morning star, he will forever gleam brightly out of the skies of eternal grace. But if he show the slightest taint of selfish desires and self love, his efforts will lead to nothing and he will be destroyed and left hopeless at the last." [28]

So what can we gather from this? Perhaps that it makes no difference if someone is expending all his energies in serving the Faith selflessly with no hints of impure motive or doing it for his ego, striving only for the sake of God to do his part. If the slightest hint of selfishness creeps in, all efforts will be a waste and he will be lost in the end. It is as if 'Abdu'l-Bahá is saying in this passage that man may start off well in terms of being spiritually attuned and he later succumbs to selfishness or self-interest; his ego becomes bloated perhaps through praise or acknowledgement for his efforts or the desire for praise or acknowledgement or he is disappointed that his efforts go unnoticed. All will come to naught because others won't listen to him but will turn away, noting his selfishness. And he will become hopeless because he will become sceptical, begin to have doubts about the Faith, perhaps argue with other believers and he is *"left hopeless at the last"*.

'Abdu'l-Bahá states that it is very difficult once the habit of pursuing one's own selfish interests has become entrenched.

"As long as man is a captive of habit, pursuing the dictates of self and desire, he is vanquished and defeated. This passionate personal ego takes the reins from his hands, crowds out the qualities of the divine ego and changes him into an animal, a creature unable to judge good from evil or to distinguish light from darkness. He becomes blind to divine attributes, for this acquired individuality, the result of an evil routine of thought, becomes the dominant note of his life." [29]

This means to me that we need to learn about self and gain self-knowledge, but if we become obsessed with our self and satisfying the self, our personal growth can be delayed. Spiritual development requires the constant struggle against the insistent self.

". . . the pursuit of passion and desire will wrap the eyes in a thousand veils that rise out of the heart to blind the sight and the insight as well.

Desire and self come in the door
And blot out virtue bright before,
And a hundred veils will rise
from the heart, to blind the eyes." [30]

'Abdu'l-Bahá clarifies in the following passage that we have two kinds of personality: "individuality", our natural or God-given personality and the personality that can reflect the divine attributes through the acquisition of sciences, arts, "real knowledge" and the practice of praiseworthy deeds. Character is the result.

"The individuality of each created thing is based upon divine wisdom, for in the creation of God there is no defect. However, personality has no element of permanence. It is a slightly changeable quality in man which can be turned in either direction. For if he acquire praiseworthy virtues

these strengthen the individuality of man and call forth his hidden forces; but if he acquire defects, the beauty and simplicity of the individual will be stifled in the foul atmosphere of self." [31]

'Abdu'l-Bahá states:

"Today, in this world, every people is wandering astray in its own desert, moving here and there according to the dictates of its fancies and whims, pursuing its own particular caprice." [32]

Caprice means a tendency to change one's mind, without any motive. To me 'Abdu'l-Bahá is saying that individuals are living their lives without purpose or even much planning, doing things on the spur of the moment, at someone else's suggestion, rather like the wind blowing them from one direction to another aimlessly. They stumble through their lives blindly, working to make money, consuming, and having a family without any self-reflection, merely eking out an existence.

"How debased the soul which can find enjoyment in this darkness, occupied with itself, the captive of self and passion, wallowing in the mire of the material world." [33]

So we can conclude that our animal nature is our fall-back position. We naturally respond at the level of this animal nature. So we have to strive daily to prevent the insistent self from asserting itself in everything we do.

Shoghi Effendi clarifies this:

"Life is a constant struggle, not only against forces around us, but above all against our own 'ego'. We can never afford to rest our oars, for if we do, we soon see ourselves carried down stream again. Many of those who drift from the course do so for the reasons that they had ceased to go on developing. They became complacent, or indifferent, and consequently ceased to draw the spiritual strength and vitality from the Cause which they should have. . . . " [34]

I would comment that we would consider serving others a noble act, one that brings out our divine nature. But what if we serve others for recognition or we are constantly seeking praise for our efforts? We recognize that our motives are not pure at least some of the time and then we know that we are following our lower nature. Awareness is a first step to making changes in our lives. As Taherzadeh points out, *"There can be no greater bounty in this life than serving the Cause, provided one's motive is pure. If service is rendered in the hope of securing fame, influence and other personal gains in this world or even in the next, then such a service becomes a great burden on the soul. It fills one's life with sadness and frustration and as Bahá'u'lláh has declared in His Writings, it will not be pleasing to God, for nothing but pure deeds and pure motives can be acceptable in His sight."* [35]

Generally, people don't want to be selfish or perceived as selfish and they are attracted to spiritual teachings about love and unity and serving mankind. And they may recognize the degree to which they are cut off from their Creator and their own spiritual growth- when encompassed by self. Again from the Bahá'í Writings:

"Behold how the sun shines upon all creation; but only surfaces that are pure and polished can reflect its glow and light. The darkened soul has no portion of the revelation of the glorious effulgence of reality and the soil of self, unable to take advantage of that light, does not produce growth." [36]

"This test is just as thou hast written: it removeth the rust of egotism from the mirror of the heart until the Sun of Truth may shine therein. For, no veil is greater than egotism and no matter how thin that covering may be, yet it will finally veil man entirely and prevent him from receiving a portion from the eternal bounty." [37]

'Abdu'l-Bahá emphasizes the "subtlety" of the ego in this passage:

"They must do as they wish; they must solve their own problems; they are grown-ups. We do not like to tell people what they should do in these matters. My work is universal; my time and thoughts are for the whole world on the most important problems relating to affairs that concern the spiritual welfare of nations and individuals. When the believers are insistent, 'Abdu'l-Bahá must give them answers, and it is their wish always that 'Abdu'l-Bahá grants them. He knows what their wish in reality is. They must make mistakes to learn, and to unfold the higher which is within themselves. The initial wish does not come from 'Abdu'l-Bahá. It comes from them. It is generally clothed with such words as these: 'We only wish to do that which 'Abdu'l-Bahá wishes us to do.' And they are sincere in this, for they do not know the subtlety of the ego of man. It is the Tempter (the subtle serpent of the mind), and the poor soul not entirely emancipated from its suggestions is deceived until entirely severed from all save God." [38]

The following quotation from the Universal House of Justice, the supreme body governing the affairs of the Bahá'í community all over the world, summarizes references to the ego that have already been made and stresses the need to keep striving to "subdue our egos":

"Your concern about the overemphasis upon the self and ego echoes a central theme of the Manifestation Himself [Bahá'u'lláh], *and it is the subject of many allusions in the Writings wherein, for example, He speaks of 'the evil of egotism' and of those who are 'captives of egotism'. The Master* ['Abdu'l-Bahá] *refers to 'the rust of egotism' and tells of '. . . the subtlety of the ego of man. It is the Tempter (the subtle serpent of the mind) and the poor soul not entirely emancipated from its suggestions is deceived until entirely severed from all else save God.' In another passage He says, 'As long as the ego is subjected to carnal desires, sin and error continue'. And He promised that with assiduous effort, 'Man will become free from egotism; he will be released from the material world.' . . .*

Extracts from letters written on behalf of the beloved Guardian [Shoghi Effendi] *by his secretaries will be most helpful in clarifying certain of your questions. . . .*

Regarding the question you asked in your letter: The only people who are truly free of the 'dross of self' are the Prophets, for to be free of one's ego is a hallmark of perfection. We humans are never going to become perfect, for perfection belongs to a realm we are not destined to enter. However, we must constantly mount higher, seek to be more perfect.

The ego is the animal in us, the heritage of the flesh which is full of selfish desires. By obeying the laws of God, seeking to live the life laid down in our teachings, and prayer and struggle, we can subdue our egos. We call people 'saints' who have achieved the highest degree of mastery over their ego. . . .

The believers, as we all know, should endeavour to set such an example in their personal lives and conduct that others will feel impelled to embrace a Faith which reforms human character. However, unfortunately, not everyone achieves easily and rapidly the victory over self. What every believer, new or old, should realize is that the Cause has the spiritual power to re-create us if we make the effort to let that power influence us, and the greatest help in this respect is prayer. We must supplicate Bahá'u'lláh to assist us to overcome the failings in our own characters, and also exert our own will power in mastering ourselves.
(To an individual believer dated 27 January 1945)

Regarding the points you refer to in your letter: the complete and entire elimination of the ego would imply perfection – which man can never completely attain – but the ego can and should be ever- increasingly subordinated to the enlightened soul of man. This is what spiritual progress implies. (To an individual believer dated 14 December 1941) . . . "[39]

And Shoghi Effendi reassures us:

"As we almost never attain any spiritual goal without seeing the next goal we must attain still beyond our reach, he urges you, who, have come so far already on the path of spirituality, not to fret about the distance you still have to cover! It is an indefinite journey, and, no doubt in the next world the soul is privileged to draw closer to God than is possible when bound on this physical plane" [40]

No one in current literature on spirituality has, to my knowledge, treated the subject of the ego in such depth and with such clarity as Eckhart Tolle in his book, *A New Earth*. [41] There is so much in Tolle's writings that can not be covered here, but I will share some general ideas with the purpose of clarifying patterns of behavior that we may identify in ourselves and therefore increase the level of our awareness. He explains that our general use of the term "I" is a misperception, an error, an illusion. We use "I" to refer to ourselves, but this reference is not who we are really are. Knowing that this is an illusion is a good thing because the ego can only survive if we take it seriously, that is, if we think it's our reality.[42] Here is how this "I" or our ego develops. At an early age, we begin to label things as "mine" so we begin our identification with things that will continue for a lifetime. In our consumer society, we are bombarded by advertisements telling us that we'll be happy if we buy certain products. We keep buying more and more because we are satisfied only for a short time and keep wanting more and it is a way to fill up our lives and find ourselves.[43] Having is equated with being and the more someone has, the more he is recognized for his possessions and it becomes the way he sees himself.[44] This is one identification. A story told by Taherzadeh of the king and the dervish comes to mind in discussing identification with possessions. People who are rich can be attached to their possessions but sometimes those with few possessions can become attached to their things:

"Once there was a king who had many spiritual qualities and whose deeds were based on justice and loving-kindness. He often envied the dervish who had renounced the world and appeared to be free from the cares of this material life, for he roamed the country, slept in any place when night fell and chanted the praises of his Lord during the day. He lived in poverty, yet

thought he owned the whole world. His only possessions were his clothes and a basket in which he carried the food donated by his well-wishers. The king was attracted to this way of life.

Once he invited the well-known dervish to his palace, sat at his feet and begged him for some lessons about detachment. The dervish was delighted with the invitation. He stayed a few days in the palace and whenever the king was free preached the virtues of a mendicant's life to him. At last the king was converted. One day, dressed in the garb of a poor man, he left his palace in the company of the dervish. They had walked together some distance when the dervish realized that he had left his basket behind in the palace. This disturbed him greatly and, informing the king that he could not go without his basket, he begged permission to return for it. But the king admonished him, saying that he himself had left behind his palaces, his wealth and power, whereas the dervish, who had preached for a lifetime the virtues of detachment, had at last been tested and was found to be attached to this world—his small basket." [45]

Continuing our discussion of Tolle's ideas, other identifications include our gender, our nationality, our religion and our careers. We also identify ourselves with our roles, for example, wife, mother and career woman, as well as our knowledge, opinions and our memories. The ego also identifies with the body and in our North American society we are told by the media that our physical appearance and level of fitness are extremely important and contribute to a positive sense of self. Unfortunately, individuals who are bombarded by messages of what constitutes positive physical attributes may feel unworthy in this respect and may not perceive themselves accurately. An example of this is the all too common experience of a woman who feels that she is overweight and starves herself to the point of anorexia. She is totally identifying with the mind in its faulty perception of her body. How we all suffer as we age if good looks and physical strength are crucial to our identity! Of course, we need to take care of our bodies throughout our lives but our physical appearance does not need to be equated with who we are. Someone can also have a problem with his body such as a physical disability and identify with the disability, receiving lots of attention for his struggles. [46]

Tolle explains that all these identifications become part of our thought patterns and we identify strongly with those thoughts and feelings, with this *"incessant stream of mind"*,[47] this compulsive, repetitive thinking. We have all experienced being unable to shut down our minds, often filled with worrying thoughts and persistent thoughts, preoccupied with one thing and unable to let it go. We are unaware that our mind possesses us.

Our thoughts and emotions are fleeting and we are continuously struggling to survive and protect our egos. And to maintain our "I" thoughts we need an opposite, an "other" who is often perceived as the enemy. Fault-finding, name-calling and complaining about an "other" or a situation serves to strengthen the ego because it feels superior to others – you are right and the person or situation is wrong.[48] Facts become distorted and opinions are confused with facts; an event and a reaction to an event become the same leading to resentment, bitterness, becoming defensive and then taking things personally and becoming offended. When this behavior becomes habitual, the person is not generally conscious of doing it. We often see this mind-set in nations who are in conflict, often based on religious differences.[49] The mind-set is *"We are right and they are wrong."* [50] War, greed and exploitation are collective manifestations of the ego.[51] We need to be clear that it is the ego in others, not their true identities, that is ruling them and also be conscious that our egos don't use those misperceptions of others to strengthen themselves in taking a superior position and reacting with anger and condemnation to what they perceive as the enemy.

The ego wants fame and recognition, according to Tolle.[52] The ego also needs attention from others. Interestingly enough, Tolle explains that a shy person who fears attention still has ego, an ambivalent ego that wants but also fears attention.[53] This person worries that he may get negative attention in the form of criticism or disapproval. So the fear of attention supersedes the need for attention. Shyness is generally equated with a negative self-concept and feelings of inadequacy but any sense of self is ego, positive or negative. Someone with a positive self-concept may secretly feel he may not be "good enough" and someone with a negative self-concept may desire to be greater than others. Egos who can't get praise get attention in other ways by playing certain roles.[54] Being a victim is a common role, seeking sympathy or pity. Once someone identifies himself as a victim, he wants it to continue and if no- one will listen to his story he can tell it to himself over and over and feel self-pity, maintaining the identify of someone who is treated unfairly. It is a dangerous place to be in terms of our spiritual development. 'Abdu'l-Bahá says,

"Despair, both here and hereafter, is all you will gain from self-indulgence..."[55]

Susan Gammage is a Bahá'í who does Life Coaching inspired by the Bahá'í Writings. She wrote several articles on her blog [56] about self-pity. I will summarize some points she has made. A clear understanding of how self-pity manifests itself may help us find our way to God and a more spiritual lifestyle.

She states that self-pity is feeling sorry for ourselves, feeling wronged, feeling like a failure, not owning up to faults and not accepting responsibility for one's life. Common phrases that identify self-pity include: *"What's the point in trying?" "I can't do anything right." "Nobody appreciates all the things I'm doing." "Why do bad things always happen to me?"* [57]

Susan explains that self-pity generally arises from something that happens in our lives and our lower nature then decides that we don't matter and life won't get better. It can start if someone breaks our heart.[58] Some of us may not have felt loved by a parent. We think that we were supposed to be loved so we come to the conclusion that there must be something wrong with us. Some people experience adversity that doesn't make sense to them and they give up, losing the opportunity to grow and overcome challenges in their lives. If we don't try to take some steps and practice coping with situations in our lives, we don't have a sense of hope, difficulties become insurmountable and we don't change. Self-pity reinforces doing nothing to change our situation. We look outside ourselves for the source of our problems and struggles and we give our power away. And if we do some things that we feel are good and they are not acknowledged, bitterness and resentment can creep in.[59] Self-pity keeps us from believing in ourselves, in others and in God. We feel inferior and unworthy and certainly don't believe that we have been created noble, as Bahá'u'lláh has told us.[60] We may all feel unworthy before God but when we face our situations and take responsibility and ask God for assistance, we can move on. We may wallow in self-pity to get attention, for example, for sickness. We do not want love or friendship – we want to complain and be a "martyr" to gain sympathy. Self-pity traps us in the prison of self. We see only the negative and blame everyone else and we pull others down with us. We cannot help someone mired in self-pity. They can't listen if you try to bolster them up and point out the positive in their lives. And we are told that we shouldn't take on the suffering of others. Shoghi Effendi states:

"We cannot bear the burden of suffering of others, and we should not try to." [61]

Susan Gammage feels that all we can do is to encourage them to turn to God in prayer, to ask for His guidance and to read the Bahá'í Writings.[62] Taking some action for themselves is also a good plan. We can pray for them and accompany them in their actions. We can do something with them that entices them to laugh and have fun and we can be their partner in doing some service for others. But, as she says, self-pity is a veil between us and God.[63] We need to stop feeling sorry for ourselves. 'Abdu'l-Bahá provides the answer:

"Do not feel sorry; do not brood over the loss; do not sit down depressed; do not be silent; but, on the contrary, day and night be engaged in the commemoration of thy Lord in the greatest joy and gladness." [64]

So it would seem to me that awareness is the first step. And we need to be patient and understand that it is a process, taking it day by day, learning to be thankful and grateful for our progress and for our station as creatures of God.

Shoghi Effendi advices us to move on:

He urges you to grasp firmly the teachings of our Faith, the love of your family and many Bahá'í friends, to put the past behind entirely, realising that it can do you no more harm; on the contrary, through changing you and making you spiritually aware, this very past can be a means of enriching your life in the future! He will certainly ardently pray for your happiness, your victory over yourself, and that you may become an exemplary and active Bahá'í. [65]

Susan Gammage's descriptions of self-pity match a helplessness that we can also see in society today. We can see people who are self-indulgent; who experience paralysis and an inability to cope; perceive themselves as victims; are full of fear; take pride in their suffering and resist any assistance; manipulate others to create guilty feelings, resorting to anger when it doesn't work.

Before leaving this topic, I want to outline some characteristics of the ego from Wayne Dyer's book, *Your Sacred Self.* [66] Again, I am providing more description of our lower nature in action to help us identify it when it arises. Wayne Dyer has written many books about finding our spiritual path. In this book, he comments that the ego is our long-time companion and it doesn't want to be abandoned. It keeps us separate from others and considers itself better. The ego thrives on our feelings of incompleteness and fear of inadequacy. It keeps its attention on self and is reluctant to give to others or be aware of others' needs and wants. The ego is threatened by any service to others but it can get the focus back on itself by pushing for acknowledgement for its contributions. It is important for the ego to dominate others and guarantee conflict. Winning the conflict demonstrates its superiority. Dyer quotes Tagore in his book:

"He whom I enclose with my name is weeping in this dungeon. I am ever busy building this wall all around; as this wall goes up into the sky day by day I lose sight of my true being in its dark shadow. I take pride in this great wall, and I plaster it with dust and sand lest a least hole should be left in this name; and for all the care I take I lose sight of my true being." [67]

Marianne Williamson has written many books based on *A Course in Miracles*, a study program of spirituality. In *The Gift of Change* she gives a graphic description of the relative unimportance of the ego, our *"small and separated self"*. [68] She states that identifying with the ego is *"like looking at a hangnail and thinking, 'That's who I am."* [69] It is not our real self but an imposter. It masquerades as who we are but really it's the *"embodiment of our own self-hatred. It is the power of our own minds turned against us, pretending to be our champion yet in reality undermining all our hopes and dreams. The ego is a delusional splinter that has cut itself off from our larger spiritual reality. It sets up a parallel mental kingdom in which it sees itself as different and special, always justified in keeping the rest of the world at bay. Seeing ourselves as separate, we subconsciously attract and interpret circumstances that seem to bear out that belief. That delusional kingdom is hell on earth."* [70]

I recently experienced what I feel portrays the epitome of such a captive life in an individual. These characteristics are espoused in Wayne Dyer's *Your Sacred Self*:

1) The excessive use of self-reference to bring conversations back to oneself.
2) Preoccupation with one's own concerns, accomplishments, daily experiences
3) A desire to win a conversation rather than sharing; using the time while someone is talking to get prepared instead of listening and then responding
4) Giving in order to get rather than being able to give unconditionally
5) Ordering people around and demanding perfection from family and coworkers
6) Correcting others' mistakes in public to demonstrate the superiority of one's knowledge
7) Withholding intimacy if people don't meet your expectations and blaming others for a lack of closeness
8) Building one's self up by boasting and bragging
9) Setting up standards that others should conform to
10) Dictating to others who may be younger, smaller or less educated.
11) Taking a hurry-up approach to life with no time for quiet or contemplation

C.S. Lewis was an influential Christian author. In his unusual book, *The Screwtape Letters*, [71] his main character was an assistant to the Devil. From the letters, I identified a few common characteristics that have not been mentioned specifically yet, that we may see in ourselves and others when we are following our ego. One is the fact of not enjoying something for its own sake, but *"in order to make clever remarks about it"* [72] to friends. Another example relates to the comment, *"my time is my own"* [73] as if people consider time their personal birthright. They start each day *"as the lawful possessor of 24 hours"* [74] then of course they feel that it's unfair that they have to devote so much of it to their work. Another interesting example C.S. Lewis mentions is the *"horror of the Same Old Thing."* [75] We tend to need change and crave novelty in our lives. Lewis also mentions the difficulty in acquiring and maintaining virtues in his humorous example of someone who, noticing that he is becoming humble, reflects about it and *"almost immediately"* pride appears. [76] This little volume is a fitting testament to the dangers of being under the influence of ego and its all-pervasive influence.

Now, having established the need to make great efforts to subdue our material natures on an everyday basis and to strive ever more deeply to attain our potential as spiritual beings, let us examine the things that obstruct us from reaching our potential, referred to in the Bahá'í Writings as veils and barriers. A clear understanding of these veils and barriers may increase our awareness and indicate the extent of the battle we need to wage if we are truly to become spiritual beings. For this topic I am relying on Taherzadeh's discussion of some of Bahá'u'lláh's untranslated Tablets.[77] Bahá'u'lláh explains that we have all the attributes of God within us but we are veiled from them.[78] Veils identified by Taherzadeh include tradition, knowledge, prejudice, materialism, wealth, power, attachment to the mortal world, attachment to the spiritual world, attachment to the Kingdom of Names and the veil of ego. But I would also include the veils of vain imaginings, pride; unkindness; dishonesty and deceitfulness; association with the unrighteous; fear and anxiety; addictions and dependencies (the need to have something on a daily basis); anger; pettiness; hate; greed, all the things that exist in the material world and come in between us and God and His Manifestation.

Taherzadeh addresses the first set of veils mentioned in his discussion of Bahá'u'lláh's book *Mathnavi*.[79] Bahá'u'lláh tells us that we need to make efforts to purify our hearts so that God's powers and attributes become manifested in us, that it is possible to reflect God's light.[80] But we need to see with a new eye (a spiritual eye) and hear with a new ear (a spiritual ear). If our eyes are fixated on the material world and if the veils prevent the inner eye from perceiving the true reality, we will not see His Revelation and if our ears are turned to the voices of the wayward we won't hear the celestial melodies. Bahá'u'lláh says:

"O Son of Dust!

Blind thine eyes, that thou mayest behold My beauty; stop thine ears, that thou mayest hearken unto the sweet melody of My voice; empty thyself of all learning, that thou mayest partake of My knowledge; and sanctify thyself from riches, that thou mayest obtain a lasting share from the ocean of My eternal wealth. Blind thine eyes, that is, to all save My beauty; stop thine ears to all save My word; empty thyself of all learning save the knowledge of Me; that with a clear vision, a pure heart and an attentive ear thou mayest enter the court of My holiness." [81]

And 'Abdu'l-Bahá reiterates the need to lift these veils in two of his talks:

"My prayer for you is that your spiritual faculties and aspirations may daily increase, and that you will never allow the material senses to veil from your eyes the glories of the Heavenly Illumination." [82]

"The bestowals of God which are manifest in all phenomenal life are sometimes hidden by intervening veils of mental and mortal vision which render man spiritually blind and incapable, but when those scales are removed and the veils rent asunder, then the great signs of God will become visible, and he will witness the eternal light filling the world. The bestowals of God are all and always manifest. The promises of heaven are ever present. The favors of God are all-surrounding, but should the conscious eye of the soul of man remain veiled and darkened, he will be led to deny these universal signs and remain deprived of these manifestations of divine bounty. Therefore, we must endeavor with heart and soul in order that the veil covering the eye of inner vision may be removed, that we may behold the manifestations of the signs of God, discern His mysterious graces and realize that material blessings as compared with spiritual bounties are as nothing." [83]

Bahá'u'lláh indicates that the eye of our spirit obtains its light from God and it is therefore shameful to allow it to turn towards a stranger.[84] Taherzadeh reminds us that Bahá'u'lláh said that *"only a tiny impediment can prevent the eyes from seeing, the ears from hearing and hearts from understanding."* [85]

Now let's consider the veil of tradition, as depicted in the Bahá'í Writings:

"Verily I beseech God, with all humbleness, to remove the covering from thine insight and to show unto thee His great signs, and to make thee a banner of guidance, severed from all else save Him, enkindled with the

fire of His love, engaged in His praise and apprehending the realities of things; so that thou mayest see with thine eyes, hear with thine ears and not imitate any of the fathers and ancestors; have perception in the matter of thy Lord, for the people are in dark veils." [86]

One of Bahá'u'lláh's most important Teachings is the independent investigation of truth.

"Nay, each must see with his own eyes, hear with his own ears and investigate independently in order that he may find the truth." [87]

It occurs to me that Bahá'ís may think that they believe in and follow this principle in their lives because they have researched the Bahá'í Faith and determined that it is the religion that they want in their lives, that they are therefore immune to this veil. But I believe that Bahá'ís still need to continue to investigate their Faith and the wealth of knowledge available to them. And they may also have traditions borne of their family and their cultures and the religious traditions with which they were raised that bar them from others and their own spiritual development.

Another veil related to this is literal interpretation:

"One of the veils is literal interpretation. To penetrate the inner significances a mighty effort is needed." [88]

We know that the followers of every religion have rejected the next Manifestation because of literal interpretation of the prophecies about His Coming. We must not look to a literal interpretation of the Bahá'í Writings because as we are told, this Revelation is like an ocean *"in whose depths are concealed innumerable pearls"*. It is our responsibility to *"strive to attain the shores of this ocean . . ."* and *"partake of . . . benefits."* [89]

In Chapter 3 there are more quotations from the Writings that indicate the myriad of meanings contained in the Word of God.

Another veil which keeps people from recognizing the latest Manifestation is knowledge. Being knowledgeable can lead to pride and a man may not realize it and may then close his eyes to truth. Knowledge is a *"veritable treasure for man"* [90] and it is important for us to gain knowledge in this world but it is a *"veil of glory"* if someone becomes *"vain and egotistical"* [91] as a result of gaining knowledge. Taherzadeh tells the story of Mirza Abu'l-Fadl who had to learn to become detached from his knowledge.[92] This is a very short summary of his words. Mirza Abu'l-Fadl was a well-known scholar and head of one of the theological colleges in Tehran. One of his students asked for assistance in responding to arguments from some of the Bahá'ís he knew. The first Bahá'í he encountered was a lowly blacksmith who utterly confounded him with his arguments. In another meeting with an uneducated Bahá'í, every subject he addressed or objections he brought forth were discussed in a simple manner and in such a way that Mirza Abu'l-Fadl could not argue the validity of the Bahá'í's arguments. The knowledge of God and the ability to understand religious truth are not dependent upon any academic education, but are bestowed by God to an individual whose heart is pure. An esteemed scholar may not discover these inner realities unless he can become detached from his knowledge. Many times Mirza Abu'l-Fadl was confounded by the simple proofs given to him regarding the Faith by uneducated men and he became humbled by his inability to refute their arguments. He experienced great intellectual struggle before he attained certitude and embraced the Bahá'í Faith. He could not reject the truth before him but his heart needed to be affected. At one point he felt that Bahá'u'lláh needed to demonstrate a miracle so that he would be satisfied. Bahá'u'lláh did not perform a miracle but he prophesized the demise of the Sultan and it happened. The Sultan was assassinated. After a year of meeting with the Bahá'ís and investigating Bahá'u'lláh's Writings, he lost his pride and became a pure spirit. I will tell another story about Mirza Abu'l-Fadl later in the chapter.

Another veil is prejudice.

Quoting from 'Abdu'l-Bahá's talks and Writings:

"Beware of prejudice; light is good in whatsoever lamp it is burning. A rose is beautiful in whatsoever garden it may bloom. A star has the same radiance if it shines from the east or the west." [93]

Bahá'u'lláh has rent the veil of prejudice and superstition which was stifling the souls of men. [94]

"I hope that you will turn with unclouded eyes towards the Sun of Truth, beholding not the things of earth, lest your hearts be attracted to the worthless and passing pleasures of the world; let that Sun give you of His strength, then will not the clouds of prejudice veil His illumination from your eyes!" [95]

"Then the awning of the mercy of thy Lord will be hoisted and those souls who are free from the filth of prejudice, contradictions and presumption

and are filled with a love that imparts affinity, intimacy, affection, meekness and humbleness will be sheltered under it." [96]

And from Shoghi Effendi:

Of these spiritual prerequisites of success, which constitute the bedrock on which the security of all teaching plans, Temple projects, and financial schemes, must ultimately rest, the following stand out as preeminent and vital, which the members of the American Bahá'í community will do well to ponder. Upon the extent to which these basic requirements are met, and the manner in which the American believers fulfill them in their individual lives, administrative activities, and social relationships, must depend the measure of the manifold blessings which the All-Bountiful Possessor can vouchsafe to them all. These requirements are none other than a high sense of moral rectitude in their social and administrative activities, absolute chastity in their individual lives, and complete freedom from prejudice in their dealings with peoples of a different race, class, creed, or color. [97]

Wealth can also be a veil that keeps us from God and a spiritual life.[98] Of course, it is part of man's nature to be attracted to material things. Wealth and attachment to the things of this world are great tests for man. Here are two passages from Bahá'u'lláh's Hidden Words on this theme:

"O Son of Being!

Busy not thyself with this world, for with fire We test the gold, and with gold We test Our servants. [99]

"O Son of Man!

Thou dost wish for gold and I desire thy freedom from it. Thou thinkest thyself rich in its possession, and I recognize thy wealth in thy sanctity therefrom. By My life! This is My knowledge, and that is thy fancy; how can My way accord with thine?" [100]

Taherzadeh explains that there is nothing wrong with wealth as long as it does not come between man and God.[101] Detachment is the criterion for nearness to God. Man can possess all the material things of this world and live a life of luxury and still be detached from them. Bahá'u'lláh states in many Tablets that it is man's greatest achievement to detach himself from all save God. We can only gain faith and progress in our path to God to the extent that we are detached from the world. God has given us His creation so that we can enjoy the beautiful things of life and the little luxuries and this does not mean that we are attached. But we know that they are transitory and we shouldn't place our affection on them and certainly not allow things to possess us. In Chapter 5, I discuss the subject of detachment in detail.

Another veil is that of vain imaginings. 'Abdu'l-Bahá says:

"Praise thou God that thou hast found thy way into the Kingdom of Splendors, and hast rent asunder the veil of vain imaginings, and that the core of the inner mystery hath been made known unto thee. This people, all of them have pictured a god in the realm of the mind, and worship that image which they have made for themselves. And yet that image is comprehended, the human mind being the comprehender thereof, and certainly the comprehender is greater than that which lieth within its grasp; for imagination is but the branch, while mind is the root; and certainly the root is greater than the branch. Consider then, how all the peoples of the world are bowing the knee to a fancy of their own contriving, how they have created a creator within their own minds, and they call it the Fashioner of all that is – whereas in truth it is but an illusion. Thus are the people worshipping only an error of perception." [102]

So it seems to me that we need to be careful not to barter our spiritual destiny for material trifling. Bahá'u'lláh says:

"O SON OF MAN!
Many a day hath passed over thee whilst thou hast busied thyself with thy fancies and idle imaginings. How long art thou to slumber on thy bed? Lift up thy head from slumber, for the Sun hath risen to the zenith, haply it may shine upon thee with the light of beauty." [103]

What are vain imaginings? Here is a clarification of all this term encompasses from the website: http://onenessbecomesus.com.

"This topic of "Vain Imaginings" is more than what it appears on the surface. Not only is it simply believing or imagining something to be true that is not; such as the earth being flat or at the center of the solar system; it pervades our whole state of perception, our assumptions; how we reason and how we "see" the world to be. Culture, Authority, upbringing, personal likes and dislikes, style and degree of education; all this and more have a combined profound impact on an individual's viewpoint and life issues.
... All humanity fails to truly understand the many levels of meaning woven into Revealed Scripture. People become attracted to what authority figures

confidently say is true. They become enamored with the fellowship of likeminded believers, which, in turn, only reinforces what they themselves, are led to believe. Instead of independently investigating, the majority remains content to simply accept what they are taught. Perhaps this can have a temporary seemingly positive effect but the long-term result is truly being captivated. It is imagined needs are met by participating in religious or social events, involvement with competition (whether it be business, gaming, dating etc.), or being entertained (and influenced) by the world of the media, and commercialism. Yet, it is evident many are looking for something more; more than the status quo; more than what is deemed 'satisfying' or 'successful'. It is also imagined, in our arrogance, that we are capable of apprehending, of grasping, Divine Truth; that somehow, God neatly fits into a package of teachings or tradition. Of course, it is surely unarguably true that God and creation are infinitely beyond our ability to understand. The best we can do is study Inspired Scripture and, independent of what we have been taught, seek for ourselves what best enables us to serve God and Man."

Again I will now rely on Taherzadeh's explanation in this paragraph. Attachment to this world and attachment to the next world are barriers between man and God.[104] Our deeds are praiseworthy to God when performed only for His love, not for a reward in our next life, only for God's sake. This seems easy to comprehend but we are so used in our society to expect rewards for our actions and to focus on our own interests that when we consider our spiritual life, we may look for what primarily satisfies our needs. We may join a religion for our own spiritual assistance but this is not a pure motive. Religion is about love and lovers don't have ulterior motives or care only for themselves. Everything is for the beloved. It is natural for us because of our animal natures and tendency to be selfish, to reach for what will benefit us. So we add our Faith to our accumulated treasures, considering it on par with all else we possess and we expect benefits as we would from other possessions. Our Faith is supposed to serve us and bring us joy. This idea and practice is attachment to this mortal world and is not part of the law of creation. God does not send down His Revelation to satisfy our selfish interests. It is quite the opposite – we are asked to arrange our lives so that we serve the Revelation. If we are able to follow His Teachings unselfishly with pure motives, our lives will be blessed because we will acquire the attributes of God within our souls. Anyone seeking the attributes of God to satisfy his ego will be deprived of God's grace. A true believer turns to the Manifestation and puts aside his interests and his own desires to seek His good pleasure and, in so doing, he attains virtues and powers. In actual fact a believer is the only one who experiences genuine happiness and acquires the qualities of God. He recognizes the glory of the new Revelation and understands that man's primary reason for being is to serve it. This is the only pure motive for being a follower of God's faith.

A third attachment that is mentioned by Bahá'u'lláh and explained by Taherzadeh's *The Revelation of Bahá'u'lláh*, is related to the "Kingdom of Names". [105] All created things manifest the names or attributes of God, including the world of mankind'; in our human world, they appear as the "Kingdom of Names" and man can often become attached to them.

"The Pen of the Most High is unceasingly calling, and yet, how few are those that have inclined their ear to its voice! The dwellers of the kingdom of names have busied themselves with the gay livery of the world, forgetful that every man that hath eyes to perceive and ears to hear cannot but readily recognize how evanescent are its colours." [106]

In many Tablets Bahá'u'lláh warns His followers about becoming the "bond-slaves" of the Kingdom of Names.[107] As Taherzadeh explains, God's attributes are given names in this world and every name reveals the characteristics of the attribute. Generosity is one of God's attributes and it is manifested in humans. But a person has to be careful because he may be proud of being known to be generous. It makes him happy when others acknowledge it and unhappy if others ignore it. The same applies to all the attributes of God that man can manifest. The other difficulty is that man usually neglects to ascribe such positive attributes as generosity to God rather than himself and his ego is therefore exalted. Or someone may become famous for his knowledge and he feels proud of the publicity, of hearing the mention of his name and being admired.

Taherzadeh goes on to explain that at the present time, society is exerting a damaging influence on man's soul.[108] Rather than emphasizing the importance of service and of making sacrifices, society teaches man to be proud of his accomplishments. He is taught while young to compete with others and surpass them to feel self-important and successful, and even powerful. But The Revelation of Bahá'u'lláh teaches the opposite of this, centering on the need for man to be humble and self-effacing and therefore to become detached from the Kingdom of Names. 'Abdu'l-Bahá was our example of detachment. He did not want publicity for Himself and disliked being photographed. He only consented to photographs because newspaper reporters and the friends wanted them. Bahá'u'lláh conferred exalted titles upon 'Abdu'l-Bahá, which described His lofty station but He chose the title of 'Abdu'l-Bahá (Servant of Bahá) and urged the friends to use this name:

"My name is 'Abdu'l-Bahá. My qualification is 'Abdu'l-Bahá. My reality is 'Abdu'l-Bahá. My praise is 'Abdu'l-Bahá. **Thraldom to the Blessed Perfection is my glorious and refulgent diadem, and servitude to all the human race my perpetual religion . . . No name, no title, no mention, no commendation have I, not will ever have, except 'Abdu'l-Bahá. This is my longing. This is my greatest yearning. This is my eternal life. This is my everlasting glory."** [109]

Taherzadeh states that severance from the Kingdom of Names may be the hardest task and it may require a lifetime of struggle.[110] If we can only internalize the concept that our virtues are not ours but instead are manifestations of God's attributes, we will then turn away from the Kingdom of Names and become the epitome of humility, bestowing the heavenly perfections upon the world. This is truly the station to which we should aspire!

We are naturally weak, ignorant, powerless and imperfect. All the virtues and goodness come from God. So man should see himself as ignorant, far from perfect, caught in the clutches of self and passion and it should not depress or hurt him when others point out these characteristics in him because of course they are part of his nature.[111] Instead he should be grateful to them for letting him know how far he is from demonstrating his spiritual qualities and also disappointed in himself, taking refuge with God and begging protection from his animal nature.

I have already written extensively about the ego, both from the Bahá'í Writings and from other sources that may help us to be aware more clearly of the ego at work. Taherzadeh explains that the ego is a veil that comes between us and God. Every veil prevents man from drawing closer to God. Bahá'u'lláh exhorts us to burn away all traces of the self to the extent that he forgets the the very idea of self and the word "I".[112] This is a profound teaching of Bahá'u'lláh. Exalting oneself, celebrating one's name and wanting fame go against creation's plan. These characteristics hinder us from receiving God's bounties. He may seem to be an amazing success in the material world, but such a man has failed in fulfilling the purpose of his creation. When someone achieves genuine greatness, he recognizes how helpless, unworthy and impotent he really is. And if he attains to a high station in terms of true learning, he discovers his ignorance. Then he can manifest God's attributes within himself and can impart these attributes to others.

Aziz'u'lláh Misbah, one of the great scholars of the Faith, said, *"To relinquish one's love for oneself and to destroy every trace of self, is a proof that one has comprehended the meaning of existence and the purpose of life. The difference between true knowledge and formal learning is that the former creates lowliness and humility within the soul; the latter drives irrationally towards the search for glory and exaltation."* [113]

Now I am going to relate a different story about Mirza Abu'l-Fadl who had truly attained a station of true knowledge, relying once more on Taherzadeh's volumes. This story clearly demonstrates the state of selflessness to which we should aspire. He had just returned from the United States where he was helping the Bahá'ís to learn more about their Faith. He was seated with 'Abdu'l-Bahá and a number of American Bahá'ís in Akka. The Bahá'ís praised him for his help in the United States and they reported on many things he had done – teaching the Faith to many, defending the Cause against those who were its adversaries, and helping the believers to build a united Bahá'í community. They continued for some time in their praise of Mirza Abu'l-Fadl and he became more and more dejected and unhappy until he began to weep loudly. The Bahá'ís couldn't understand and even thought that perhaps they hadn't praised his efforts enough. 'Abdu'l-Bahá explained that they had hurt him by giving him so much praise because MIrza Abu'l-Fadl thought of himself as utter nothingness and truly believed he was unworthy of mention, let alone praise. He was really an example for the Bahá'ís to follow as he never used "I" in referring to anything of merit that he had done.[114] Also, he recognized that the station of Bahá'u'lláh was so exalted and he was completely unworthy that he could not ask permission to be in His presence. So he did not ever meet Bahá'u'lláh. But he did meet 'Abdu'l-Bahá and spent ten months with him, demonstrating such self-effacement and humility in front of all the other Bahá'ís. He prayed deeply and with great weeping at the thought of God's greatness and his utter nothingness. 'Abdu'l-Bahá referred to him as *"a supreme exemplar for the Bahá'ís to follow, a lamp of this Cause, the light of guidance, a brilliant star and a billowing ocean."* [115]

So let me summarize. Why do we need to work hard to develop our spiritual natures? If we are selfish, all other virtues will fade and we will grow worse. All efforts will lead to nothing. We will be in despair. We will not grow spiritually and we will not be of service to others, because we will see no need to extend to others. We will not be worshipping the divine reality, not involved in the world of mankind. We will not grow spiritually and will be unprepared for the next world. We will be veiled, shut out and deprived of eternal grace. And we will not be pleasing

God. The soil of self doesn't produce growth. The soul is debased and wallowing in the mire of the material world. We don't attract blessings and don't benefit. The soul is not fed and becomes atrophied and the ego becomes bloated. If we don't shine, others don't see the light. We may have doubts about our faith. It is so easy to fall into our "natural" way, to move away from our spiritual self, to lose our spiritual perception and begin thinking in an egoic manner. That is why we need concrete steps to keep moving us towards His Holy Threshold and that is what the following chapters will address.

We cannot leave this chapter on the insistent self without the concept of materialism and its effect on us and our spiritual growth. The information presented here is taken from the book *Materialism: Moral and Social Consequences* by Dr. Abdu'l-Missagh Ghadirian, a Bahá'í writer, psychiatrist and professor at McGill University, Faculty of Medicine, who has also published extensively in academic journals.

Materialism can be defined as a *"desire to consume and acquire material goods. It is often bound up with a value system which regards social status as being determined by affluence as well as the perception that happiness can be increased through buying, spending, and accumulating material wealth."* [116] Ghadirian explains that for some individuals material consumption alone is the goal of their lives, for others acquiring and possessing wealth gives pride and pleasure and is equated with happiness and for others their possessions determine their success and their claim to fame.[117] But in every case individuals who pursue material things remain dissatisfied because there are always more and better goods to be had and they compare themselves to others and want more. And achieving a material goal doesn't lead to a lasting feeling of contentment because nothing can quench the eternal thirst for more. Added to the acquisition of the material and the constant pursuit of more is the need for instant gratification. But things can never be as fast as we'd like or good enough.[118] Material consumption also includes leisure activities so that the pursuit of pleasure and self-indulgence in pleasure-seeking are embraced as values.[119] Ghadirian refers to materialism as a *"state of mind and a lifestyle some people consciously choose- but many more possess it, unaware of its consuming effect on their daily life."* [120] Our materialistic culture is also marked by permissiveness and freedom, by doing one's thing without any regard to consequences, a view that what feels good right now is worth doing. As a society this results in social and environmental problems that are not addressed.[121] Rewards become more important than the intrinsic nature of activities.[122] Altruism – the ability to sacrifice one's own interests for that of others, a sense of responsibility for one's fellow-man, caring, empathy and compassion are destroyed. Relationships suffer because people with an interest in material things have little loyalty to others and the nature of relationships is one of conflict, competition and strong emotion, rather than joy, trust and cooperation.[123]

'Abdu'l-Bahá describes it well:

"Today all the peoples of the world are indulging in self-interest and exert the utmost effort and endeavor to promote their own material interests. They are worshipping themselves and not the divine reality, nor the world of mankind. They seek diligently their own benefit and not the common weal. This is because they are captives of the world of nature and unaware of the divine teachings, of the bounty of the Kingdom and of the Sun of Truth." [124]

It would seem to me, then, that this aggressive, materialistic culture seems to be invading every segment of society and we are facing moral bankruptcy. As Ghadirian points out, the standards that guided human beings for centuries are steadily losing their influence and have been replaced by the value of rampant materialism, of an ideology built on extreme relativism and of the demands of unbridled individualism.[125] If we are also unsure or thirsting for something to assuage an inner emptiness, we may turn to wealth and material things to feel better about ourselves.[126] Possession brings power and a sense of entitlement and self-importance which breeds a sense of superiority.[127] A quick Google search defines a sense of entitlement as a belief that one is deserving of or entitled to certain privileges which others believe should be obtained through effort, and unrealistic expectations of favorable treatment or automatic compliance with one's expectations. It is the prioritization of one's needs above the needs of others because of a sense of elevated self-importance and self-absorption. Many believe that a sense of entitlement exists in societies like North America where few people have experienced want. We've developed an appetite for the finer things of life and the sense of being able to have whatever we want whenever we want it.

Children are directly exposed to materialism through socialization and modelling and it is readily internalized. As the Universal House of Justice points out:

"In the current state of society, children face a cruel fate. Millions and millions in country after country are dislocated socially. Children

find themselves alienated by parents and other adults whether they live in conditions of wealth or poverty. This alienation has its roots in a selfishness that is born of materialism that is at the core of the godlessness seizing the hearts of people everywhere." [128]

Ghadirian notes that the need and craving for money and possessions is promoted through marketing.[129] If this publicity is reinforced by peers or parents, it is internalized as lifestyle. Consumer behavior tends to be automatic.[130] People tend not to think about their needs and level of consumption and the advertising industry takes advantage of this lack of mindfulness. We're too busy to stop to examine the bombardment of messages thrown at us. The materialistic lifestyle and attachment to things consumes so much of one's life that it leaves no room for reflecting on life beyond it.[131] The more people are drawn into such behavior, the less they become interested in other aspirations or alternatives with more meaning.

Shoghi Effendi clearly points this out:

"Indeed, the chief reason for the evils now rampant in society is the lack of spirituality. The materialistic civilization of our age has so much absorbed the energy and interest of mankind that people in general do no longer feel the necessity of raising themselves above the forces and conditions of their daily material existence. There is not sufficient demand for things that we should call spiritual to differentiate them from the needs and requirements of our physical existence. The universal crisis affecting mankind is, therefore, essentially spiritual in its causes. The spirit of the age, taken on the whole, is irreligious. Man's outlook on life is too crude and materialistic to enable him to elevate himself into the higher realms of the spirit." [132]

'Abdu'l-Bahá said:

"The fountain of divine generosity is gushing forth, but we must have thirst for the living waters. Unless there be thirst, the salutary waters will not assuage." [133]

So to me all the effort that goes into satisfying the body affects the mind – it is in a whirlwind of thoughts in an attempt to get satisfaction but at some point the pleasure centres are saturated and it will become meaningless. Even if a life seems comfortable in the eyes of others, there is a sense of emptiness and a general discontent and even despair that can only be satisfied through spirituality.

This is described very well by 'Abdu'l-Bahá:

"Every soul seeketh an object and cherisheth a desire, and day and night striveth to attain his aim. One craveth riches, another thirsteth for glory and still another yearneth for fame, for art, for prosperity and the like. Yet finally all are doomed to loss and disappointment. One and all they leave behind them all that is theirs and empty-handed hasten to the realm beyond, and all their labours shall be in vain. To dust they shall all return, denuded, depressed, disheartened and in utter despair. ... [134]

Shoghi Effendi described the challenges of living in such a materialistic environment *"pervading all departments of life ... the crass materialism, which lays excessive and ever-increasing emphasis on material well-being, forgetful of those things of the spirit on which alone a sure and stable foundation can be laid for human society. It is this same cancerous materialism born originally in Europe, carried to excess in the North American continent, contaminating the Asiatic peoples and nations, spreading its ominous tentacles to the borders of Africa, and now invading its very heart, which Bahá'u'lláh in unequivocal and emphatic language denounced in His Writings, comparing it to a devouring flame and regarding it as the chief factor in precipitating the dire ordeals and world-shaking crises that must necessarily involve the burning of cities and the spread of terror and consternation in the hearts of men. ... It is this same all-pervasive, pernicious materialism against which the voice of the Center of Bahá'u'lláh's Covenant* ['Abdu'l-Bahá] *was raised, with pathetic persistence, from platform and pulpit, in His addresses to the heedless multitudes. ..."* [135]

He also emphasized how difficult it is for us to struggle against the forces of materialism:

"The gross materialism that engulfs the entire nation at the present hour; the attachment to worldly things that enshrouds the souls of men; the fear and anxieties that distract their minds; the pleasure and dissipations that fill their time, the prejudices and animosities that darken their outlook, the apathy and lethargy that paralyze their spiritual faculties -- these are among the formidable obstacles that stand in the path of every world-be warrior in the service of Bahá'u'lláh, obstacles which he must battle against to surmount in his crusade for the redemption of his own countrymen." [136]

"People are so markedly lacking in spirituality these days that the Bahá'ís should consciously guard themselves against being caught in

what one might call the undertow of materialism and atheism, sweeping the world these days. Skepticism, cynicism, disbelief, immorality and hard-heartedness are rife, and as friends are those who stand for the antithesis of all these things they should beware lest the atmosphere of the present world affects them without their being conscious of it." [137]

Shoghi Effendi predicted that the "cancer of materialism" would be devastating to society. Ghadirian explains that cancer is the result of abnormal cells multiplying and proliferating out of control.[138] They grow differently from normal cells because they don't have limits; they multiply and invade their neighbouring cells until they form a malignant tumor, which can then spread to other parts of the body. Cancer develops in a quiet manner but eventually destroys. Materialism also grows in an abnormal manner and expands and destroys insidiously. Every one of us can potentially develop this insidious behavior or, in contrast, evolve into spiritual beings. Cancer also grows. We may be unaware of cancer growing within us until it has overtaken our bodies. Materialism similarly can grow in us and we are unaware of the changes in ourselves.

Ghadirian cites studies that have indicated an obsession with money and possessions can be like an addiction and that our brains with such an obsession react differently from those who perceive money as a necessity for material well-being.[139] In studying the reactions of the pleasure centre of the brain through magnetic resonance imaging, researchers discovered that monetary gain mimics the use of cocaine and stimulates the release of dopamine, a "feel-good" neurotransmitter. Being overly attached to financial gain may lead to addiction because of the recurring stimulation of the pleasure centre of the brain.

It seems then extremely important for us to cultivate an awareness of how we can be affected by materialism, to ever strive to regard the world as an illusion, *"a show, vain and empty, a mere nothing, bearing the semblance of reality"* [140] *"a mirage rising over the sands, that the thirsty mistaketh for water"*, [141] *"worth as much as the black in the eye of a dead ant"* [142]

"By the righteousness of God! The world, its vanities and its glory, and whatever delights it can offer, are all, in the sight of God, as worthless as, nay even more contemptible than dust and ashes." [143]

"Arise, O people, and, by the power of God's might, resolve to gain the victory over your own selves, that haply the whole earth may be freed

and sanctified from its servitude to the gods of its idle fancies – gods that have inflicted such loss upon, and are responsible for the misery of, their wretched worshipers. These idols form the obstacle that impedeth man in his efforts to advance in the path of perfection. We cherish the hope that the Hand of Divine power may lend its assistance to mankind, and deliver it from its state of grievous abasement." [144]

REFERENCES

1 'Abdu'l-Bahá, *Selections from the Writings of 'Abdu'l-Bahá* (Wilmette, IL: Bahá'í Publishing Trust, 1997), 206,p. 256
2 Honnold, Annamarie, *Vignettes from the Life of 'Abdu'l-Bahá* (Oxford: George Ronald, 1982), 3, p. 10
3 Shoghi Effendi, *The Compilation of Compilations* Vol.II, prepared by the Universal House of Justice 1963-1990 (Victoria, Australia: Bahá'í Publications, 1991), 1318, 10 December 1947, p. 18-19
4 Honnold, Annamarie, *Vignettes from the Life of 'Abdu'l-Bahá*, 4, p.10
5 Shoghi Effendi, *The Compilation of Compilations* Vol.II, 1318, 10 December 1947, p. 18
6 'Abdu'l-Bahá, *Paris Talks* (London: Bahá'í Publishing Trust, 1995), The Two Natures in Man, [2], p. 60
7 Taherzadeh, Adib, *The Revelation of Bahá'u'lláh* Vol. 3 (Oxford: George Ronald, 1988), p.35
8 Bahá'u'lláh, *The Summons of the Lord of Hosts* (Haifa, Israel: Bahá'í World Centre, 2002), Lawh-i-Rais, [23] p.170)
9 Bahá'u'lláh, *The Hidden Words* (Wilmette, IL: Bahá'í Publishing Trust, 2003), Persian no. 40, p.36
10 Bahá'u'llah, *Gleanings from the Writings of Bahá'u'lláh* (Wilmette, IL: Bahá'í Publishing Trust, 1976), CLIII, p. 326-327
11 Taherzadeh, Adib, *The Revelation of Bahá'u'lláh* Vol. 3, p. 35
12 Esslemont, Dr. J.E. *Bahá'u'lláh and the New Era* (Wilmette, IL: Bahá'í Publishing Trust, 1980), p.195
13 Bahá'u'lláh, *Gleanings from the Writings of Bahá'u'lláh*, XLIII, p. 94
14 Bahá'u'lláh, *The Hidden Words*, Persian no. 72, p.47
15 Gautama Buddha, http://www.goodreads.com/quotes
16 'Abdu'l-Bahá, *Tablets of the Divine Plan* (Wilmette, IL: Bahá'í Publishing Trust, 1977), April 11, 1916, p. 42-43
17 'Abdu'l-Bahá, *Foundations of World Unity* (Wilmette, IL: Bahá'í Publishing Trust, 1968), Continuity of Revelation, p. 110-111
18 'Abdu'l-Bahá, *The Promulgation of Universal Peace* (Wilmette, IL: Bahá'í Publishing Trust, 1982), 25 July 1912, [1], p. 244
19 Ibid., 6 July 1912, [3], p. 226
20 'Abdu'l-Bahá, *Foundations of World Unity*, Spiritual Springtime, p. 64
21 Bahá'u'lláh, *Gleanings from the Writings of Bahá'u'lláh*, CXLVII, p. 316
22 'Abdu'l-Bahá, *Tablets of 'Abdu'l-Bahá 'Abbás* Vol. I (New York: Bahá'í Publishing Committee, The National Spiritual Assembly of the Bahá'ís of the United States, 1980), p. 141
23 'Abdu'l-Bahá, *Paris Talks*, Spiritual Aspiration in the West, [7], p. 72
24 Ibid., There can be no True Happiness and Progress without

Spirituality, [7], p. 108
25 'Abdu'l-Bahá, *Tablets of 'Abdu'l-Bahá 'Abbás* Vol. III (New York: Bahá'í Publishing Committee, The National Spiritual Assembly of the Bahá'ís of the United States, 1980) p. 673-674
26 'Abdu'l-Bahá, *Tablets of 'Abdu'l-Bahá 'Abbás* Vol. I, p. 135-136
27 Ibid, p. 42
28 'Abdu'l-Bahá, *Selections from the Writings of 'Abdu'l-Bahá*, 35, p. 71-72
29 'Abdu'l-Bahá, *Divine Philosophy* (Boston, MA: Tudor Press, 1918), p. 134
30 'Abdu'l-Bahá, *The Secret of Divine Civilization* (Wilmette, IL: Bahá'í Publishing Trust, 1990), p.64
31 'Abdu'l-Bahá, *Divine Philosophy*, p. 131-132
32 'Abdu'l-Bahá, *Selections from the Writings of 'Abdu'l-Bahá*, 35, p.70
33 'Abdu'l-Bahá, *The Promulgation of Universal Peace*, 11 June 1912, [4], p. 185
34 Shoghi Effendi, *Principles of Bahá'í Administration* (London: Bahá'í Publishing Trust, 1976), p. 87-88
35 Taherzadeh, Adib, *The Revelation of Bahá'u'lláh* Vol. 3, p. 396
36 'Abdu'l-Bahá, *The Promulgation of Universal Peace*, 26 May 1912, [3], p. 148
37 'Abdu'l-Bahá, *Bahá'í World Faith-*'Abdu'l-Bahá Section (Wilmette, IL: Bahá'í Publishing Trust, 1976), p. 371-372
38 'Abdu'l-Bahá, *Bahá'í Scriptures* (New York: Bahá'í Publishing Committee, 1928), 936, p. 487
39 The Universal House of Justice, *Child Abuse, Psychology and Knowledge of Self* (1985, December 2), 20
40 Shoghi Effendi, *The Unfolding Destiny of the British Bahá'í Community* (London: Bahá'í Publishing Trust, 1981), 3rd March 1955, p.461
41 Tolle, Eckhart, *A New Earth, Awakening to your Life's Purpose* (New York, New York: Penguin Group (USA), 2005)
42 Ibid., p. 27-28
43 Ibid., p. 35-36
44 Ibid., p. 45
45 Taherzadeh, Adib, *The Revelation of Bahá'u'lláh* Vol.1 (Oxford: George Ronald, 2001), p. 76-77
46 Tolle, Eckhart, *A New Earth*, p. 49-51
47 Ibid., p. 30
48 Ibid., p. 59-61
49 Ibid., p. 68-71
50 Ibid., p. 72
51 Ibid., p. 73
52 Ibid., p. 85
53 Ibid., p. 86
54 Ibid., p. 87
55 'Abdu'l-Bahá, *The Secret of Divine Civilization*, p. 105
56 Gammage, Susan, http://susangammage.com/blog

57 Ibid. (2010, December 18), How Do We Know If We've Fallen Victim To Self Pity?
58 Ibid. (2010, December 18), Where Does Self Pity Come From?
59 Ibid. (2010, December 19), The Effects of Self Pity
60 Bahá'u'lláh, *The Hidden Words*, Arabic no. 22, p.9
61 Shoghi Effendi, *Lights of Guidance* (New Delhi, India: Bahá'í Publishing Trust, 1994), 791, p. 237
62 Gammage, Susan, http://susangammage.com/blog (2010, December 19), 16 Steps to Overcome Self Pity
63 Ibid. (2010, December 19), Why Should We Stop Feeling Sorry For Ourselves?
64 'Abdu'l-Bahá, *Tablets of 'Abdu'l-Bahá 'Abbás* Vol.I, p. 133
65 Shoghi Effendi, *The Unfolding Destiny of the British Bahá'í Community* (London: Bahá'í Publishing Trust, 1981), 8th April 1948, p. 450
66 Dyer, Dr. Wayne W., *Your Sacred Self* (New York: HarperPaperbacks, 1995)
67 Ibid., p. 179
68 Williamson, Marianne, *The Gift of Change* (New York: HarperCollins Publishers, 2004), p. 27
69 Ibid., p. 27
70 Ibid., p. 28
71 Lewis, C.S., *The Screwtape Letters* (San Francisco: HarperSanFrancisco, 2001)
72 Ibid., p. 64
73 Ibid., p. 112
74 Ibid.
75 Ibid., p. 135
76 Ibid., p. 64
77 Taherzadeh, Adib, *The Revelation of Bahá'u'lláh* Vol. 2 (Oxford: George Ronald, 1988)
78 Ibid., p. 31
79 Ibid., p. 32-44
80 Ibid., p. 31
81 Bahá'u'lláh, *The Hidden Words*, Persian no. 11, p.25
82 'Abdu'l-Bahá, *Paris Talks*, The Evolution of the Spirit, [41], p. 94
83 'Abdu'l-Bahá, *The Promulgation of Universal Peace*, 4 May 1912, [8], p. 90
84 Taherzadeh, *The Revelation of Bahá'u'lláh* Vol. 2, p. 31
85 Ibid., p. 32
86 'Abdu'l-Bahá, *Tablets of 'Abdu'l-Bahá 'Abbás* Vol. I, p. 63
87 'Abdu'l-Bahá, *Divine Philosophy*, p. 25
88 Ibid., p. 29
89 Bahá'u'lláh, *Gleanings from the Writings of Bahá'u'lláh*, CLIII, p. 326
90 Bahá'u'lláh, *Tablets of Bahá'u'lláh* (Haifa, Israel: Research Department of the Universal House of Justice, 1978), p. 52

91 Taherzadeh, Adib, *The Revelation of Bahá'u'lláh* Vol. 2, p. 33
92 Taherzadeh, Adib, *The Revelation of Bahá'u'lláh* Vol. 3, p. 91-104
93 'Abdu'l-Bahá, *Divine Philosophy*, p. 25
94 'Abdu'l-Bahá, *Paris Talks*, The Light of Truth is Now Shining upon the East and West, [7],p. 34
95 Ibid.,The Clouds that Obscure the Sun of Truth, [8], p. 44
96 'Abdu'l-Bahá, *Tablets of 'Abdu'l-Bahá 'Abbás* Vol. II, (New York: Bahá'í Publishing Committee, The National Spiritual Assembly of the Bahá'ís of the United States, 1980), p. 424
97 Shoghi Effendi, *The Advent of Divine Justice* (Wilmette, IL: Bahá'í Publishing Trust, 1971), Spiritual Prerequisites, p. 18
98 Taherzadeh, Adib, *The Revelation of Bahá'u'lláh* Vol. 2, p. 280
99 Bahá'u'lláh, *The Hidden Words*, Arabic no. 55, p.16
100 Ibid., Arabic no. 56, p.16-17
101 Taherzadeh, Adib, *The Revelation of Bahá'u'lláh* Vol. 2, p. 34-35
102 'Abdu'l-Bahá, *Selections from the Writings of 'Abdu'l-Bahá*, 24, p. 53-54
103 Bahá'u'lláh, *The Hidden Words*, Arabic no. 62, p.18
104 Taherzadeh, Adib, *The Revelation of Bahá'u'lláh* Vol. 2, p. 36-38
105 Ibid., p. 39
106 Bahá'u'lláh, *Gleanings from the Writings of Bahá'u'lláh*, XCVI, p. 195-196
107 Taherzadeh, Adib, *The Revelation of Bahá'u'lláh* Vol. 2, p. 40 108 Ibid., p. 40-41
109 Shoghi Effendi, *The World Order of Bahá'u'lláh* (Wilmette, IL: Bahá'í Publishing Trust, 1982), p. 139
110 Taherzadeh, Adib, *The Revelation of Bahá'u'lláh* Vol. 2, p. 42
111 Ibid., p. 43
112 Ibid., p. 43-44
113 Ibid., p. 44
114 Ibid., p. 45
115 Taherzadeh, Adib, *The Revelation of Bahá'u'lláh*, Vol. 3, p. 106
116 See http://em/wikipedia.org/wiki/Economic%20Materialism
117 Ghadirian, Abdu'l-Missagh, M.D., *Materialism, Moral and Social Consequences* (Oxford: George Ronald), p. 5
118 Ibid., p. 27
119 Ibid., p. 17
120 Ibid., p.2
121 Ibid., p. 65-66
122 Ibid., p. 11
123 Ibid., p. 65
124 'Abdu'l-Bahá, *Selections from the Writings of 'Abdu'l-Bahá*, 68, p. 103-104
125 Ghadirian, Abdu'l-Missagh, M.D., *Materialism, Moral and Social Consequences*, p. 134-135

126 Ibid., p. 49
127 Ibid., p. 79
128 The Universal House of Justice, *Message to the Bahá'ís of the World, Ridvan 2000*, p. 8
129 Ghadirian, Abdu'l-Missagh, M.D., *Materialism, Moral and Social Consequences*, p. 10
130 Ibid., p. 18-19
131 Ibid., p. 26
132 Shoghi Effendi, *The Compilation of Compilations* Vol.II, 1762, 8 December 1935, p. 238
133 'Abdu'l-Bahá, *The Promulgation of Universal Peace*, 16 June 1912, [1], p. 195
134 'Abdu'l-Bahá, *Selections from the Writings of 'Abdu'l-Bahá*, 176, p. 204
135 Shoghi Effendi, *Citadel of Faith: Messages to America 1947-1957* (Wilmette, IL: Bahá'í Publishing Trust, 1980), America Passing through Crisis, p. 124-125
136 Shoghi Effendi, Ibid., The Individual Bahá'í Must Arise, p. 149
137 Shoghi Effendi, *Lights of Guidance*, 1842, p. 542
138 Guadirian, Abdu'l-Missagh, M.D., *Materialism, Moral and Social Consequences*, p. 136
139 Ibid., p. 70
140 Bahá'u'lláh, *Gleanings from the Writings of Bahá'u'lláh*, CLIII, p. 328
141 'Abdu'l-Bahá, *Selections from the Writings of 'Abdu'l-Bahá*, 157, p. 186
142 Bahá'u'lláh, *Epistle to the Son of the Wolf* (Wilmette, IL: Bahá'í Publishing Trust, 1979), p. 56
143 Bahá'u'lláh, *Gleanings from the Writings of Bahá'u'lláh*, CXXXIX, p. 304
144 Ibid., XLIII, p. 93

Chapter 2
Turning to God

Chapter 2
Turning to God

Now it's time to explore how we can make concentrated efforts to allow our higher natures to supercede our selfish inclinations and to live more fully in the spiritual realm. Because the writings of the Bahá'í Faith provide a wealth of information about the "tools" we need to live a spiritual life and because they provide the answers for the conditions of the world today, I will quote extensively from them and from Bahá'í writers who have delved into the Message of Bahá'u'lláh. Other resources will be included with the aim of increasing our understanding of the subject at hand.

We will first examine the concept of prayer in some depth: the need for prayer and its benefits, obstacles to prayer and how to pray. I could also have included meditation in this chapter because prayer and meditation are so closely intertwined. As Gail Sheehy, the well-known author of the book, *Passages*, related to stages in our lives indicates, "To pray without meditation is like calling up God to tell Him your problem and hanging up before you get the answer."[1] But we will concentrate on meditation in the next chapter.

Our spiritual destiny depends upon our connection to God. 'Abdu'l-Bahá explains, *"It is incumbent upon thee to turn to the Kingdom of God and to pray, supplicate and invoke during all times because this is the means by which thy soul shall ascend upward to the apex of the gift of God."* [2]

Shoghi Effendi elaborates on this. (Shoghi Effendi was the Guardian of the Bahá'í Faith, great-grandson of Bahá'u'lláh and authorized interpreter of His Teachings.)

... The core of religious faith is that mystic feeling which unites man with God. This state of spiritual communion can be brought about and maintained by means of meditation and prayer. And that is the reason why Bahá'u'lláh has so much stressed the importance of worship. It is not sufficient for a believer merely to accept and observe the teachings. He should, in addition, cultivate the sense of spirituality which he can acquire chiefly by means of prayer. The Bahá'í Faith, like all other Divine religions, is thus fundamentally mystic in character. Its chief goal is the development of the individual and society, through the acquisition of spiritual virtues and powers. It is the soul of man which has first to be fed. And this spiritual nourishment prayer can best provide ... The

believers . . . should, therefore, fully realize the necessity of praying. For prayer is absolutely indispensable to their inner spiritual development, and this . . . is the very foundation and purpose of the Religion of God. ³

Taherzadeh points out that it is natural for us to turn to God in prayer.⁴ We are like plants turning toward the sun. The sun provides the light and warmth the plant needs to grow and the plant naturally stretches in the sun's direction. 'Abdu'l-Bahá tells us:

"There is nothing sweeter in the world of existence than prayer. Man must live in a state of prayer. The most blessed condition is the condition of prayer and supplication. Prayer is conversation with God. The greatest attainment or the sweetest state is none other than conversation with God. It creates spirituality, creates mindfulness and celestial feelings, begets new attractions of the Kingdom and engenders the susceptibilities of the higher intelligence . . . While man prays he sees himself in the presence of God. If he concentrates his attention he will surely at the time of prayer realize that he is conversing with God . . . Prayer and supplication are so effective that they inspire one's heart for the whole day with high ideals and supreme sanctity and calmness. One's heart must be sensitive to the music of prayer. He must feel the effect of prayer. He must not be like an organ from which softest notes stream forth without having consciousness of sensation in itself." ⁵

Nathan Rutstein, a Bahá'í writer and educator who has written extensively about spirituality, states that *"prayer is a sacred rite that is absolutely essential to the spiritual development process. It is a ladder to the Kingdom, a God-given aid to help us to discover, release and develop our reality or true self."* ⁶ If we don't pray, we need to rely on our instincts to cope with life and we do not get divine assistance. And we don't make progress. Madeline and William Hellaby, also Bahá'ís, in their book on prayer stated in their book on prayer that we cannot rise above our materialistic society without developing the mystic feeling uniting us with God to fill our souls with the *"spirit of life"*.⁷ We have nothing to offer humanity if we don't receive spiritual nourishment through prayer.

In response to a question about prayer, 'Abdu'l-Bahá wrote:

"O thou spiritual friend! Thou hast asked the wisdom of prayer. Know thou that prayer is indispensable and obligatory and man under no pretext whatsoever is excused from performing the prayer unless he be mentally unsound, or an insurmountable obstacle prevent him. The

wisdom of prayer is this: That it causeth a connection between the servant and the True One, because in that state man with all heart and soul turneth his face towards His Highness the Almighty, seeking His association and desiring His love and compassion. The greatest happiness for a lover is to converse with his beloved, and the greatest gift for a seeker is to become familiar with the object of his longing; that is why with every soul who is attracted to the Kingdom of God, his greatest hope is to find an opportunity to entreat and supplicate before his Beloved, appeal for His mercy and grace and be immersed in the ocean of His utterance, goodness and generosity " [8]

And again He said:

"As to thy question, 'Why pray? What is the wisdom thereof, for God has established everything and executes all affairs after the best order and He ordains everything according to a becoming measure and puts things in their places with the greatest propriety and perfection – therefore what is the wisdom in beseeching and supplicating and in stating one's wants and seeking help?' Know thou, verily, it is becoming of a weak one to beseech the glorious, bountiful One. When one supplicates to his Lord, turns to Him and seeks bounty from His ocean this supplication is by itself a light to his heart, an illumination to his sight, a life to his soul and an exaltation to his being.

Therefore during thy supplications to God and thy reciting 'Thy name is my healing,' consider how thy heart is cheered, thy soul delighted by the spirit of the love of God and thy mind attracted to the Kingdom of God! By these attractions one's ability and capacity increase. When the vessel is widened the water increaseth and when the thirst grows the bounty of the cloud becomes agreeable to the taste of man. This is the mystery of supplication and the wisdom of stating one's wants." [9]

The mystery of prayer and its power is demonstrated to us in this Writing of Bahá'u'lláh:

"Intone, O My servant, the verses of God that have been received by thee, as intoned by them who have drawn nigh unto Him, that the sweetness of thy melody may kindle thine own soul, and attract the hearts of all men. Whoso reciteth, in the privacy of his chamber, the verses revealed by God, the scattering angels of the Almighty shall scatter abroad the fragrance of the words uttered by his mouth, and shall cause the heart of every righteous man to throb. Though he may, at first, remain unaware of its effect yet the virtue of the grace vouchsafed unto him must needs sooner or later exercise its influence upon his soul. Thus have the mysteries of

the Revelation of God been decreed by virtue of the Will of Him Who is the Source of power and wisdom." [10]

And again, Bahá'u'lláh says:

"They who recite the verses of the All-Merciful in the most melodious of tones will perceive in them that with which the sovereignty of earth and heaven can never be compared. From them they will inhale the divine fragrance of My worlds -- worlds which today none can discern save those who have been endowed with vision through this sublime, this beauteous Revelation. Say: These verses draw hearts that are pure unto those spiritual worlds that can neither be expressed in words nor intimated by allusion. Blessed be those who hearken." [11]

'Abdu'l-Bahá said:

"Know that nothing will benefit thee in this life save supplication and invocation unto God, service in His vineyard, and, with a heart full of love, be in constant servitude unto Him."[12]

But how we pray, what motive and attitude we adopt in prayer are crucial. If we rely totally on the will of God, we will benefit most from prayer.

"Commit thyself to God; give up thy will and choose that of God; abandon thy desire and lay hold on that of God." [13]

We surrender and put ourselves in God's hands, beseeching His mercy, in order that His will becomes our will.

We say in the Long Obligatory Prayer: *"Behold me standing ready to do Thy will and Thy desire, and wishing naught else except Thy good pleasure. I implore Thee by the Ocean of Thy mercy and the Day-Star of Thy grace to do with Thy servant as Thou willest and pleasest . . . Whatsoever is revealed by Thee is the desire of my heart and the beloved of my soul. O God, my God! Look not upon my hopes and my doings, nay rather look upon Thy will that hath encompassed the heavens and the earth . . . I have desired only what Thou didst desire, and love only what Thou dost love.*[14]

And we are saying to God that whatever He bestows upon us we will accept with radiant acquiescence.

"In the highest prayer, men pray only for the love of God, not because they fear Him or hell, or hope for bounty or heaven . . . When a man

falls in love with a human being, it is impossible for him to keep from mentioning the name of his beloved. How much more difficult is it to keep from mentioning the Name of God when one has come to love Him ... The spiritual man finds no delight in anything save commemoration of God." [15]

The Báb was the Manifestation of God Who came before Bahá'u'lláh. These words of The Báb define the purity of motive needed for prayer to be acceptable to God:

"Worship thou God in such wise that if thy worship lead thee to the fire, no alteration in thine adoration would be produced, and so likewise if thy recompense should be paradise. Thus and thus alone should be the worship which befitteth the one True God. Shouldst thou worship Him because of fear, this would be unseemly in the sanctified Court of His presence, and could not be regarded as an act by thee dedicated to the Oneness of His Being. Or if thy gaze should be on paradise, and thou shouldst worship Him while cherishing such a hope, thou wouldst make God's creation a partner with Him, notwithstanding the fact that paradise is desired by men.

Fire and paradise both bow down and prostrate themselves before God. That which is worthy of His Essence is to worship Him for His sake, without fear of fire, or hope of paradise..." [16]

Shoghi Effendi comments on the experience of a worshipper:

"The true worshipper, while praying, should endeavour not so much to ask God to fulfil his wishes and desires, but rather to adjust these and make them conform to the Divine Will. Only through such an attitude can one derive that feeling of inner peace and contentment which the power of prayer alone can confer." [17]

As Rutstein explains, it is fitting to approach God and ask for His guidance and, in fact, we are lost without His help.[18] Many times we supplicate to God and ask Him to fulfil our wishes. Sometimes we are anxious about something and we end up bargaining with God. We are acknowledging His greatness and that He is in control of our lives, but we are also challenging His wisdom and power by begging Him to meet our request. Then we need to listen to the wisdom of these words:

"O Son of Spirit!

Ask not of Me that which We desire not for thee, then be content with what We have ordained for thy sake, for this is that which profiteth thee, if therewith thou dost content thyself." [19]

Rutstein points out that God understands our motives and subconscious desires and He may respond in a way that He feels is right for us.[20] The response may be a test or challenge. Once we have made a request, we don't need to keep asking God for His assistance. He knows what we are thinking before we are conscious of it. We need to let go, be content with His will, wait patiently for His answer and believe that it will be for the best.

Prayer that is an outpouring of our deep and abiding love for God and our appreciation of Him as the Supreme Creator is probably the "most profound expression of love a human being can express." [21] Taherzadeh states that praising God opens the channels of grace and we receive God's blessings.[22] But we must turn to God to receive His blessings. Otherwise we are *"deprived and spiritually starved"*. [23]

'Abdu'l-Bahá said:

"If the heart turns away from the blessings God offers how can it hope for happiness? If it does not put its hope and trust in God's Mercy, where can it find rest? O, trust in God! For His Bounty is everlasting, and in His Blessings, for they are superb. O, put your faith in the Almighty, for He faileth not and His goodness endureth forever! His Sun giveth Light continually, and the Clouds of His Mercy are full of the Waters of Compassion with which He waters the hearts of all who trust in Him. His refreshing Breeze ever carries healing in its wings to the parched souls of men! Is it wise to turn away from such a loving Father Who showers His blessings upon us, and to choose rather to be slaves of matter?" [24]

Bahá'u'lláh tells us, *"Love Me, that I may love thee. If thou lovest Me not, my love can in no wise reach thee, Know this, O servant."* [25]

If we investigate all religions we will find the message of the love of God. It seems to me that in the above passage, God is not saying to us that we have to love Him or He won't love us. We are always surrounded by God's love. But His love can not "reach" us unless we do our part and turn to Him, just as a plant must turn to the warmth of the sun or it will die. We will "die" also if we deprive ourselves of the rays of His love. We as a society need it desperately, now as never before because we are living in the depths of materialism and sunk in the mire of our attachments, forgetting our Source and therefore not reflecting His love. Bahá'u'lláh tells us:

"The essence of wealth is love for Me; whoso loveth Me is the possessor of all things, and he that loveth Me not is indeed of the poor and needy. This is that which the Finger of Glory and Splendour hath revealed." [26]

Many of our prayers contain words of thanksgiving as a reminder that we must always remember His bounties and approach Him in gratitude. 'Abdu'l-Bahá reminds us:

"Do you realize how much you should thank God for His blessings? If you should thank Him a thousand times with each breath it would not be sufficient, because God has created and trained you. He has protected you from every affliction and prepared every gift and bestowal. Consider what a kind Father He is ... He has given us a kind father and compassionate mother, ... refreshing water, gentle breezes and the sun shining above our heads. In brief, He has supplied all the necessities of life although we did not ask for any of these great gifts ...

... You must appreciate the value of this bounty and engage your time in mentioning and thanking the True One." [27]

Ruth Moffett, an American Bahá'í educator wrote a book on prayer in obedience to Shoghi Effendi's wish that she convey the importance of prayer to her fellow Bahá'ís. In her book she discusses the hindrances that keep us from attaining the presence of God through prayer. One of these is indifference in our hearts to the eternal. *". . . indifference to God is itself a torment . . ."* [28]

"Indifference breeds deterioration. Silence is the cause of retrogression. Thoughtlessness leads to forgetfulness. Passivity, inaction, produce oblivion. Consequently do ye not seek one moment of rest by day or by night. Nay, rather strive after composure of heart in the heaven of Unity." [29]

It occurs to me that indifference can often be a way of protecting ourselves from hurt, a long-held attitude or behavior that has worked for us in the past to keep us out of harm's way, at least we thought. It may not be a conscious thing. If we hold ourselves aloof a little from God, it may be a protection learned at some point in our lives. Or we may feel unworthy. Indifference must become spiritual attraction – love for God and genuine reaching out to Him in supplication and love for all of His creatures. Doubt is another hindrance mentioned by Moffett that may also be a protective device. If we are not quite sure about our Faith, we may hesitate, we may lack conviction. If we already doubt, then perhaps the behavior of some of our friends who profess to be spiritual and don't demonstrate it in their actions will test us and make us question our faith. And, as Moffett points out, if we are content to linger in this state, we will remain hesitant and will not resolve our doubts.[30] Bahá'u'lláh explains the consequences of doubt:

"Whoso hath not recognized this sublime and fundamental verity, and hath failed to attain this most exalted station [the recognition that 'He shall not be asked of His doings], the winds of doubt will agitate him, and the sayings of the infidels will distract his soul. He that hath acknowledged this principle will be endowed with the most perfect constancy . . . Such is the teaching which God bestoweth on you, a teaching that will deliver you from all manner of doubt and perplexity, and enable you to attain unto salvation in both this world and in the next." [31]

And He tells us:

"O FLEETING SHADOW!

Pass beyond the baser stages of doubt and rise to the exalted heights of certainty. Open the eye of truth, that thou mayest behold the veilless Beauty and exclaim: Hallowed be the Lord, the most excellent of all creators!" [32]

"And be not of those who doubt." [33]

And from The Bible:

"If any of you lack wisdom, let him ask of God, that giveth to all men liberally, and upbraideth not and it shall be given him. But let him ask in faith, nothing wavering. For he that wavereth is like a wave of the sea driven with the wind and tossed." [34]

At times we wander far from the right conduct and demonstrate waywardness, another of Moffett's "hindrances".[35] Bahá'u'lláh explains,

"It is the waywardness of the heart that removeth it far from God, and condemneth it to remoteness from Him." [36]

We also need steadfastness in order to approach God. It seems to me that it is common in our materialistic society to experience the hindrance of restlessness, as Moffett describes, to feel uneasy or unsure, searching for novelty and with our thoughts scattered in many directions.[37] We have to work hard and ask God daily for tranquility, its antidote. According to 'Abdu'l-Bahá, *"The greatest bestowal in the world of existence is a tranquil heart . . . This station is joy succeeded by joy, confidence after confidence and Paradise after Paradise."* [38]

Similarly, impatience deters us and is often reflected in irritation, a tendency towards petulance in relation to events and circumstances but it can develop into a habit of chronic complaint over small things that "poisons the entire system." [39] We can never attain spiritual perception without patience, according to Moffett.[40] In the Bahá'í Writings we are told, *"He, verily, shall increase the reward of them that endure with patience . . . Blessed are the steadfastly enduring, they that are patient under ills and hardships, who lament not over anything that befalleth them, and they who tread the path of resignation."* [41]

"It behooveth whosoever hath set his face towards the Most Sublime Horizon to cleave tenaciously unto the cord of patience, and to put his reliance in God, the Help in Peril, the Unconstrained." [42]

And Muhammad says:

"Therefore, remember me: I will remember you; and give me thanks and be not ungrateful. O ye who believe! Seek help with patience and with prayer, for God is with the patient." [43]

We are continuing our discussion of the hindrances to prayer that Moffett discusses in her book. Closely aligned with impatience is discontent, and dissatisfaction even when it is not possible to change things.[44] Acquiescence to God's will is the opposite of this hindrance. Or we may be irresolute in character and lack determination and will, so we need to learn decisiveness. And, of course, we need to guard against exalting our own selves as we strive towards the quality of selflessness and draw closer to God. As 'Abdu'l-Bahá tells us, *"The 'master-key' to self-mastery is self-forgetting. The road to the palace of life is through the path of renunciation."* [45]

And He advised us:

"Turn your faces away from the contemplation of your own finite selves and fix your eyes upon the Everlasting Radiance; then will your souls receive in full measure the Divine power of the Spirit and the blessings of the Infinite Bounty." [46]

The last hindrance mentioned by Moffett is ignorance.[47] Of course we are all ignorant about many things but we should not be satisfied to live in ignorance. We should strive to gain the knowledge of spiritual teachings and to immerse ourselves in the Word of God.

It is not always easy to set aside time to pray and it requires discipline on our part. It is so important because without prayer, it is difficult for us to leave behind our selfish desires and we can then make decisions based on self-interest.

'Abdu'l-Bahá says," *Man becomes a stone unless he continually supplicates to God. The heart of man is like a mirror which is covered with dust and to cleanse it one must continually pray to God that it may become clean. The act of supplication is the polish which erases all worldly desires."* [48]

Prayer does not come easily to many of us who have felt unworthy of conversation with God. Moffett feels that those who hesitate to pray are "standing in the station of pride" [49] or haven't realized their need for prayer or its great value. Hellaby tells us that if we don't feel "good enough" we may be really saying that we don't feel the need to change our habits and we then choose to hold ourselves back from God. [50] We remain wrapped in the veil of self and do not feel close to God, as Bahá'u'lláh tells us:

"O SON OF DESIRE!

The learned and the wise have for long years striven and failed to attain the presence of the All- Glorious; they have spent their lives in search of Him, yet did not behold the beauty of His countenance. Thou without the least effort didst attain thy goal, and without search hast obtained the object of thy quest. Yet, notwithstanding, thou didst remain so wrapt in the veil of self, that thine eyes beheld not the beauty of the Beloved, nor did thy hand touch the hem of His robe. Ye that have eyes, behold and wonder." [51]

It occurs to me that God can't take anything away from us if we don't let it go. Once we reach an understanding of our issues and the reasons for our behavior, we can then ask God to help us change. As Hellaby suggests, we need to humble ourselves totally and remove all traces of self and then we need to shake ourselves off and try and try again.[52] True repentance requires our ability to see our actions as wrong, *"to be struck by the sense of our wrong-doing"*, [53] to feel shame and then resolve to battle and eventually master it. Some people say they can't pray because it is too difficult for them to admit their wrong-doings and they know they can't pray to be forgiven if they are truly not repenting.[54] But how do we deal with our sins through prayer? We don't need to wallow in our wrong-doings but we need to bring ourselves to account each day.

"O SON OF BEING!

Bring thyself to account each day ere thou art summoned to a reckoning; for death, unheralded, shall come upon thee and thou shalt be called to give account for thy deeds." [55]

By noting the events of our days either by writing them out in a journal or reflecting upon them in our minds before bedtime, we can examine our behavior and determine where we stand from a spiritual viewpoint, in other words find examples of the insistent self and determine to do better. Rutstein devotes a chapter to this topic in his book, *A Way out of the Trap*. He explains the process in detail with some specific suggestions that are very beneficial. I highly recommend it. He feels that this is a way of purifying our hearts and helping us understand our behavior and gives us the knowledge and determination to make changes. It is important, according to Rutstein, that it be approached in a prayerful condition, so that we don't rationalize and make excuses for our actions (lower nature behavior) and so that it does not become an exercise in self-flagellation. Saying prayers beforehand is helpful. We always need to remind ourselves that we are noble beings trying to live up to a spiritual standard but we have shortcomings. We keep a spiritual focus and review our good actions and progress made. Then in our prayer sessions, we can express our gratitude to God for His assistance in helping us to make progress and ask for His guidance to continue helping us to cope with our difficulties.[56] And here is 'Abdu'l-Bahá's advice:

"Every day in the morning when arising you should compare today with yesterday and see in what condition you are. If you see your belief is stronger and your heart more occupied with God and your love increased and your freedom from the world greater then thank God and ask for the increase of these qualities. You must begin to pray and repent for all that you have done which is wrong and you must implore and ask for help and assistance that you may become better than yesterday so that you may continue to make progress." [57]

Hellaby recommends that the way to deal with our sins is to so fill our minds with our Lord so there's no room for thinking of sins.[58] We are then contemplating God's perfections rather than our faults. Bahá'u'lláh tells us:

"Remembrance of Me cleanseth all things from defilement" and asks us to *"remember My days"* and *"recall to mind My sorrows."* [59]

It is helpful to me to think of a sin as "missing the mark, an error in perception", a term used by some theologians these days. Perhaps this definition allows us to let go of some of our guilt and shame and see ourselves in a more forgiving light, particularly those, like me, who when we heard the word "sin" tended to "shrivel" in shame.

Perhaps, I feel, a lack of self-confidence may also be a reason why some resist a true communion with God. They feel inadequate in the sight of God because of the things they did or continue to do that plague them. Even the awareness of the power of prayer and the need for it in their lives, even their love for God, doesn't help them to turn regularly to Him in fervent prayer. Some of us grew up feeling that we were defective in some way, as I mentioned in my introduction. I believed that at some fundamental level I was not worthy of God's attention and to approach him humbly in prayer was not really possible. Thus a rote reading of prayers sufficed my prayer sessions. This was really a sense of false pride. Who was I to stand apart from My Creator who loves me and wants to help me? The awareness that God does love all of us is a big part of my healing journey and the realization that God has an impersonal, detached love for all life and my life is no more or less precious to Him than anyone else's allows me to experience a deep humility.

". . . Thou art the All-Bountiful, the overflowing showers of Whose mercy have rained down upon high and low alike, and the splendors of Whose grace have been shed over both the obedient and the rebellious . . ." [60]

We know that God is the All-Merciful, that He knows us as we are and loves us anyway, and understands how difficult it may be to progress spiritually in this materialistic society. We also know that we're human and prone to make mistakes but these mistakes help us to find our spiritual path. We need never be ashamed to admit our weaknesses and mistakes. And we are given prayers for forgiveness so that we can approach God in contrition and remorse.

I remember being on Bahá'í pilgrimage in Israel and listening to a talk. The speaker reminded her audience that we have all been chosen by God for our capacity and ability. We need to figure out what that is and pray for it to be developed. We are asked by 'Abdu'l-Bahá to develop our own spiritual qualities, to guide others and to train souls. But we need to lose our self, our insistent self! We need to use the prayers for forgiveness, clean our slate and stop focusing on our shortcomings. Who are we to decide how much God can forgive? We need to leave the past and ask God to help us move forward. We need to learn to forgive ourselves, to realize that not forgiving ourselves is holding back many of our efforts and that we need to know that God will forgive us over and over again, that His mercy is infinite.

"What outpouring flood can compare with the stream of His all-embracing grace, and what blessing can excel the evidences of so great and pervasive a mercy? There can be no doubt whatever that if for one moment the tide of His mercy and grace were to be withheld from the world, it would completely perish. For this reason, from the beginning

that hath no beginning the portals of Divine mercy have been flung open to the face of all created things, and the clouds of Truth will continue to the end that hath no end to rain on the soil of human capacity, reality and personality their favors and bounties. Such hath been God's method continued from everlasting to everlasting." [61]

But God knows our difficulty in forgiving ourselves and seeking His mercy:

"Glorified art Thou, O Lord my God. Every time I venture to make mention of Thee, I am held back by my mighty sins and grievous trespasses against Thee, and find myself wholly deprived of Thy grace, and utterly powerless to celebrate Thy praise. My great confidence in Thy bounty, however, reviveth My hope in Thee, and my certitude that Thou wilt bountifully deal with me emboldeneth me to extol Thee, and to ask of Thee the things Thou dost possess . . ." [62]

I urge my readers who are dealing with difficult issues in their life and therefore feel that they are blocked in their ability to reach out to God to seek professional help. Rutstein openly discusses his journey in *The Way out of the Trap.* This is in addition to turning to God in total selflessness and humility, Our Beloved who knows us as no one else can, and asking Him to release us from these burdens and to develop our true spiritual selves. We surrender our situation to God and ask God to save our lives. We do it for ourselves so that we can become "channels" for God's love to reach others and become more spiritually developed. We also do it for our fellow-humans, struggling to accept us with all our glaring shortcomings, and for our friends and family, and for those who will become attracted to a life of faith when they see us in our spiritual garment.

Let us now move on from this highly personal section of the chapter.

'Abdu'l-Bahá encourages us to say our prayers out loud:

". . . Why should it be necessary for him to repeat prayers aloud and with the tongue? One reason for this is that if the heart alone is speaking the mind can be more easily disturbed. But repeating the words so that the tongue and heart act together enables the mind to become concentrated. Then the whole man is surrounded by the spirit of prayer and the act is more perfect." [63]

But just repeating the prayers is not enough:

"Prayer and supplication are two wings whereby man soars toward the heavenly mansion of the True One. However, verbal repetition of prayer does not suffice. One must live in a perennial attitude of prayer. When man is spiritually free his mind becomes the altar and his heart the sanctuary of prayer. Then the meaning of the verse 'He will lift up from before his eyes the veil' will become fulfilled in man." [64]

We need to feel the prayers given to us by Bahá'u'lláh, The Báb and 'Abdu'l-Bahá and, according to Moffett, *"let the spiritual power of each word surround us as we dwell within the spirit of prayer"*.[65] Hellaby explains that we need to have love in our hearts and faith when we turn to God and reach out to Him in a state of humility and pure devotion, consecrating ourselves to Him with a pure heart with no malice towards another. So we need to let go of any irritations or anger, any feelings of being offended and, if we are in the wrong, to right that wrong so that we are not blocked from reaching God.[66] If we are not overcome by emotion when we pray, if we do not feel that closeness to God, we need to examine ourselves, try harder to move away from any self-centeredness, pride and immaturity, any absorption in our problems that hinders us from lifting our spirits to God, to put ourselves in His hands and ask Him to help us draw closer.[67]

"Waft, then, unto me, O my God and my Beloved, from the right hand of Thy mercy and loving- kindness, the holy breaths of Thy favors, that they may draw me away from myself and from the world unto the courts of Thy nearness and Thy presence. Potent art Thou to do what pleaseth Thee…" [68]

We need to develop a prayerful attitude:

"The prayerful attitude is attained by two means. Just as a man who is going to deliver a lecture prepares therefore and his preparation consists of certain meditations and notations, so the preparation for the prayerful attitude is detaching one's mind from all other thoughts save the thought of God at the time of prayer and then praying when the prayerful attitude shall be attained." [69]

Rutstein states that *"every thought that springs from a love for God is a prayer"*.[70] By considering every thought as a prayer we are aware of our connection to God and we become more confident and positive in our lives, despite any difficulties we have to face because we are sure of God's assistance no matter what happens and we feel secure in our *"divine sanctuary"*. [71] As we begin to make progress, we'll be better able to face and learn from tests so that eventually we'll reach the conclusion that our greatest mistake is to turn away from God.[72] We'll be ready to rely on Him no matter what difficulties or disappointments we face, no matter how inadequate we feel and the depth to which we sink spiritually. If we continue to reach out to God in all circumstances, we'll learn to turn to Him first and depend totally on Him. We have to believe that He will answer our prayers and provide the guidance we need. Maybe he will give us signs but even sincere souls praying ardently for assistance may miss the signs.[73] It occurs to me that if we are uncertain if something is a sign, we can ask God to confirm it somehow and explain that we're not too bright and we need more direction!

In the following story, 'Abdu'l-Bahá teaches a girl about prayer:

"One day a despondent little Jewish girl, all in black, was brought into the Master's presence. With tears flowing, she told Him her tale of woes: her brother had been unjustly imprisoned three years before – he had four more years to serve; her parents were constantly depressed; her brother-in-law, who was their support, had just died. She claimed the more she trusted in God the worse matters became. She complained, '. . . my mother reads the Psalms all the time; she doesn't deserve that God should desert her so. I read the Psalms myself, - the ninety-first Psalm and the twenty-third Psalm every night before I go to bed. I pray too.'

Comforting and advising her, 'Abdu'l-Bahá replied, 'To pray is not to read Psalms. To pray is to trust in God, and to be submissive in all things to Him. Be submissive, then things will change for you. Put your family in God's hands. Love God's will. Strong ships are not conquered by the sea, - they ride the waves. Now be a strong ship, not a battered one." [74]

Shoghi Effendi gave to Ruth Moffett five steps to use in prayer *"if we have a problem of any kind for which we desire a solution or wish help"*.[75]

"First Step. Pray and meditate about it. Use the prayers of the Manifestations as they have the greatest power. Then remain in the silence of contemplation for a few minutes.

Second Step. Arrive at a decision and hold to this. This decision is usually born during the contemplation. It may seem almost impossible of accomplishment but if it seems to be an answer to a prayer or a way of solving the problem, then immediately take the next step.

Third Step. Have determination to carry the decision through. Many fail here. The decision, budding into determination, is blighted and instead becomes a wish or a vague longing. When determination is born, immediately take the next step.

Fourth Step. Have faith and confidence that the power will flow through you, the right way will appear, the door will open, the right thought, the right message, the right principle, or the right book will be given to you. Have confidence, and the right thing will come to your need. Then, as you rise from prayer, take at once the fifth step.

Fifth Step. Act as though it had all been answered. And as you act, you, yourself, will become a magnet, which will attract more power to your being, until you become an unobstructed channel for the Divine Power to flow through you. Many pray but do not remain for the last half of the first step. Some who meditate arrive at a decision, but fail to hold it. Few have the determination to carry the decision through, and still fewer have the confidence that the right thing will come to their need. But how many remember to act as though it had all been answered? How true are those words – 'Greater than the prayer is the spirit in which it is uttered, but greater than the way it is uttered is the spirit in which it is carried out.'" [76]

In clarifying these 5 steps Shoghi Effendi indicated that they were only personal suggestions. He stated, **"The Master said guidance was when the doors opened after we tried. We can pray, ask to do God's will only, try hard, and then if we find our plan is not working out, assume it is not the right one, at least for the moment."** [77]

Rutstein feels that the most important thing is to schedule prayer and depend on it as we do on food and drink.[78] Dorothy Baker, an American Bahá'í, who served on her National Spiritual Assembly and became a "Hand of the Cause" (see introduction), stated that *"we cannot be anything but emaciated if we take it only spasmodically"*.[79] It is a necessity in our lives. I think that once we become aware that God is closer to us than our own hands and feet and we learn to turn to Him regularly, then prayer will become an integral part of our lives that we cannot live without because we cannot be far from Him.

Bahá'u'lláh commands us in the Kitab-i-Aqdas, the Book of Laws, **"Recite ye the verses of God every morn and eventide. Whoso faileth to recite them hath not been faithful to the Covenant of God and His Testament, and whoso turneth away from these holy verses in this Day is of those who throughout eternity have turned away from God."** [80]

And He says,

"At the dawn of every day he [the true seeker] should commune with God, and with all his soul persevere in the quest of his Beloved." [81]

This is 'Abdu'l-Bahá's guidance:

"When a soul rises in the morning from sleep, before everything else, he must commemorate the name of God in order that he may obtain spirituality and illumination." [82]

"Supplicate unto Him and beseech in the middle of the night and at early morn just as a needy and captive one beseeches. . . ." [83]

"Automatic, formalistic prayers which do not touch the core of the heart are of no avail. How sweet, how delicious, how satisfying, how spiritual is the prayer in the middle of the night! . . . While the majority of the people are fast asleep the adorer of the Ideal beloved is wakeful. All around him there is a rare and delicate silence, deep, airy, ethereal silence, calm, magical and subtle – and there is the worshiper, communing with nature and the Author of nature." [84] 'Abdu'l-Bahá also said: *"Often at night I do not sleep, and the thoughts of this world weigh heavily on my mind. I toss uneasily in my bed. Then in the darkness of the night I get up and pray – converse with God. It is most sweet and uplifting."* [85]

Moffett tells us that when we turn to God in prayer our thoughts should be clear cut, intense and sincere.[86] As Gilbert said in her popular novel *"Prayer is a relationship; half the job is mine. If I want transformation, but can't even be bothered to articulate what, exactly, I'm aiming for, how will it ever occur? Half the benefit of prayer is in the asking itself, in the offering of a clearly posed and well-considered intention. If you don't have this, all your pleas and desires are boneless, floppy, inert; they swirl at your feet in a cold fog and never lift."* [87]

Sincerity is a prerequisite for prayer. As Rutstein indicates, a beautifully worded prayer that does not come from a sincere heart does not constitute communion with God, whereas prayer given with few and crude words from a pure heart will receive blessings.[88]

'Abdu'l-Bahá says:

"... it is incumbent upon thee to be purely sincere, to turn to the holy Kingdom and to generously give the spirit in the cause of the Lord of Might." [89]

Secondly, the more we have faith, the more we will get results, as Bahá'u'lláh explains:

"It bestoweth wealth without gold, and conferreth immortality without death." [90]

'Abdu'l-Bahá emphasizes it:

". . . nothing shall be impossible to you if you have faith. . . . As ye have faith so shall your powers and blessings be." [91]

And Shoghi Effendi tells us to pray to Bahá'u'lláh:

"While praying it would be better to turn one's thoughts to the Manifestation as He continues, in the other world, to be our means of contact with the Almighty . . ." [92]

However, we can also turn to 'Abdu'l-Bahá or Shoghi Effendi:

"If you find you need to visualize someone when you pray, think of the Master. Through Him you can address Bahá'u'lláh. Gradually try to think of the qualities of the Manifestation, and in that way a mental form will fade out, for after all the body is not the thing. His Spirit is there and is the essential, everlasting element." [93]

"In regard to your question: we must not be rigid about praying; there is not a set of rules governing it; the main thing is we must start out with the right concept of God, the Manifestation, the Master ['Abdu'l-Bahá], *the Guardian* [Shoghi Effendi] *– we can turn, in thought, to any one of them when we pray. For instance you can ask Bahá'u'lláh for something, or, thinking of Him, ask God for it. The same is true of the Master or the Guardian. You can turn in thought to either of them and then ask their intercession, or pray direct to God. As long as you don't confuse their stations, and make them all equal, it does not matter much how you orient your thoughts."* [94]

Shoghi Effendi also gave us three conditions of prayer: concentration, purity of intention, and lastly, detachment from the outcome.[95]

We need to persevere in our efforts, according to 'Abdu'l-Bahá:

"Draw nigh unto God and persevere in communion with thy Lord so that the fire of God's love may glow more luminously in the heart, its heat

grow stronger and give warmth to that region and its sound reach the Supreme Concourse." [96]

And we need to listen to God, as well as talking to Him. Conversation has to go both ways. 'Abdu'l-Bahá has told us how to listen to God:

"We should speak in the language of heaven – in the language of the spirit – for there is a language of the spirit and heart. It is as different from our language as our own language is different from that of the animals, who express themselves only by cries and sounds.

It is the language of the spirit which speaks to God. When, in prayer, we are freed from all outward things and turn to God, then it is as if in our hearts we hear the voice of God. Without words we speak, we communicate, we converse with God and hear the answer . . . All of us, when we attain to a truly spiritual condition, can hear the Voice of God." [97]

Dorothy Baker gave many talks about prayer. She said in one of her talks, "Talk, listen to the inner silences. Hear the voice of God. Yearning opens the recesses of the heart . . ." [98]

And it is important to have privacy, to have quiet. The Báb explains:

"The reason why privacy hath been enjoined in moments of devotion is this, that thou mayest give thy best attention to the remembrance of God, that thy heart may at all times be animated with His Spirit, and not be shut out as by a veil from thy Best Beloved. Let not thy tongue pay lip service in praise of God while thy heart be not attuned to the exalted Summit of Glory, and the Focal Point of communion. Thus if haply thou dost live in the Day of Resurrection, the mirror of thy heart will be set towards Him Who is the Day-Star of Truth and no sooner will His light shine forth than the splendor thereof shall forthwith be reflected in thy heart " [99]

What about the length of our prayer sessions?

Bahá'u'lláh tells us:

"Take heed lest excessive reading and too many acts of piety in the daytime and in the night season make you vainglorious. Should a person recite but a single verse from the Holy Writings in a spirit of joy and radiance, this would be better for him than reciting wearily all the scriptures of God, the Help in Peril, the Self-Subsisting. Recite ye the verses of God in

such measure that ye be not overtaken with fatigue or boredom. Burden not your souls so as to cause exhaustion and weigh them down, but rather endeavour to lighten them, that they may soar on the wings of revealed verses unto the dawning-place of His signs. This is conducive to nearer access unto God, were ye to comprehend." [100]

Shoghi Effendi said to a believer who had been ill:

"We don't have to pray and meditate for hours in order to be spiritual." [101]

St. Augustine said, *"A short prayer pierceth heaven."* [102]

We do not have to say a long prayer and even saying "Alláh-u-Abhá" with joy is enough, according to Hellaby.[103] "Alláh-u-Abhá" is a phrase used by Bahá'ís which means "God is the Most-Glorious" and is referred to as "The Greatest Name". Shoghi Effendi advises:

"He feels more emphasis should be laid on the importance and power of prayer, including the use of The Greatest Name, but not over-emphasizing. It is the spirit behind the words which is really important." [104]

The repetition of the Greatest Name is one of Bahá'u'lláh's ordinances: *"It hath been ordained that every believer in God, the Lord of Judgement, shall, each day, having washed his hands and then his face, seat himself and, turning unto God, repeat 'Allah-u-Abha' ninety-five times. Such was the decree of the Maker of the Heavens when, with majesty and power, He established Himself upon the thrones of His Names . . .* [105]

Inasmuch as we do not become exhausted but are refreshed and joyful from our prayers, they can of course be as long as we want!

Because it does not come easily to pray, we are asked to say an obligatory prayer and given a time- frame for it. Hellaby noted that by using the obligatory prayer we create a *"ring of prayer"* [106] around the world at any one time. And in saying our obligatory prayer we demonstrate our obedience to God, as Bahá'u'lláh indicates:

"We, verily, have set forth all things in Our Book, as a token of grace unto those who have believed in God, the Almighty, the Protector, the Self-Subsisting. And we have ordained obligatory prayer and fasting so that all may by these means draw nigh unto God, the Most Powerful, the Well-Beloved. We have written down these two laws and expounded every irrevocable decree. We have forbidden men from following whatsoever might cause them to stray

from the Truth, and have commanded them to observe that which will draw them nearer unto Him Who is the Almighty, the All-Loving. Say: Observe ye the commandments of God for love of His beauty, and be not of those who follow in the ways of the abject and foolish." [107]

Many of the quotations from Bahá'u'lláh's and 'Abdu'l-Bahá's Writings on obligatory prayer refer both to obligatory prayer and fasting. We will consider the commandment of fasting in another chapter. 'Abdu'l-Bahá explains:

"Thou hast written concerning obligatory prayer. Such prayer is binding and mandatory for everyone. Most certainly guide all to its observance, because it is like a ladder for the souls, a lamp unto the hearts of the righteous and the waters of life from the garden of paradise. It is a clear duty prescribed by the All-Merciful, in the observance of which it is in no wise permissible to be dilatory or neglectful." [108]

It is important to obey God's Commands for us and we only benefit by drawing nearer to Him and following a spiritual path. We also obey His injunctions for love of His beauty. And in His infinite Mercy, He bestows upon us His bounties and blessings when we say our obligatory prayers. Bahá'u'lláh tells us:

"As for obligatory prayer, it hath been sent down by the Pen of the Most High in such wise that it setteth ablaze the hearts and captivateth the souls and minds of men." [109]

"Concerning obligatory prayer, it hath been revealed in such wise that whosoever reciteth it, even one time, with a detached heart, will find himself wholly severed from the world." [110]

"Of the new Obligatory Prayers that were later revealed, the long Obligatory Prayer should be said at those times when one feeleth himself in a prayerful mood. In truth, it hath been revealed in such wise that if it be recited to a rock, that rock would stir and speak forth; and if it be recited to a mountain, that mountain would move and flow. Well is it with the one who reciteth it and fulfilleth God's precepts. Whichever prayer is read will suffice." [111]

And in the words of 'Abdu'l-Bahá:

"The obligatory prayers are binding inasmuch as they are conducive to humility and submissiveness, to setting one's face towards God and expressing devotion to Him. Through such prayer man holdeth communion with God, seeketh to draw near unto Him, converseth with the true Beloved of one's heart, and attaineth spiritual stations." [112]

"Know thou that in every word and movement of the obligatory prayer there are allusions, mysteries and a wisdom that man is unable to comprehend, and letters and scrolls cannot contain." [113]

Even though we will never really understand, Taherzadeh explains that the movements in the two longer prayers convey our attitude towards God so that we are humbled before Him.[114] Because Bahá'u'lláh, despite being a Manifestation, lived in Persia, He would express Himself as a Persian. The gestures therefore reflect His culture. Raising hands to heaven signified supplication to God, bending the body demonstrated humility and prostrating the body before God expressed man's utter nothingness in His presence. Considering the meaning of these gestures while we pray may assist us to say our prayers more fervently.

We are also asked to wash our face and hands prior to reciting our obligatory prayers:

". . . Perform ye, likewise, ablutions for the Obligatory Prayer; this is the command of God, the Incomparable, the Unrestrained." [115]

But we do not need to say the longer obligatory prayers, as Shoghi Effendi explains:

"Bahá'u'lláh has reduced all ritual and form to an absolute minimum in His Faith. The few forms that there are – like those associated with the two longer obligatory daily prayers, are only symbols of the inner attitude. There is a wisdom in them, and a great blessing, but we cannot force ourselves to understand or feel these things, that is why He gave us also the very short and simple prayer, for those who did not feel the desire to perform the acts associated with the other two." [116]

When we say the obligatory prayers, we turn to the Qiblih, the Point of Adoration, Bahá'u'lláh's resting place on earth in Israel. Shoghi Effendi explains:

"He would advise you to only use the short midday Obligatory Prayer. This has no genuflections and only requires that when saying it the believer turn his face towards Akka where Bahá'u'lláh is buried. This is a physical symbol of an inner reality, just as the plant stretches out to the sunlight – from which it receives life and growth – so we turn our hearts to the Manifestation of God, Bahá'u'lláh, when we pray; and we turn our faces, during this short prayer, to where His dust lies on this earth as a symbol of the inner act" [117]

Here is the short obligatory prayer:

"I bear witness, O my God, that Thou hast created me to know Thee and to worship Thee. I testify, at this moment, to my powerlessness and to Thy might, to my poverty and to Thy wealth. There is none other God but Thee, the Help in Peril, the Self-Subsisting." [118]

In this prayer, Bahá'u'lláh tells us that our purpose in life and the reason for our creation is knowing and loving God, worshipping and serving Him, obeying Him and drawing near to His presence.

And if we turn to God with purity of motive and humility, we will experience the power of the obligatory prayers, as Bahá'u'lláh and 'Abdu'l-Bahá have written:

"O My brother! How great, how very great, can the law of obligatory prayer be, when through His mercy and loving kindness, one is enabled to observe it. When a man commenceth the recitation of the Obligatory Prayer, he should see himself severed from all created things and regard himself as utter nothingness before the will and purpose of God, in such wise that he seeth naught but Him in the world of being. This is the station of God's well-favored ones and those who are wholly devoted to Him. Should one perform the Obligatory Prayer in this manner, he will be accounted by God and the Concourse on high among those who have truly offered the prayer." [119]

"Obligatory prayer causeth the heart to become attentive to the Divine Kingdom. One is alone with God, converseth with Him, and acquireth bounties. Likewise, if one performeth the Obligatory Prayer with his heart in a state of utmost purity, he will obtain the confirmations of the Holy Spirit, and this will entirely obliterate love of self. I hope that thou wilt persevere in the recitation of the Obligatory Prayer, and thus will come to witness the power of entreaty and supplication." [120]

"Obligatory prayer is the very foundation of the Cause of God. Through it joy and vitality infuse the heart. Even if every grief should surround Me, as soon as I engage in conversing with God in obligatory prayer, all My sorrows disappear and I attain joy and gladness. A condition descendeth upon Me which I am unable to describe or express. Whenever, with full awareness and humility, we undertake to perform the Obligatory Prayer before God, and recite it with heartfelt tenderness, we shall taste such sweetness as to endow all existence with eternal life." [121]

'Abdu'l-Bahá gives us some direction about saying our obligatory prayer in conjunction with other prayers:

"O thou servant of the True Lord! Obligatory prayer and other supplications are essential to servitude unto Him Who is the All-Sufficing ... When the obligatory prayers and other prayers are joined together and follow each other, worship attaineth its perfection. It can be seen that these two are spiritual companions and are like one soul in two bodies. May God assist you all to thrive in love and fellowship." [122]

"O servant of the holy threshold! Thou hast asked about those prayers that are beyond what is prescribed, those that are recommended, invocations, and devotions honored by tradition. In this Dispensation that which hath been expressly prescribed is obligatory. But individual worship, invocations, supererogatory prayers, and specially recommended prayers are not binding. Nonetheless, the saying of any prayer individually after the Obligatory Prayers is well-pleasing and acceptable, but no particular ones have been singled out." [123]

The term "supererogatory" refers to prayers that are performed over and above those prescribed as obligatory.

But Bahá'u'lláh explains that other prayers, in addition to the obligatory prayers, have special potency and include the Tablet of Ahmad and the Long Healing Prayer.

"These daily obligatory prayers, together with a few other specific ones, such as the Healing Prayer, the Tablet of Ahmad, have been invested by Bahá'u'lláh with a special potency and significance, and should therefore be accepted as such and be recited by the believers with unquestioned faith and confidence, that through them they may enter into a much closer communion with God, and identify themselves more fully with His laws and precepts." [124]

Dorothy Baker suggested that *"you can lose contact ... through your own veils and clouds if you do not pray every day [and] if there are clouds around, use the Tablet of Ahmad as it never fails."* [125] Martha Root told Dorothy, *"when I am faced with a difficulty, I use the Tablet of Ahmad every day for nine days, asking God, in the name of that Holy Tablet, to remove the difficulty. If I am faced with an extremely difficult problem, I recite the Tablet of Ahmad three times a day for nine days. And when I am faced with a problem that is completely impossible and there is and can be no solution, I use the Tablet of Ahmad nine times a day for nine days and the problem is always solved."* [126]

She also suggested that we wake up and pray at dawn for someone for 19 days and thank the person for the privilege of doing it because it increases our own connection to the power that sustains us. I highly recommend Dorothy Baker's biography, *From Copper to Gold*, to get a glimpse of the power of prayer in her life.

'Abdu'l-Bahá also asks us to pray for those who have ascended to the spiritual world:

"Those who have ascended have different attributes from those who are still on earth, yet there is no real separation. In prayer there is a mingling of station, a mingling of condition. Pray for them as they pray for you." [127]

And we are asked to pray for our parents. The Báb tells us:

"It is seemly that the servant should, after each prayer, supplicate God to bestow mercy and forgiveness upon his parents. Thereupon God's call will be raised: 'Thousand upon thousand of what thou hast asked for thy parents shall be thy recompense!' Blessed is he who remembereth his parents when communing with God. There is, verily, no God but Him, the Mighty, the Well-Beloved." [128]

And so to summarize. We pray to know and to love God, and thereby our faith and conviction increase and we are motivated to continue our relationship with God through prayer. With self-discipline and perseverance prayer becomes our habit. We notice if we don't pray one day and our consciousness of the need to turn to God regularly is heightened. Once we acquire the habit of saying our obligatory prayers and other prayers regularly, it becomes as important to us as the other routines of life. And we need to understand, as Hellaby says, that obedience itself makes us a recipient of His grace and aids our progress spiritually.[129]

It seems to me that we may feel some vague feeling about God's presence or we may feel that no one is there listening to our words. We may feel that others seem to be good at connecting and living in His presence. We should not expect to feel the presence of God every time we pray. Learning how to pray requires work and effort, resolve and willpower. We may have to just keep praying and gradually we'll feel that we're actually communing with God.

"Let not thy tongue pay lip service in praise of God while thy heart be not attuned to the exalted Summit of Glory, and the Focal Point of communion..." [130]

When thoughts wander in all directions, Hellaby advises us to gently bring them back to our prayers.[131] I know for myself that I dutifully said prayers, and many of them at one time, for many years, trying to get the "feelings", a connection, a spiritual experience, to be carried away from self, but all the time my mind was chattering, wondering about my day, what I'd do about something that was happening in my life, everything except turning humbly to God and focusing totally on God and His will for me.

We should not even expect benefits for ourselves from praying but leave it all to God to utilize our prayers as He desires. Our prayers may seem rote and lacking in emotion and God may seem far away. Perhaps at this time, God is testing our faith to see if we will continue to turn to Him. Even if we feel that we are not "good" at praying, God is still working in us and we only have to look within:

"Turn thy sight unto thyself, that thou mayest find Me standing within thee, Mighty, Powerful and Self-Subsisting." [132]

Maybe, as Hellaby suggests, we try too hard. Maybe we need to stop our search and relax and agree to be found, knowing that He is seeking us.[133]

"Be still and know that I am God." [134]

And if we consider our prayer to be our last one, we may put our heart and soul into it:

"When you stand up to pray, perform your prayer as if it were your last. Do not say anything you will have to make excuses for tomorrow and resolve to give up all hopes of what men possess." [135]

We must leave our self-will at the door and reach a stage described by 'Abdu'l-Bahá:

"Man is eternally in a state of communion and prayer with the source of all good. The highest and most elevating state is the state of prayer. Prayer is communion with God . . . Its efficacy is conditional upon the freedom of the heart from extraneous suggestions and mundane thoughts. The worshiper must pray <u>with a detached spirit, unconditional surrender of the will, concentrated attention and a magnetic spiritual passion.</u> [my underlining] *His innermost being must be stirred with the ethereal breeze of holiness. If the mirror of his life is polished from the dross of all desires, the heavenly pictures and star-like images of the Kingdom of God will become fully reflected therein. Then he will be given power*

to translate these celestial forms into his own daily life and the lives of many thousands . . ." [136]

'Abdu'l-Bahá Himself taught us how to pray:

"When 'Abdu'l-Bahá was in New York He called to Him an ardent Bahá'í and said, 'If you will come to Me at dawn tomorrow, I will teach you to pray.' Delighted, Mr. M arose at four and crossed the city, arriving for his lesson at six. With what exultant expectation he must have greeted this opportunity! He found 'Abdu'l-Bahá already at prayer, kneeling by the side of the bed. Mr. M followed suit, taking care to place himself directly across.

Seeing that 'Abdu'l-Bahá was quite lost in His own reverie, Mr. M began to pray silently for his friend, his family and finally for the crowned heads of Europe. No word was uttered by the quiet Man before him. He went over all the prayers he knew then, and repeated them twice, three times – still no sound broke the expectant hush.

Mr M surreptiously rubbed one knee and wondered vaguely about his back. He began again, hearing as he did so, the birds heralding the dawn outside the window. An hour passed, and finally two. Mr. M was quite numb now. His eyes, roving along the wall, caught sight of a large crack. He dallied with a touch of indignation but let his gaze pass again to the still figure across the bed.

The ecstasy that he saw arrested him and he drank deeply of the sight. Suddenly he wanted to pray like that. Selfish desires were forgotten. Sorrow, conflict, and even his immediate surroundings were as if they had never been. He was conscious of only one thing, a passionate desire to draw near to God.

Closing his eyes again he set the world firmly aside, and amazingly his heart teemed with prayer, eager, joyous, tumultuous prayer. He felt cleansed by humility and lifted by a new peace. 'Abdu'l-Bahá had taught him to pray!

The Master of Akka immediately arose and came to him. His eyes rested smilingly upon the newly humbled Mr. M. 'When you pray,' He said, 'You must not think of your aching body, nor of the birds outside the window, nor of the cracks in the wall!' He became very serious then, and added, 'When you wish to pray you must first know that you are standing in the presence of the Almighty!'" [137]

We can be assured that our prayers are always answered:

"But we ask for things which the divine wisdom does not desire for us and there is no answer to our prayer . . . We pray,'O God! make me wealthy!'

If this prayer were universally answered, human affairs would be at a standstill. There would be none left to work in the streets, none to till the soil, none to build, none to run the trains ... The affairs of the world would be interfered with, energies crippled and progress hindered. But whatever we ask for, which is in accord with divine wisdom, God will answer.

For instance, a very feeble patient may ask the doctor to give him food which would be positively dangerous to his life and condition. He may beg for roast meat. The doctor is kind and wise. He knows it would be dangerous to his patient so he refuses to allow it. The doctor is merciful; the patient ignorant. Through the doctor's kindness the patient recovers; his life is saved. Yet the patient may cry out that the doctor is unkind, not good, because he refuses to answer his pleading.

God is merciful. In His mercy He answers the prayers of all His servants when according to His supreme wisdom it is necessary." [138]

We may not understand the answer to our prayer. Or the answer may be disguised. Hellaby explains that we may want to develop a specific virtue and God provides a situation to help us develop it.[139] Sometimes we can answer the request ourselves. Sometimes we don't give God enough time or the answer is to wait.[140] Sometimes the words of our prayers do not reflect what we want in our hearts.[141] We only get in God's way by not being ready or receptive to Him, by closing our hearts and being unresponsive and by worrying and trying to do it all on our own.[142] We give God the opportunity and follow His will through our plea in the Long Obligatory Prayer:

"O God, my God! Look not upon my hopes and doings, nay rather look upon Thy will that hath encompassed the heavens and the earth."

It seems to me that we may not wish to take the responsibility, to take the hard road to let go of bad habits or our treatment of another. Or, as Hellaby points out, sometimes we need to demonstrate perseverance by continuing to pray for something because only prayer can bring it about and we may have to sacrifice our selfish desires to receive it, while maintaining hope and faith. Our spiritual needs will be answered by a change in our circumstances or a change in us.[143] Patience is always needed to deal with situations in our lives and we need to have trust and confidence that God will lead the way.[144] Being in the presence of God and offering our supplications is only the beginning point. Through prayer we learn to serve others. We reflect our highest form of prayer in our interactions with others.

"... strive that your actions day by day may be beautiful prayers. Turn towards God, and seek always to do that which is right and noble." [145]

As Rutstein concludes, prayer then becomes what we do conscious of the nearness of God and His wish to help us in our lives.[146] If we have this awareness of God's presence within our hearts, we will call on Him constantly as we go about our lives and this love of God becomes a magnet that attracts others as we demonstrate our devotion in our interactions with others.

"Woe to those who pray, But in their prayer are careless; Who make a shew of devotion; But refuse to help the needy." [147]

Prayer must necessarily result in action. When we pray for others, do we also demonstrate thoughtfulness in our actions towards them? Unselfishness in prayer bestows a heart ready to serve.[148] It also affects the one who is being prayed for. Knowing someone is praying for you is empowering and may assist them to cope. According to Hellaby, *"great praying requires great living and this, in turn, requires great service, culminating when necessary, in great sacrifice."* [149] Our prayers can't help but be effective when we ***"sacrifice all our conditions for the divine station of God"*** [150] and pray for others and serve them. Our sacrifice becomes the channel for the grace of God to flow to others.

"To turn to God at all times with true love, to commune with Him in spirit, to regard Him as always present, to praise and glorify Him by word and by deed, to pray ardently for His confirmations to promote His Cause, to carry out His teachings and to serve mankind in one's daily work- all these acts constitute the main features of worshipping God. Prayer alone will not be conducive to the good- pleasure of God if it is not followed by service to the Cause" [151]

But we need to start with prayer, as 'Abdu'l-Bahá reminds us:

"It has been revealed in the Teachings that work is worship, but this does not mean that worship and the prescribed mentionings of God should be abandoned, for such worship is a requirement set forth in the book of God. Prayer makes the heart mindful, it spiritualizes the soul, it causes the spirit to exult, it gladdens the breast, till Divine love appears and a man leans trustingly on the Lord and bows in lowliness at the Threshold of Grandeur." [152]

In closing, here is a description of 'Abdu'l-Bahá's prayerfulness:

"'Abdu'l-Bahá's prayerfulness aided Him to sustain an equanimity even in times of deep sorrow and dire anguish. His 'love for God was the

ground and cause of an equanimity which no circumstance could shake and of an inner happiness which no adversity affected . . . ' To be sure, in times of severe stress – when Bahá'u'lláh was away in the wilderness of Sulaymaniyyih and again when the Master Himself was in grave danger in Akka due to false accusations brought against Him – 'Abdu'l-Bahá was known to pray, and perhaps also to chant, throughout an entire night. The death of His beloved Father, Bahá'u'lláh, made Him momentarily almost lifeless – but He rallied and was sustained by His abiding love of God. Indeed it is reported that the Master 'often prayed that His conditions might become more severe in order that His strength to meet them might be increased.'" [153]

REFERENCES

1 Sheehy, Gail, *Passages in Caregiving: Turning Chaos into Confidence* (New York: Harper Collins, 2010), p. 255
2 'Abdu'l-Bahá, *The Divine Art of Living* (Wilmette, IL: Bahá'í Publishing Trust, 1974), p. 33
3 Shoghi Effendi, *The Compilation of Compilations* Vol.II, 1762, 8 December, 1935, p. 238
4 Taherzadeh, Adib, *The Revelation of Bahá'u'lláh*, Vol. 2, p. 233
5 'Abdu'l-Bahá, *Star of the West* Vol. 8, no. 4 (1917, May 17), p. 41
6 Rutstein, Nathan, *A Way out of the Trap* (Springfield, MA: Whitcomb Publishing, 1995), p. 114 7 Hellaby, William and Madeline, *Prayer, A Bahá'í Approach* (Oxford: George Ronald, 1985), p. 4- 5
8 'Abdu'l-Bahá, *Bahá'í World Faith*, p. 368
9 'Abdu'l-Bahá, *The Divine Art of Living*, p. 26
10 Bahá'u'lláh, *Gleanings from the Writings of Bahá'u'lláh*, CXXXVI, p. 295
11 Bahá'u'lláh, *The Kitab-i-Aqdas, The Most Holy Book* (Bahá'í World Centre, Haifa, Israel: The Universal House of Justice, 1992), 116, p. 61
12 'Abdu'l-Bahá, *Bahá'í World Faith*, p. 375
13 'Abdu'l-Bahá, *The Divine Art of Living*, p. 28
14 Bahá'u'lláh, *Prayers and Meditations by Bahá'u'lláh* (Wilmette, IL: Bahá'í Publishing Trust, 1987), CLXXXIII, p. 317-318
15 Esslemont, Dr. J.E., *Bahá'u'lláh and the New Era*, p.94-95
16 The Báb, *Selections from the Writings of The Báb*, compiled by the Research Department of the Universal House of Justice (Haifa, Israel: Bahá'í World Centre, 1976), p. 78
17 Shoghi Effendi, *The Compilation of Compilations* Vol. II, 1768,26 October 1938,p. 240
18 Rutstein, Nathan, *A Way out of the Trap*, p. 116-117
19 Bahá'u'lláh, *The Hidden Words*, Arabic no. 18, p.8
20 Rutstein, Nathan, *A Way out of the Trap*, p. 117
21 Ibid., p. 116
22 Taherzadeh, Adib, *The Revelation of Bahá'u'lláh* Vol. 2, p. 232-233
23 Ibid., p. 233
24 'Abdu'l-Bahá, *Paris Talks*, There can be no True Happiness and Progress without Spirituality, [8], p. 108-109
25 Bahá'u'lláh, *The Hidden Words*, Arabic no. 5, p.4
26 Bahá'u'lláh, *Tablets of Bahá'u'lláh*, p. 156
27 'Abdu'l-Bahá, *The Divine Art of Living*, p. 35-36
28 'Abdu'l-Bahá, *Some Answered Questions* (Wilmette, IL: Bahá'í Publishing Trust, 1981), 75, p. 265
29 'Abdu'l-Bahá, *Bahá'í Scriptures*, 798, p. 439

30 Moffett, Ruth J. *DU'A: On Wings of Prayer* (Happy Camp, CA: Naturegraph Publishers, 1984), p. 24
31 Bahá'u'lláh, *Gleanings from the Writings of Bahá'u'lláh*, XXXVII, p. 87
32 Bahá'u'lláh, *The Hidden Words*, Persian no. 9, p. 24-25
33 Bahá'u'lláh, *Bahá'í Prayers* (Wilmette, IL: Bahá'í Publishing Trust, 2002), p. 309
34 Moffett, Ruth J., *DU'A: On Wings of Prayer*, p.46
35 Ibid., p. 24
36 Bahá'u'lláh, *Gleanings from the Writings of Bahá'u'lláh*, XCIII,p. 186
37 Moffett, Ruth J., *DU'A: On Wings of Prayer*, p. 24
38 Ibid., p. 24
39 Ibid., p. 24-25
40 Ibid., p. 25
41 Bahá'u'lláh, *Gleanings from the Writings of Bahá'u'lláh*, LXVI, p. 129
42 Bahá'u'lláh, *Epistle to the Son of the Wolf*, p. 99
43 Moffett, Ruth J., *DU'A: On Wings of Prayer*, p. 47 44 Ibid., p. 25
45 Ibid.
46 'Abdu'l-Bahá, *The Divine Art of Living*, p. 28
47 Moffett, Ruth J., *DU'A: On Wings of Prayer*, p. 26
48 Ibid., p. 16
49 Moffett, Ruth J., *DU'A: On Wings of Prayer*, p. 30
50 Hellaby, William and Madeline, *Prayer, A Bahá'í Approach*, p. 82
51 Bahá'u'lláh, *The Hidden Words*, Persian no. 22, p. 29
52 Hellaby, William and Madeline, *Prayer, A Bahá'í Approach*, p. 82
53 Ibid., p. 83
54 Ibid.
55 Bahá'u'lláh, *The Hidden Words*, Arabic no. 31, p. 11
56 Rutstein, Nathan, *A Way out of the Trap*, p. 132-133
57 'Abdu'l-Bahá, *Lights of Guidance*, 1485, p. 456
58 Hellaby, William and Madeline, *Prayer, A Bahá'í Approach*, p. 91-92
59 Ibid., p. 92
60 Bahá'u'lláh, *Prayers and Meditations by Bahá'u'lláh*, CLVII, p. 250
61 Bahá'u'lláh, *Gleanings from the Writings of Bahá'u'lláh*, XXVII, p. 68-69
62 Bahá'u'lláh, *Bahá'í Prayers*, p. 76
63 Moffett, Ruth J. *DU'A: On Wings of Prayer*, p. 61-62
64 'Abdu'l-Bahá, *Bahá'í Scriptures*, 796, p. 438
65 Moffett, Ruth J., *DU'A: On Wings of Prayer*, p. 30
66 Hellaby, William and Madeline, *Prayer, A Bahá'í Approach*, p. 53-54
67 Moffett, Ruth J., *DU'A: On Wings of Prayer*, p. 32
68 Bahá'u'lláh, *The Divine Art of Living*, p. 31
69 Moffett, Ruth J., *DU'A: On Wings of Prayer*, p. 55
70 Rutstein, Nathan, *A Way out of the Trap*, p. 120
71 Ibid.

72 Ibid., p. 118
73 Ibid.
74 Honnold, Annamarie, *Vignettes from the Life of 'Abdu'l-Bahá*, 10, p. 115-116
75 Moffett, Ruth J., *DU'A: On Wings of Prayer*, p. 27
76 Ibid., p. 28
77 Ibid., p. 27
78 Rutstein, Nathan, *A Way out of the Trap*, p. 119
79 Gilstrap, Dorothy Freeman, *From Copper to Gold, The Life of Dorothy Baker* (Wilmette, IL: Bahá'í Publishing Trust, 1999), p. 545
80 Bahá'u'lláh, *The Kitab-i-Aqdas, The Most Holy Book*, 149, p. 73
81 Bahá'u'lláh, *Gleanings from the Writings of Bahá'u'lláh*, CXXV, p. 265
82 Moffett, Ruth J., *DU'A: On Wings of Prayer*, p. 57
83 Ibid., p. 55
84 Ibid., p. 60-61
85 Ibid., p. 57
86 Ibid., p. 26
87 Gilbert, Elizabeth, *Eat, Pray, Love* (New York: Penguin Group, 2006), p. 177
88 Rutstein, Nathan, *A Way out of the Trap*, p. 116
89 'Abdu'l-Bahá, *Tablets of 'Abdu'l-Bahá 'Abbás* Vol. III, p. 620
90 Bahá'u'lláh, *Gleanings from the Writings of Bahá'u'lláh*, CXXV, p. 269
91 'Abdu'l-Bahá, *Bahá'í Scriptures*, 970, p. 504
92 Shoghi Effendi, *The Compilation of Compilations* Vol. II, 1764, 27 April 1937, p. 239
93 Ibid., 1779, 31 January 1949, p. 242
94 Ibid., 1776, 24 July 1946, p. 242
95 McKay, Doris, *Fires in Many Hearts* (Manotick, Ontario: Nine Pines Publishing, 1993), p. 63
96 'Abdu'l-Bahá, *The Divine Art of Living*, p. 28
97 Esslemont, Dr. J.E., *Bahá'u'lláh and the New Era*, p. 88-89
98 Gilstrap, Dorothy Freeman, *From Copper to God, The Life of Dorothy Baker*, p. 252
99 The Báb, *Selections from the Writings of The Báb*, p. 93-94
100 Bahá'u'lláh, *The Compilation of Compilations* Vol. II, 1723, p. 225
101 Shoghi Effendi, Ibid., 1777, 23 November 1947, p. 242
102 Hellaby, William and Madeline, *Prayer, A Bahá'í Approach*, p. 20
103 Ibid., p. 8
104 Shoghi Effendi, *The Compilation of Compilations* Vol. II, 1775, 16 March 1946, p. 241
105 Bahá'u'lláh, *The Kitab-i-Aqdas, The Most Holy Book*, 18, p. 26
106 Hellaby, William and Madeline, *Prayer, A Bahá'í Approach*, p. 29
107 Bahá'u'lláh, *The Importance of Obligatory Prayer and Fasting*, (compiled by the Research Department of the Universal House of Justice, 2000), I

108 'Abdu'l-Bahá, *The Importance of Obligatory Prayer and Fasting*, XII
109 Bahá'u'lláh, Ibid., VII
110 Ibid., VIII
111 Ibid., XI
112 'Abdu'l-Bahá, *The Compilation of Compilations* Vol. II, 1744, p. 232
113 Ibid., 1748, p. 233
114 Taherzadeh, Adib, *The Revelation of Bahá'u'lláh* Vol. 3, p. 349-350
115 Bahá'u'lláh, *The Kitab-i-Aqdas, The Most Holy Book*, 18, p. 26
116 Shoghi Effendi, *The Compilation of Compilations* Vol. II, 1780, 24 June 1949, p. 243
117 Ibid., p. 242-243
118 Bahá'u'lláh, *Prayers and Meditations of Bahá'u'lláh*, CLXXXI, p. 314
119 Bahá'u'lláh, *The Importance of Obligatory Prayer and Fasting*, IX
120 'Abdu'l-Bahá, Ibid., XI
121 Ibid., XIV
122 Ibid., XIX
123 Ibid., XXIII
124 Shoghi Effendi, *Principles of Bahá'í Administration*, p. 7
125 Gilstrap, Dorothy Freeman, *From Copper to God, The Life of Dorothy Baker,* p. 252-253
126 Ibid., p. 251-252
127 'Abdu'l-Bahá, *'Abdu'l-Bahá in London* (Oakham: Bahá'í Publishing Trust, 1982), p. 96
128 The Báb, *Selections from the Writings of The Báb*, p. 94
129 Hellaby, William and Madeline, *Prayer, A Bahá'í Approach*, p. 31
130 The Báb, *Selections from the Writings of The Báb*, p. 94
131 Hellaby, William and Madeline, *Prayer, A Bahá'í Approach*, p. 51
132 Bahá'u'lláh, *The Hidden Words*, Arabic no. 13, p. 7
133 Hellaby, William and Madeline, *Prayer, A Bahá'í Approach*, p. 57
134 Ibid.
135 Moffett, Ruth J. *DU'A: On Wings of Prayer*, p. 48
136 Ibid., p. 60
137 Honnold, Annamarie, *Vignettes from the Life of 'Abdu'l-Bahá*, 27, p. 131-132
138 'Abdu'l-Bahá, *The Divine Art of Living*, p. 31-32
139 Hellaby, William and Madeline, *Prayer, A Bahá'í Approach*, p. 76
140 Ibid., p. 77
141 Ibid., p. 81
142 Ibid., p. 75
143 Ibid., p. 80
144 Ibid., p. 77
145 'Abdu'l-Bahá, *Paris Talks*, Good Ideas must be Carried into Action, [7], p. 81
146 Rutstein, Nathan, *A Way out of the Trap*, p. 120
147 *The Koran*, Sura 107: 4-7, p. 31

148 Hellaby, William and Madeline, *Prayer, A Bahá'í Approach*, p. 105
149 Ibid., p. 107
150 'Abdu'l-Bahá, *The Divine Art of Living*, p. 73
151 Taherzadeh, Adib. *The Revelation of Bahá'u'lláh* Vol. 4 (Oxford: George Ronald, 1988), p. 36
152 Moffett, Ruth J., *DU'A: On Wings of Prayer*, p. 63
153 Honnold, Annamarie, *Vignettes from the Life of 'Abdu'l-Bahá*, 24, p. 128-129

Chapter 3
Meditation

Chapter 3
Meditation

Bahá'ís, like those of other faiths and those who practice a spiritual way of life, are asked to meditate, to ponder and reflect:

"One hour's reflection is preferable to seventy years of pious worship." [1]

One of the six essential requisites for our spiritual growth, summarized by the Universal House of Justice, is prayerful meditation on the teachings. And we know that when we pray to God, we need to listen and wait for a response, which can best be received through meditation. So it is important to know how to meditate and to spend some time in meditation. Bahá'u'lláh did not specify any particular methods of meditation or any rituals concerning meditation, but he did reveal meditations for us to use.

Perhaps we would do well first to consider what meditation is.

The website www.mikefinch.com defines meditation as *"a practice in which an individual trains the mind and/or induces a mode of consciousness to realize some benefit."*

The 1913 edition of Webster's dictionary defines meditation as: *The act of meditating; close or continued thought; the turning or revolving of a subject in the mind; serious contemplation; reflection; musing*

And the Merriam-Webster dictionary online, defines meditation as: *a discourse intended to express its author's reflections or to guide others in contemplation . . .*

Below is a selection of definitions (culled from Google at random) of meditation:

Meditation is the process of conscious, controlled focus of the mind which may take place when the thinking processes, both in pictures and in words, have been stopped.

Meditation is a set of attentional practices leading to an altered state or trait of consciousness characterized by expanded awareness, greater presence, and a more integrated sense of self.

Meditation is effortless concentration.

Meditation is to still the mind, focus it away from the everyday concerns of your talking self, and to listen inward.

Meditation is a way to evoke the relaxation response and at the same time a way to train and strengthen awareness; a method for centering and focusing the self; a way to halt constant verbal thinking and relax the bodymind; a technique for calming the central nervous system; a way to relieve stress, bolster self-esteem, reduce anxiety, and alleviate depression. . . . But I would like to emphasize that meditation itself is, and always has been, a spiritual practice.

The goal of all forms of meditation is single-mindedness -- to let go of all distractions and focus on one object of attention or devotion.

Meditation is simply witnessing your mind without any involvement at all.

Meditation is to seek inner silence and losing the sense of separateness.

Meditation is a spiritual practice that bonds the mind, body and soul together.

Prayer is when you speak . . . Meditation is when you listen.

Meditation is the intentional self-regulation of attention, in the service of self-inquiry, in the here and now.

Yang meditation is the concentrated focusing of the mind on something. The 'something' can have almost infinite variety. Common subjects of this type of meditation are: mantras, chakras, colors, shapes, prayers, and affirmations. Yin meditation is the clearing of the mind of all thought, both pictures and words, and the holding of that mind in a focused and alert state . . .

So we have a beginning. Meditation is related to "reflection", "serious contemplation" a "conscious controlled focus of the mind", "leading to an altered state", "effortless concentration," "single- mindedness". It's about listening "inward", seeking "inner silence" and "losing a sense of separateness". It requires the ability to "halt constant verbal thinking" and "still the mind" or hold it "in a focused and alert state". It involves "expanded awareness, greater presence and a more integrated sense of self." And it is "a spiritual practice that bonds mind, body and soul together." So how do these ideas about meditation relate to meditation as described in the Bahá'í Writings:

Bahá'u'lláh stated:

"Do thou meditate on that which We have revealed unto thee, that thou mayest discover the purpose of God, thy Lord, and the Lord of all worlds." ²

And from *The Hidden Words* of Bahá'u'lláh, those gems containing the very essence of His instructions for mankind:

"O Man of Two Visions!
Close one eye and open the other. Close one to the world and all that is therein, and open the other to the hallowed beauty of the Beloved." ³

'Abdu'l-Bahá tells us:

"Bahá'u'lláh says there is a sign (from God) in every phenomenon: the sign of the intellect is contemplation and the sign of contemplation is silence, because it is impossible for a man to do two things at one time – he cannot both speak and meditate.

It is an axiomatic fact that while you meditate you are speaking with your own spirit. In that state of mind you put certain questions to your spirit and the spirit answers: the light breaks forth and the reality is revealed.

You cannot apply the name 'man' to any being void of this faculty of meditation; without it he would be a mere animal, lower than the beasts.

Through the faculty of meditation man attains to eternal life; through it he receives the breath of the Holy Spirit – the bestowal of the Spirit is given in reflection and meditation.

The spirit of man is itself informed and strengthened during meditation; through it affairs of which man knew nothing are unfolded before his view. Through it he receives Divine inspiration, through it he receives heavenly food.

Meditation is the key for opening the doors of mysteries. In that state man abstracts himself: in that state man withdraws himself from all outside objects; in that subjective mood he is immersed in the ocean of spiritual life and can unfold the secrets of things-in-themselves. To illustrate this, think of man as endowed with two kinds of sight; when the power of insight is being used the outward power of vision does not see.

This faculty of meditation frees man from the animal nature, discerns the reality of things, puts man in touch with God.

This faculty brings forth from the invisible plane the sciences and arts. Through the meditative faculty inventions are made possible, colossal undertakings are carried out; through it governments can run smoothly. Through this faculty man enters into the very Kingdom of God.

Nevertheless some thoughts are useless to man; they are like waves moving in the sea without result. But if the faculty of meditation is bathed in the inner light and characterized with divine attributes, the results will be confirmed.

The meditative faculty is akin to the mirror; if you put it before earthly objects it will reflect them. Therefore if the spirit of man is contemplating earthly subjects he will be informed of these.

But if you turn the mirror of your spirits heavenwards, the heavenly constellations and the rays of the Sun of Reality will be reflected in your hearts, and the virtues of the Kingdom will be obtained.

Therefore let us keep this faculty rightly directed – turning it to the heavenly Sun and not to earthly objects – so that we may discover the secrets of the Kingdom, and comprehend the allegories of the Bible and the mysteries of the spirit.

May we indeed become mirrors reflecting the heavenly realities, and may we become so pure as to reflect the stars of heaven." [4]

So what does 'Abdu'l-Bahá tell us are the requirements for meditation? First, we need to be quiet. Then we need to withdraw our self. We then do not use our vision, our outward sight, but we use insight. We put questions to our spirit and it answers.

Through meditation we can attain:

- Eternal life
- The breath of the Holy Spirit
- The unfoldment of affairs of which we knew nothing
- Divine inspiration and heavenly food
- Freedom from the animal nature
- The ability to discern the reality of things
- The ability to be in touch with God
- Sciences and arts brought forth from the invisible realm

- New inventions
- The achievement of colossal undertakings
- Smooth-running governments
- Entrance into the Kingdom of God
- The virtues of the Kingdom

And we are asked to keep our thoughts on heavenly things and turn the mirror of our spirits heavenwards to *"discover the secrets of the Kingdom . . ."*

After studying this passage, it is clear how important it is for us to learn how to meditate and to practice it regularly in our lives.

Here is another passage about the benefits of meditation:

"Through meditation the doors of deeper knowledge and inspiration may be opened. Naturally, if one meditates as a Bahá'í he is connected with the Source; if a man believing in God meditates he is tuning in to the power and mercy of God; but we cannot say that any inspiration which a person, not knowing Bahá'u'lláh or not believing in God, receives is merely from his own ego . . ." [5]

And so we see the power of meditation that pulls us away from our lower nature to another realm.

Bahá'u'lláh says that *"the deepest meditations are but reflections of that which is created within ourselves by the Revelations of God."* [6]

"O Salman! All that the sages and mystics have said or written have never exceeded, nor can they ever hope to exceed, the limitations to which man's finite mind hath been strictly subjected. To whatever heights the mind of the most exalted of men may soar, however great the depths which the detached and understanding heart can penetrate, such mind and heart can never transcend that which is the creature of their own conceptions and the product of their own thoughts. The meditations of the profoundest thinker, the devotions of the holiest of saints, the highest expressions of praise from either human pen or tongue, are but a reflection of that which hath been created within themselves, through the revelation of the Lord, their God. Whoever pondereth this truth in his heart will readily admit that there are certain limits which no human being can possibly transgress. Every attempt which, from the beginning that hath no beginning, hath been made to visualize and know God is limited by the exigencies of His own creation - a creation which He, through the operation of His own Will and for the purposes of none other but His own Self, hath called into being.

Immeasurably exalted is He above the strivings of human mind to grasp His Essence, or of human tongue to describe His mystery." [7]

"One day the Guardian said to a prominent pilgrim in Haifa, 'Do you pray?' Of course, beloved Guardian, I pray every morning.' 'Do you meditate?' The man paused a bit and said slowly, 'No, I guess I do not.'

The Guardian replied that prayer is of no use without meditation and that meditation must be centered on the Holy Writings. He continued very earnestly that meditation is of no use unless it is followed by action. He thus made clear another step in this most important process in the life of the soul.

The Guardian then explained further that meditation is not just sitting down, closing your eyes, keeping silent in a silent atmosphere, and being blank. That is not meditation. We must concentrate on the Teachings . . . and their implications. Prayer is of no consequence if it remains the murmur of syllables and sounds – of what use is that? God knows already. We are not saying the prayers for God, we are saying them for our own selves. If the words do not strengthen us, if we do not reflect upon the Writings we read, if we do not make the Writings part of our daily action, we are wasting our time." [8]

Shoghi Effendi stated that *"inspiration received through meditation is of a nature that one cannot measure or determine. God can inspire into our minds things that we had no previous knowledge of, if He desires to do so."* [9]

He also said, *"Prayer and meditation are very important factors in deepening the spiritual life of the individual, but with them must go also action and example, as these are the tangible results of the former. Both are essential."* [10]

'Abdu'l-Bahá explained, *"As in a dream one talks with a friend while the mouth is silent, so is it in the conversation of the spirit. A man may converse with the ego within him saying: 'May I do this? Would it be advisable for me to do this work?' Such is the conversation with the higher self."* [11]

And 'Abdu'l-Bahá said:

The first thing to do is to acquire a thirst for Spirituality, then Live the Life! Live the Life! Live the Life! The way to acquire this thirst is to meditate upon the future life. Study the Holy Words, read your Bible, read the Holy Books, especially study the Holy Utterances of Bahá'u'lláh; Prayer and Meditation, take much time for these two. Then will you know this Great Thirst, and then only can you begin to Live the Life! [12]

So if we *"meditate upon the future life"* it will help to awaken our souls from the stupor of self- absorption and egotism.

But how do we meditate? Shoghi Effendi advised us:

"As to meditation: This also is a field in which the individual is free. There are no set forms of meditation prescribed in the teachings, no plan as such, for inner development. The friends are urged —nay enjoined to pray, and they also should meditate, but the manner of doing the latter is left entirely to the individual." [13]

". . . the Guardian sees no reason why the friends should not be taught to meditate, but they should guard against superstitious or foolish ideas creeping into it." [14]

And in this letter the Universal House of Justice provides us with more guidelines:

"It is striking how private and personal the most fundamental spiritual exercises of prayer and meditation are in the Faith. Bahá'ís do, of course, have meetings for devotions, as in the Mashriqu'l- Adhkar [Bahá'í House of Worship] or at Nineteen Day Feasts, but the daily obligatory prayers are ordained to be said in the privacy of one's chamber, and meditation on the Teachings is, likewise, a private individual activity, not a form of group therapy.

In His talks 'Abdu'l-Bahá describes prayer as 'conversation with God' and concerning meditation He says that 'while you meditate you are speaking with your own spirit. In that state of mind you put certain questions to your spirit and the spirit answers: the light breaks forth and the reality is revealed.

There are, of course, other things that one can do to increase one's spirituality. For example, Bahá'u'lláh has specified no procedures to be followed in meditation, and individual believers are free to do as they wish in this area, provided that they remain in harmony with the Teachings, but such activities are purely personal and should under no circumstances be confused with those actions which Bahá'u'lláh Himself considered to be of fundamental importance for our spiritual growth.

Some believers may find it beneficial to them to follow a particular method of meditation, and they may certainly do so, but such methods should not be taught at Bahá'í Summer Schools or be carried out during a session of the School because, while they may appeal to some people, they may repel others. They have nothing to do with the Faith and should be kept quite separate so that enquirers will not be confused.

It would seem that there are in Norway many believers who draw particular benefit from meditation. The House of Justice suggests that for their private meditations they may wish to use the repetition of the Greatest Name, Allah-u-Abha, ninety-five times a day . . ." [15]

This requirement to repeat the Greatest Name every day was mentioned in the last chapter and it is clear from this letter that we have a form of meditation that is ready to use.

But the Bahá'í teachings indicate that we are free to determine a method of meditation on the Creative Word that works for us. If we do not know how to meditate we can learn through reading books or attending workshops to master some basics. I have been taught that learning to concentrate on one's breathing aids meditation. When your mind wanders, observe your thoughts, allow them to pass and gently bring them back to your breathing (In some techniques you count your breath, for example, counting to 10 and beginning again). Some practitioners ask their learners to focus on an object with a steady gaze, in some techniques eyes are open but gazing at a point in the distance, some meditate with eyes closed. Some forms of meditation include repetition of a mantra. And Bahá'ís can consider the Greatest Name their mantra.

There are other phrases repeated in the Bahá'í Prayers that can be used in meditation, as outlined by Wendi Momen in her excellent book *Meditation*[16] :

"Is there any Remover of difficulties save God? Say: Praised be God! He is God! All are His servants, and all abide by His bidding!

He [Bahá'u'lláh] said,"Bid them recite: 'Is there any Remover of difficulties save God? Say: Praised be God! He is God! All are His servants, and all abide by His bidding!' Tell them to repeat it five hundred times, nay, a thousand times, by day and by night, sleeping and waking, that haply the Countenance of Glory may be unveiled to their eyes, and tiers of light descend upon them." [17]

(Bahá'u'lláh wrote this in the midst of great sorrow and sadness because of the machinations of his brother).

"Greater is God than every great one!"

"Glorified be my Lord, the All-Glorious!"

"Thou the Sufficing, Thou the Healing, Thou the Abiding, O Thou Abiding One!"

"Thou seest me, O my God, holding to Thy Name, the Most Holy, the Most Luminous, the Most Mighty, the Most Great, the Most Exalted, the Most Glorious, and clinging to the hem of the robe to which have clung all in this world and the world to come."

In her book, Momen also outlines various meditation techniques and demonstrates how aspects of the techniques and their goals are found in the Bahá'í Writings. She also provides short verses and longer meditations from the Writings that can be used in meditation.

Referring back to one of the requisites for spiritual growth, prayerful meditation on the teachings, it may be beneficial while reading the Writings every day to choose a phrase or quotation for meditation and to carry it with us, keeping it in mind to hopefully assist us as we go about our day.

Later in this chapter I would like to describe some meditations that I have found useful in terms of drawing me deeper into a spiritual state.

But first, what do we meditate on?

According to Shoghi Effendi:

". . . to always use and read, during your hours of meditation and prayer, the words revealed by Bahá'u'lláh and the Master." [18]

"He thinks it would be wiser for the Bahá'ís to use the Meditations given by Bahá'u'lláh, and not any set form of meditation recommended by someone else; but the believers must be left free in these details and allowed to have personal latitude in finding their own level of communion with God." [19]

Rutstein defines meditation on the Writings as *"reflective reading"* or *"spiritual daydreaming."*[20] We need to read and meditate about the Word of God or we will *"shrivel up spiritually."*[21] Bahá'ís refer to prayerful study of the Writings as deepening maybe because we need to immerse ourselves in Holy Writings to appreciate them.

"Immerse yourselves in the ocean of My words, that ye may unravel its secrets, and discover all the pearls of wisdom that lie hid in its depths."[22]

We need to read the Word of God with care and thought. We may experience *"brilliant flashes of insight"* [23] or we may not, but it is our efforts that matter. We may not attain understanding immediately, but it will come to us later in the day or the next time we meditate. Of course, when we are feeling refreshed and can concentrate readily without having our minds full of problems, understanding comes more quickly. The process is not automatic and we can't expect that it will happen every time. We can't expect our minds to remain free of clutter even with practice. But if we practice meditation on a regular basis, we will eventually be able to gain insights more often.[24] Perhaps it may help us to be more patient with ourselves when we realize that our brains are scanning continually for threats. Rick Hanson, a neuropsychologist and best-selling author [25] explains that our vigilance may at times be warranted but often it's excessive and driven by reactions to events from our past that may no longer be relevant. We become anxious unnecessarily and our bodies and brains are primed to overreact even to little things. Therefore it is understandable that maintaining a state of mindfulness is difficult. So it seems that we have to just keep doing it, laugh about our struggles to clear our mind and persist. Marianne Williamson explains that *"One moment of enlightened awareness doesn't transform your life. The spiritual path is slow and arduous at times as every single circumstance becomes the ground on which both ego and spirit seek to make their stand. Spiritual practice is like physical exercise; it has a cumulative effect, and if we want to enjoy its benefits, we can never stop doing it."* [26] Some of us resist meditation because we feel we cannot possibly learn how to do it, others because we don't feel worthy spiritually but we need to do it *"to become worthy"*, as Rutstein points out. [27] My understanding is that we can only change through prayer, meditation and plunging into Holy Writings regularly, replacing any negative attitudes and actions with positive qualities and steps. We need to be patient because such significant change does not happen overnight. And sometimes when we pray and meditate, an answer doesn't come. Instead of trying frantically to make things happen, we may need to wait and have faith that God will eventually reveal the answer to us. If we continue to delve into the Holy Writings, we gain insight into ourselves as spiritual beings. We become rooted spiritually and then are able to use this spiritual energy to take action and solve problems. And this is possible because of the power of the Word of God, as Bahá'u'lláh tells us:

"Know thou, moreover, that the Word of God- exalted be His glory – is higher and far superior to that which the senses can perceive, for it is sanctified from any property or substance. It transcendeth the limitations of known elements and is exalted above all the essential and recognized substances. It became manifest without any syllable or sound and is none

but the Command of God which pervadeth all created things. It hath never been withheld from the world of being. It is God's all-pervasive grace, from which all grace doth emanate. It is an entity far removed above all that hath been and shall be." [28]

In Chapter 2 I mentioned that there are many meanings contained in the Word of God. Here are passages from the Bahá'í Writings about the depth of meanings:

"O My servants! My holy, My divinely ordained Revelation may be likened unto an ocean in whose depths are concealed innumerable pearls of great price, of surpassing luster. It is the duty of every seeker to bestir himself and strive to attain the shores of this ocean, so that he may, in proportion to the eagerness of his search and the efforts he hath exerted, partake of such benefits as have been pre- ordained in God's irrevocable and hidden Tablets." [29]

"Blessed is the one who discovereth the fragrance of inner meanings from the traces of this Pen through whose movement the breezes of God are wafted over the entire creation, and through whose stillness the very essence of tranquillity appeareth in the realm of being." [30]

"The object of reading and reciting is to understand the inner significances of the verses and mysteries of the Book." [31]

". . . Number me not with them who read Thy words and fail to find Thy hidden gift which, as decreed by Thee, is contained therein, and which quickeneth the souls of Thy creatures and the hearts of Thy servants." [32]

". . . investigate and study the Holy Scriptures word by word so that you may attain knowledge of the mysteries hidden therein. Be not satisfied with words, but seek to understand the spiritual meanings hidden in the heart of the words . . .

"For instance . . . consider the symbolical meanings of the words and teachings of Christ. His Holiness said, 'I am the living bread which came down from heaven; if any man eat of this bread he shall live forever.' When the Jews heard this they took it literally and failed to understand the significance of His meaning and teaching. The spiritual truth which Christ wished to convey to them was that the reality of Divinity within Him was like a blessing which had come down from heaven and that he who partook of this blessing should never die. That is to say, 'bread' was the symbol of the perfections which had descended upon Him from God, and he who ate of this bread or endowed himself with the perfections

of Christ would undoubtedly attain to life everlasting. The Jews did not understand Him, and taking the words literally said,' How can this man give us his flesh to eat?' Had they understood the real meaning of the Holy Book they would have become believers in Christ.

All the texts and teachings of the Holy Testaments have intrinsic spiritual meanings. They are not to be taken literally . . . These are the mysteries of God . . . I therefore pray in your behalf that you may be given the power of understanding these inner real meanings of the Holy Scriptures and may become informed of the mysteries deposited in the words of the Holy Bible so that you may attain eternal life and that your hearts may be attracted to the Kingdom of God. May your souls be illumined by the light of the words of God and may you become repositories of the mysteries of God, for no comfort is greater and no happiness is sweeter than spiritual comprehension of the divine teachings." [33]

Now I thought it would be helpful to study *The Seven Valleys*, written by Bahá'u'lláh, to ponder its depths about traversing the planes of existence. *The Seven Valleys* is a guide to the development of our spiritual nature and a fruitful source for meditation on our inner essence and path towards transformation, since it is a mystical composition. Its theme is the soul's journey in stages from this world to the realms of God's nearness and it was written in response to a Sufi's questions. (Sufism is a mystical dimension of Islam wherein the transcendence of the soul is pursued through repetition of the names of God and the verses of the *Qur'an*). For this discussion, I am depending upon Jenabe Caldwell's book *Reflections, Commentary on The Seven Valleys*,[34] which he was requested to compile because of the many insights he gained as a result of his classes on *The Seven Valleys* over a thirty-five year period. I will also rely on Taherzadeh's commentary on *The Seven Valleys*.[35] We know that as human beings we cannot ever to hope to gain more than a faint glimmering into the depth of *The Seven Valleys*. But perhaps through meditation on each of thee Valleys of the wayfarer's journey, we can gain valuable insights and become more immersed in God's light.

In the introduction of *The Seven Valleys*, Bahá'u'lláh calls upon us to surrender to God's will and to make His Teachings the top priority of our lives. Bahá'u'lláh's Teachings provide the answers for living our lives and dealing with work, family and friends.[36] Caldwell explains that a person who crosses the Seven Valleys will attain a station in which nothing can be mentioned besides God, because he is in a state of absolute certainty.[37] His former self is sacrificed for his true station, which is attained by absolute obedience to God's will.[38] The secrets of eternity are engraved on men and even though we are living and walking on this earth, our souls are soaring *"on the wings of longing"*[39] in the Revelation of God. The Word of God gives life to our souls and when the light of His knowledge enters us, it pulls us away from the emptiness of the world to our heavenly home.[40] Summarizing from Caldwell's book, there are seven stages to the maturing of souls. To progress through the Seven Valleys, we must detach from vain and selfish desires; materialism; excess baggage (ourselves); ideas; acquired knowledge; greed; self-centeredness; friends, relatives and work; imagination; imitating others; following the footsteps of our ancestors without checking out the truth for ourselves; enemies; preconceived ideas; prejudices; magic; material and spiritual gains. What we need for our journey is to be patient; to clean and purify our hearts; to take steps; to be single-minded; to have a pure motive and an open mind and heart; to detach from the things of pleasure and enjoyment on earth.

Until we acquire patience, we can't hope to get close to God but if we ***"strive for a hundred thousand years and yet fail to behold the beauty of the Friend,"*** [41] we should not get discouraged but continue to make the effort.[42] In the last chapter on prayer, we discussed impatience as a hindrance to prayer, emphasizing the need for patience in our supplications to God. Bahá'u'lláh teaches us the importance of patience in His Tablet about patience and the example of Job, as recounted by Taherzadeh.[43] The life of Job, the prophet, of course, is a marvelous example to us of patience. Job was a wealthy man living in luxury and comfort. God had entrusted him to guide his people and he was dedicated to his mission. But many were jealous and said he was devoted to God only because he was so wealthy. So God gave him many tribulations to prove his sincerity. He lost his sons, all his possessions and his crops. Then he became very ill. Throughout these ordeals he remained patient, resigned and thankful to God. Then he was forced from his village with only his wife to help him. He became destitute and had no food for days. Bahá'u'lláh tells us that Job was *"so patient and resigned to the will of God that his thankfulness and devotion to his Lord increased with his trials."* [44] He proved his detachment from possessions and God gave everything back to him. The people recognized his station and his words then penetrated their hearts. Bahá'u'lláh extols those who endure hardships patiently and with resignation.[45] Their fortitude and constancy, long-suffering and patience demonstrate the loftiness of their station. It occurs to me that we cannot fail to see that God wants us to learn patience, that as we continue on our spiritual journey we will be tested to prove ourselves worthy of being His servants and many of our tests will centre around our ability to be patient, to suffer and to withstand our misfortune in order to become transformed into spiritual beings. And we will realize how very difficult it is, particularly in our modern-day world that seems to be moving faster every day and purporting instant solutions and quick fixes. Today I was out walking and as I stopped to have a rest my eye spotted a slug slithering across the ground. I watched its progress and was surprised to see how fast it was actually able to cover the distance. Then I pondered where it was going, what was its purpose. The trail was gravel and dirt with only a few dry leaves in sight. And I threw a green leaf in its path, thinking it might be after some vegetation. But it slithered over the green leaf and continued on its way. I couldn't help thinking how difficult it was for me to watch the slug's slow progress and how much patience that slug needed to go from one point to another. But it wouldn't be aware of the distance, unlike me. Observe my lack of patience, just watching the slug and my need to intervene to throw the green leaf in its path "to get on with it." Bahá'u'lláh tells us:

"Be thou patient and quiet thyself. The things thou desirest can last but an hour." [46]

We will continue our journey through The Seven Valleys.

Service to humanity is essential upon entering the Valley of Search. Bahá'u'lláh tells us, *"In their search they have stoutly girded up the loins of service."* [47] It is *"not just service, but strong service."* [48] We will come across others like ourselves in this Valley and the mystery of our purpose in life will be revealed, as long as our hearts are removed from this world and the next.[49] Bahá'u'lláh constantly reassures us that the Invisible Realm will help us if we take steps and the fire burning in our hearts will continue to burn.[50] Our one desire is union with our Beloved. But sacrifice is needed of the things we possess, of all we've *"seen, and heard and understood,"* [51] all preconceived ideas, so that we are worthy to enter the spiritual realm.[52]

"Labor is needed if we are to seek Him; ardor is needed, if we are to drink of the honey of reunion with Him; and if we taste of this cup, we shall cast away the world." [53]

We only need to experience a little of God's nearness and we can not be satisfied with the material world.[54] The seeker needs to look in all places and investigate all leads, to be constantly on the move and ready to go wherever is needed to attain his goal. But he can't rush from place to place. He must abide in one place long enough to search out his Beloved.[55]

In the Valley of Love, a wayfarer must give up himself to become one with the love of God.[56] He becomes ecstatic in his love and only thinks of the lover. But an all-consuming love confuses the mind and reality – *"it burneth to ashes the harvest of reason."* [57]

Pain is the characteristic of this valley because we have seen the trace of God and it is painful to be separated from Him.[58] And Bahá'u'lláh tells us,"*...if there be no pain this journey will never end.*"[59] The thought of being separated increases the love we feel for Him. Bahá'u'lláh assures us that if we truly love God, we will fear nothing and can not be harmed.[60]

"Wherefore must the veils of the satanic self be burned away at the fire of love, that the spirit may be purified and cleansed and thus may know the station of the Lord of the Worlds.

*Kindle the fire of love and burn away all things,
Then set thy foot into the land of the lovers."* [61]

Each valley is progressive. When we pass out of the valley of search, we continue to search. Now that we have found the Beloved, our search is focused on how to get closer to the Beloved in order to understand and commune with Him. We have passed from the Valley of Love so our love for the beloved increases as we enter the Valley of Knowledge.[62] Taherzadeh explains that it is difficult to translate the original word "Ma'rifat" in English. *"It is a combination of true understanding, recognition and knowledge"* and is a knowledge *"not primarily based on learning . . . but the knowledge of God [that] dawns upon man through his heart."* [63]

Love without knowledge makes us fanatics.[64] In this Valley, we move from doubt to certitude.[65] The wayfarer gains a new vision and attains understanding of the mysteries of the love of God. In this valley we are *"content with the decree of God,"* [66] content to give up our own will and follow God's will. From the beginning we can see the end.[67] We know that what God does is perfect and any defects and flaws are man's doing. We do not despair when we face pain or calamities but approach them in recognition, realizing that they are part of God's mercy. We perceive wisdom in everything. We may experience injustice, but in the end there will be justice; there may be severe tests but we will learn patience and loving-kindness. In short, God's purpose for man will be accomplished. [68]

"And if he meeteth with injustice he shall have patience, and if he cometh upon wrath he shall manifest love." [69]

Up until now the Valleys were very limited but in the Valley of Unity the wayfarer *"ascendeth into the heaven of singleness,"* [70] *"from the plane of limitation into that of the absolute."* [71] Now there is no beginning or end. *"With the ear of God he heareth, with the eye of God he beholdeth the mysteries of the divine creation."* [72] He doesn't see creation subjectively with his own eyes, but objectively through God's eyes.[73] He learns that every part of creation manifests God's attributes, depending on its kingdom and to the extent that it is able. Now the wayfarer's vision has become so much wider because he isn't concerned about self or attachment to the world. He sees God's signs in everything. The ego has no place here. *"He looketh on all things with the eye of oneness ... He seeth in himself neither name nor fame nor rank, but findeth his own praise in praising God.* [74]

Bahá'u'lláh explains that *"the walls of self and passion and ... ignorance and blindness ..."* [75] keep us from God. God will not shut us out but we make the choice to shut ourselves out and therefore our punishment is self-inflicted.[76] If we fail a test we must continue to experience it until we pass it with His loving assistance.[77] In this valley, the wayfarer no longer worries about tests but depends on God with absolute faith and confidence and even prays for tests. Bahá'u'lláh explains that all men are created to reflect the light of God in relation to their capacity and efforts.[78] And in this valley we will see God in His creation and perceive the value of each person. [79]

"O My Brother! A pure heart is as a mirror; cleanse it with the burnish of love and severance from all save God, that the true sun may shine within it and the eternal morning dawn. Then wilt thou clearly see the meaning of 'Neither doth my earth nor My heaven contain Me, but the heart of My faithful servant containeth Me.' And thou wilt take up thy life in thine hand, and with infinite longing cast it before the new Beloved One." [80]

"Whensoever the Splendor of the King of the King of Oneness settleth upon the throne of the heart and soul, His shining becometh visible in every limb and member. At that time the mystery of the famed tradition gleameth out of the darkness: 'A servant is drawn unto Me in prayer until I answer him; and when I have answered him, I become the ear wherewith he heareth ... '" [81]

We find God (through His Manifestation) in our hearts. So when His light comes into our hearts to dwell, it is like a house which previously was empty and waiting for its owner to arrive home, at which time it becomes a place of invitation, of warmth and joy. [82] God created the light within us and His Teachers *"turn on the switch."* [83] Bahá'u'lláh tells us, *"Knowledge is a single point, but the ignorant have multiplied it."* [84]

The Valley of Unity is a stage that transcends words, names or attributes. To be truly in this valley, one only sees oneness. We need to impoverish ourselves – to be detached from everything. [85]

In the Valley of Contentment a wayfarer *"burneth away the veils of want"* [86] and he sees all. He leaves behind sorrow, anguish, grief and mourning and instead becomes blissful, joyful, living in *"delight and rapture."* [87] Words and feelings can't be conveyed to describe the soul's station:

"Only heart to heart can speak the bliss of mystic knowers;
No messenger can tell it and no missive bear it." [88]

"O friend, till thou enter the garden of such mysteries, thou shalt never set lip to the undying wine of this Valley. And shouldst thou taste of it, thou wilt shield thine eyes from all things else, and drink of the wine of contentment; and thou wilt loose thyself from all things else, and bind thyself to Him, and throw thy life down in His path, and cast thy soul away." [89]

The wayfarer sees God in all creation through his soul's inner vision and beholds a new creation.[90] He is content to sacrifice everything in His path. Now he is totally independent and is not worried about poverty because he is rich in spirit.[91] Only travelers who enter this valley experience true joy rather than a happiness based on the things of this world.[92] Our example is 'Abdu'l-Bahá who at the age of 9 began sharing the sufferings of His Father and spent 40 years in prison but was always cheerful and full of love for all who crossed His path.

In the Valley of Wonderment, everything is tossed into confusion because we begin to see *"wealth as poverty itself and the essence of freedom as sheer impotence."* [93] We are wearied, we are snatched by our roots, overwhelmed with the beauty of God in all creation, seeing new worlds constantly being formed in front of our inner eyes.[94] He discovers something new at every moment. The traveler now is able to see how vast creation is and how infinite and he can discover inner mysteries of the Revelation of God with clear vision and insight.[95] We are in awe as we go *"from astonishment to astonishment . . ."* [96] Meditating on God's creation, we discover a myriad wisdoms and truths.[97] God has given us signs in our dreams to teach us about the interrelatedness of all worlds as proof of the mysteries of life and our eternal destiny. Bahá'u'lláh takes us a step higher from the Valley of Unity to include the invisible worlds of God.[98] We cannot grasp the infinite worlds but through contemplation we can approach a faint glimmering of these mysteries because of His bounty. [99]

"O Lord, increase my astonishment at Thee!" [100]

Bahá'u'lláh tells us to *"reflect upon the perfection of man's creation, and that all these planes and states are folded up and hidden away within him.*

Dost thou reckon thyself only a puny form
When within thee the universe is folded?" [101]

The teaching of the world is folded up within us potentially through obedience to the Teachings and it requires prayer and hard work.[102]

"O friend, the heart is the dwelling of eternal mysteries, make it not the home of fleeting fancies; waste not the treasure of thy precious life in employment with this swiftly passing world. Thou comest from the world of holiness – bind not thine heart to the earth; thou art a dweller in the court of nearness – choose not the homeland of the dust." [103]

In the Valley of True Poverty and Absolute Nothingness, one sacrifices himself to God and leaves nothing behind – personal opinions, veils, wealth, even thoughts.[104] Nothingness is the **"dying from self and the living in God…"** [105] *"The mystery of sacrifice is that there is no sacrifice . . . the blossom is sacrificed for the fruit. The caterpillar is sacrificed for the butterfly. The worldly man is sacrificed into a heavenly being."* [106] Our first step towards God is selfish but the next step is to completely abandon self to be carried with wonder and astonishment totally unimaginable into the nearness of God.[107] Caldwell uses the following analogy.[108] He describes a man of the swamp and his journey to the river of life with his guide book, The Seven Valleys. When this man stops to enjoy his new life on a beautiful river, he is swept back into the swamp, like all the currents of life that pull us back. He learns to battle the negative currents and to feel safe and secure in his soul, truly feeling that he must be one of the chosen ones. Then his canoe is smashed on a boulder and other difficulties occur, which test his strength. He is aware of unseen forces assisting him. He is tested one day by huge rapids in front of him and he has to decide whether to give up or face the rapids and perhaps die. He progresses and his world becomes more beautiful. But he realizes that he must traverse all those miles back to the swamp to rescue his brothers and sisters. He has attained complete abandonment of self. And as he makes his way back God lifts him to a higher, inexplicable level. Caldwell is saying that if we demonstrate selfless devotion in our journey and put others before ourselves, God reaches down and lifts us up into a higher plane, a plane with no words to describe its wonder and we become one with Bahá'u'lláh; our words and feelings are as nothing. This [higher plane] cannot be reached without selfless sacrifice and plunging *"into the depths of hell fire for the sake of others."* [109] In this state one sees the face of God in every face. We must sacrifice ourselves so that only God is left and everything else save God is nothingness.

"O Brother! Not every sea hath pearls; not every branch will flower, nor will the nightingale sing thereon. Then ere the nightingale of the mystic paradise repair to the garden of God, and the rays of the heavenly morning return to the Sun of Truth – make thou an effort, that haply in this dustheap of the mortal world thou mayest catch a fragrance from the everlasting garden, and live forever in the shadow of the peoples of this city. And when thou hast attained this highest station and come to this mightiest plane, then shalt thou gaze on the Beloved, and forget all else." [110]

The wayfarer reacheth a oneness above the **"oneness of Being and Manifestation"** [111] that only ecstasy can describe. But he is told that he must obey the Laws and **"stray not the breadth of a hair from the 'Law'..."** [112] To traverse the Seven Valleys Caldwell states that we cannot break God's law. His laws are unbreakable. *"We break ourselves by disobeying the laws of God."*[113]

And so we come to the end of this journey. It seems to me that *The Seven Valleys* provides us with myriad truths and infinite wisdom to contemplate in meditation.

Now here are some meditations I can recommend to you. They come from various sources. It is to be noted once more that there are no specific techniques or meditation practices in the Bahá'í Writings. But the suggestions given here may be useful because most of them are proven methods to still the mind. As preparation prior to doing meditation, it may be useful to do relaxation. Achieving a relaxed body and mind helps us to attain a meditative state. Creating an atmosphere through the use of candles and soft music combined with the sounds of nature for example, are also helpful.

Here is a relaxation exercise with some modifications from the book *Developing Intuition* [114]:

"Sit in an alert, upright position in a comfortable chair with your lower back well supported, hands gently resting in your lap with your palms open ... Take a deep breath and exhale slowly, allowing your shoulders to be loose and relaxed. Open your mouth wide. Yawn, or pretend you are yawning. Let the areas around your eyes and forehead be relaxed and loose. Let the areas around your nose, mouth, and jaw be relaxed. Breathe slowly and easily. If ideas or feelings come into your mind at this time, pretend they are a telephone ringing in the distance, perhaps in a neighbor's house. You acknowledge that 'someone is calling' but you do not have to answer.

Take a deep breath, inhaling gently and slowly, imagining the breath entering your right nostril. Hold the breath for a moment, then exhale slowly and comfortably, imagining that you are exhaling through your left nostril. Take another deep breath, this time imagining your breath entering your left nostril and exiting your right.

Focus your attention on how your breath feels: cooling, as it enters your nostrils, perhaps gently expanding your chest as it fills your lungs, then slightly warming your nostrils as you exhale. You may wish to visualize the air as having a beautiful, vibrant color as it enters and exits your body. Repeat this breathing pattern until you have done at least four full cycles. A full cycle is one inhalation and one exhalation through each nostril . . .

[As you focus on your breathing, you are going to relax each part of your body, starting with your feet and ankles and moving towards your head. Feel the part of your body getting heavier and sinking or becoming lighter as you breathe and focus on it.]

[Now] be aware of your feet relaxing. [Then] be aware of your legs relaxing. [Then]... your buttocks. [Then]... your abdomen. Be aware of your arms and hands relaxing. [And]... your upper back. [And]... your chest. [Then]... your neck and shoulders. [And finally]... your head. Now let your breathing pattern return to normal as you enjoy the relaxed state you have created."

You may want to imagine yourself in your favourite place. Think of the sights, sounds, tastes in that place, how it feels, concentrate on using all your senses to recreate the feeling of being there. If you don't have a favourite place, create one.

Meditations:

> 1. Breathing mindfully (for grounding and centering yourself) – Observe your breath flowing in and out of the lungs. Notice the air flowing in through your nostrils, the rise and fall of your shoulders and rib cage. Let your thoughts come and go, acknowledge them and refocus on your breath. (You may last only 10 seconds at first before you 'drift off'.) You're not trying to get rid of extraneous thoughts; you may remain aware of them, but your attention is fully centered on your breathing. Now take ten slow, deep breaths. Work up to 5 or 10 minutes.[115]
>
> 2. Leaves on a Stream – *"Find a comfortable position, close your*

eyes and fix them on a spot and take a few slow, deep breaths. Imagine you're sitting by the side of a gently flowing stream. There are leaves floating on the surface of the water. For the next 5 minutes, take every thought that pops into your head, place it on a leaf, and let it float on by. Alternately, if you find visualization, just imagine a black moving strip or a moving expanse of blackness, and place each thought onto that . . . If your mind conjures up pictures rather than words, put each picture on a leaf, and let it float on by." [116]

3. Radio Mind – This exercise is good for those who predominantly hear their thoughts like voices in their heads. *"Imagine your mind is a radio. Listen to your thoughts as if you're listening to a sports commentator or news announcer. Notice where the voice seems to be located – in the direct center of your head or off to one side. Notice the speed and rhythm of the words, the volume and pitch. Notice the emotion present in the voice. Notice the pauses or gaps when the words stop or slow down. Try doing this for 5 minutes initially."* [117]

4. Using the senses – Focus your attention on your inner energy field. Become aware of the stillness. *"Use your senses fully. Be where you are. Look around. Just look, don't interpret. See the light, shapes, colors, textures. Be aware of the silent presence of each thing. Be aware of the space that allows everything to be. Listen to the sounds; don't judge them. Listen to the silence underneath the sounds. Touch something – anything – and feel and acknowledge its Being. Observe the rhythm of your breathing; feel the air flowing in and out, feel the life energy inside your body. Allow everything to be, within and without. Allow the "isness" of all things. Move deeply into the Now."* [118]

5. Inner Guidance Meditation – *"Find a quiet, peaceful place where you will be undisturbed for a few minutes. Sit . . . in a comfortable position with your spine straight and well supported. Close your eyes. Take a deep breath, and as you exhale slowly, relax your body. Take another deep breath and as you exhale, relax your body a little more. Take another deep breath and as your exhale, relax your body as deeply and completely as you can. If any place in your body feels tight and tense, gently breathe into that area and allow it to release and relax. Not take another deep breath and as you exhale, relax your mind. Let your thoughts just drift away. As each new thought comes up in your mind, let it go. There is no need to hold onto any thought. Just keep letting*

them go and bringing your attention back to breathing slowly and deeply and relaxing. Take another deep breath and as you exhale, imagine that you can move your awareness out of your mind, out of your head, and drop it slowly down into your body. Let it rest in the area of your solar plexus or your belly. Now take another deep breath and, as you exhale, let your awareness move into a very deep quiet place within. With every breath, as you exhale, move a little deeper and a little deeper until you come to rest in the deepest, quietest place you can find. Then just let yourself rest in this quiet place inside . . . [You can ask yourself a question then] *rest quietly and be open to what might come . . . Take whatever comes and be with it for a little while . It's not necessary to understand it. Just be with it in a receptive way . . . allow yourself to sit with it . . .* [Contemplate whatever comes to you.] *When you feel complete with the process for now, begin to notice your breath again. Notice how your body is feeling and become aware of your surroundings. When you are ready you can open your eyes."* [119]

6. Love's Pathway – Close your eyes and breathe deeply 3 or 4 times, while saying the following to yourself:
"I am the full expression of God's love. Just as God is love, so am I. I am love. Hold in mind the image of someone you love. Then imagine yourself holding that person in a loving embrace, while saying 'I love you' in your mind. Hold on to this feeling of love, allowing it to spread throughout your entire being. While holding on to this feeling of love, silently say to yourself, 'I feel love.' After a few moments mentally say, 'I feel God.' Then finally, in your mind, say, 'Thank you', allowing the feeling of gratitude and appreciation to wash over you. Remain in this state of being love for a few minutes, imagining the love in you radiating outward in an egg-shaped sphere of vibratory energy that flows out onto all people, encompassing the world and the universe." [120]

7. Connecting with the Inner Body – *"You may find it helpful to close your eyes . . . but later on when 'being in the body' has become natural and easy, this will no longer be necessary. Direct your attention into your body. Feel it from within. Is it alive? Is there life in your hands, arms, legs, and feet – in your abdomen, your chest? Can you feel the subtle energy field that pervades the entire body and gives vibrant life to every organ and every cell? Can you feel it simultaneously in all parts of the body as a single field of energy? Keep focusing on the feeling of your inner body for a few moments. Do not*

start to think about it. Feel it. The more attention you give it, the clearer and stronger this feeling will become. It will feel as if every cell is becoming more alive, and if you have a strong visual sense, you may get an image of your body becoming luminous. Although such an image can help you temporarily, pay more attention to the feeling than to any image that may arise . . . If you cannot feel very much at this stage, pay attention to whatever you can feel. Perhaps there is just a slight tingling in your hands and feet . . . Open your eyes . . . Keep some attention in the inner energy field of the body even as you look around the room . . .
If at any time you are finding it hard to get in touch with the inner body, it is usually easier to focus on your breathing first . . . Whenever an answer, a solution or a creative idea is needed, stop thinking for a moment by focusing attention on your inner energy field. Become aware of the stillness . . . In any thought activity, make it a habit to go back and forth every few minutes or so between thinking and an inner kind of listening, an inner stillness." [121]

8. *"Waiting" – ". . . The state of presence could be compared to waiting. Jesus used the analogy of waiting in some of his parables. This is not the usual bored or restless kind of waiting . . . There is a qualitatively different kind of waiting, one that requires your total alertness. Something could happen at any moment, and if you are not absolutely awake, absolutely still, you will miss it . . . all your attention is in the [present moment], and none is left for daydreaming, thinking, remembering, anticipating. There is no tension in it, no fear, just alert presence. 'Be like a servant waiting for the return of the master,' says Jesus. The servant does not know at what hour the master is going to come. So he stays awake, alert, poised, still, lest he miss the master's arrival."* [122]

9. *"As you breathe in, you say to yourself, 'Breathing in, I know that I am breathing in.' And as you breathe out, say, 'Breathing out, I know that I am breathing out.'" Or just say 'in'; 'out'. Or:*

*"Breathing in, I calm my body, Breathing out, I smile.
Dwelling in the present moment,
I know this is a wonderful moment."* [123]

10. *The practice of silence* – Written by monks, this little book embellishes the monastic tradition of maintaining silence.

Here are just a few snippets from this gem. *"Within each one of us there is a place where there is complete silence, free from all . . . thoughts . . . cares and desires . . . where we are totally at home with ourselves . . . the point at which the true encounter between God and humanity can take place."* [124] Spend time in silence. It can be considered a "letting go". Be confident in silence, being *"hidden in God"*, let yourself *"fall into His arms"*, abandon yourself as you are so God can take over your guidance.[125] But don't *"force any experience of God"* and don't wait impatiently for it. *"Relinquish all expectations . . . Let go of . . . images and imaginings . . . relinquish [your] very selves. We do not need to display anything to God. We are simply before God and remain silent. We hold up our empty hearts to God's presence, to be filled with God's...love."* [126] We wait and persevere in waiting. The only thing that matters is that the Spirit of God be free to operate in us. I may recoil from letting go of self because *"by nature I wish to hold on to myself and rather use God as an instrument toward my perfection, instead of abandoning myself to God with my imperfections."* [127] We take our thoughts, feelings and cares much too seriously instead of letting God have such close access to us that only God matters. When we do speak, we feel the silence we have experienced. We speak calmly and sensibly and *"say what the Spirit prompts us to say... and speak only when the Spirit prompts us to do so."* [128] Silence provides an atmosphere for prayer and it provides the growth that has been gained in prayer. *"The observance of silence . . . allows the spirit of prayer to reverberate and take root in the heart."* [129] Silence *"is not a passive inactivity but rather an active listening, a withdrawal . . . into the realm of God, when I listen to what God has to say to me during silence, when I permit myself to enter into the experience that awaits me on God's part during a genuine silence."* [130]

REFERENCES

1 Bahá'u'lláh, *The Kitab-i-Iqan, The Book of Certitude*, (Wilmette, IL: Bahá'í Publishing Trust, 1983), p. 238
2 Bahá'u'lláh, *Gleanings from the Writings of Bahá'u'lláh*, LXXX, p. 153
3 Bahá'u'lláh, *The Hidden Words*, Persian no. 12, p. 26
4 'Abdu'l-Bahá, *Paris Talks*, Address...at the Friends' Meeting House, [8-20], p. 174-176
5 Shoghi Effendi, *The Compilation of Compilations* Vol. II, 1774, 19 November 1945, p. 241
6 Hellaby, William and Madeline, *Prayer, A Bahá'í Approach*, p. 20
7 Ibid., p. 20-21
8 Moffett, Ruth J., *DU'A: On Wings of Prayer*, p. 29
9 Ibid.
10 Ibid.
11 'Abdu'l-Bahá, *Paris Talks*, The Progress of the Soul, [4], p. 179
12 'Abdu'l-Bahá, *The Compilation of Compilations* Vol. I, prepared by the Universal House of Justice 1963-1990 (Victoria, Australia: Bahá'í Publications, 1990), 425, p. 204
13 Shoghi Effendi, *Principles of Bahá'í Administration*, p. 10
14 Shoghi Effendi, *The Compilation of Compilations* Vol. II, 1774, 19 November 1945, p. 241
15 The Universal House of Justice, *Messages from the Universal House of Justice 1963-1986*
(Wilmette, IL: Bahá'í Publishing Trust, 1986), 375.7-375.9, p. 589-590
16 Momen, Wendi, *Meditation* (Oxford: George Ronald, 1999)
17 Shoghi Effendi, *God Passes By* (Wilmette, IL: Bahá'í Publishing Trust, 1974), p. 119
18 Shoghi Effendi, *The Compilation of Compilations* Vol. II, 1761, 6 December 1935, p. 237
19 Ibid., 1782, 27 January 1952, p. 243
20 Rutstein, Nathan, *A Way out of the Trap*, p. 124
21 Ibid., p. 123
22 Bahá'u'lláh, *Gleanings from the Writings of Bahá'u'lláh*, LXX, p. 136
23 Rutstein, Nathan, *A Way out of the Trap*, p. 125
24 Ibid., p. 125-126
25 Hanson, Rick. *Buddha's Brain* (Oakland, CA: New Harbinger Publications, 2009), p. 88
26 Williamson, Marianne, *The Gift of Change*, p. 80
27 Rutstein, Nathan. *A Way out of the Trap*, p. 126
28 Bahá'u'lláh, *Tablets of Bahá'u'lláh*, p. 140-141
29 Bahá'u'lláh, *Gleanings from the Writings of Bahá'u'lláh*, CLIII, p. 326

30 Bahá'u'lláh, *The Kitab-i-Aqdas, The Most Holy Book*, [158], p. 76
31 Redman, Earl, *'Abdu'l-Bahá in their Midst* (Oxford: George Ronald, 2011), p. 269
32 Bahá'u'lláh, *Prayers and Meditations by Bahá'u'lláh*, LVI, p. 83
33 'Abdu'l-Bahá, *The Promulgation of Universal Peace*, 3 December 1912, [3], p. 459-460
34 Caldwell, Jenabe, *Reflections, Commentary on the Seven Valleys* (New Delhi, India: Bahá'í Publishing Trust, 2005)
35 Taherzadeh, Adib, *The Revelation of Bahá'u'lláh* Vol. 1, p. 96-101
36 Caldwell, Jenabe, *Reflections, Commentary on the Seven Valleys*, p. 2
37 Ibid., p. 5
38 Ibid., p. 6
39 Ibid., p. 7
40 Ibid., p. 8
41 Bahá'u'lláh, *The Seven Valleys and the Four Valleys* (Wilmette, IL: Bahá'í Publishing Trust, 1991), p.5
42 Caldwell, Jenabe, *Reflections, Commentary on the Seven Valleys*, p. 10
43 Taherzadeh, Adib, *The Revelation of Bahá'u'lláh* Vol. 1, p. 270
44 Ibid., p. 271
45 Ibid.
46 Bahá'u'lláh, *Prayers and Meditations of Bahá'u'lláh*, VIII, p. 11
47 Bahá'u'lláh, *The Seven Valleys and the Four Valleys*, p. 5
48 Caldwell, Jenabe, *Reflections, Commentary on the Seven Valleys*, p. 11
49 Ibid., p. 22
50 Ibid., p. 23
51 Bahá'u'lláh, *The Seven Valleys and the Four Valleys*, p. 7
52 Caldwell, Jenabe, *Reflections, Commentary on the Seven Valleys*, p. 24
53 Bahá'u'lláh, *The Seven Valleys and the Four Valleys*, p. 7
54 Caldwell, Jenabe, *Reflections, Commentary on the Seven Valleys*, p. 24
55 Ibid., p. 25
56 Ibid.
57 Bahá'u'lláh, *The Seven Valleys and the Four Valleys*, p. 8
58 Caldwell, Jenabe, *Reflections, Commentary on the Seven Valleys*, p. 27
59 Bahá'u'lláh, *The Seven Valleys and the Four Valleys*, p. 8
60 Caldwell, Jenabe, *Reflections, Commentary on the Seven Valleys*, p. 27
61 Bahá'u'lláh, *The Seven Valleys and the Four Valleys*, p. 11
62 Caldwell, Jenabe, *Reflections, Commentary on the Seven Valleys*, p. 30
63 Taherzadeh, Adib, *The Revelation of Bahá'u'lláh* Vol. 1, p. 98
64 Caldwell, Jenabe, *Reflections, Commentary on the Seven Valleys*, p. 30
65 Ibid., p. 32
66 Bahá'u'lláh, *The Seven Valleys and the Four Valleys*, p. 12
67 Caldwell, Jenabe, *Reflections, Commentary on the Seven Valleys*, p. 32
68 Ibid., p. 37

69 Bahá'u'lláh, *The Seven Valleys and the Four Valleys*, p. 13
70 Ibid., p. 17
71 Taherzadeh, Adib, *The Revelation of Bahá'u'lláh* Vol. 1, p. 99
72 Bahá'u'lláh, *The Seven Valleys and the Four Valleys*, p. 17
73 Taherzadeh, Adib, *The Revelation of Bahá'u'lláh* Vol. 1, p. 99
74 Bahá'u'lláh, *The Seven Valleys and the Four Valleys*, p. 18
75 Ibid., p. 19
76 Caldwell, Jenabe, *Reflections, Commentary on the Seven Valleys*, p. 59
77 Ibid., p. 56
78 Ibid., p. 57
79 Ibid., p. 58
80 Bahá'u'lláh, *The Seven Valleys and the Four Valleys*, p. 21-22
81 Ibid., p. 22
82 Caldwell, Jenabe, *Reflections, Commentary on the Seven Valleys*, p. 66
83 Ibid., p. 68
84 Bahá'u'lláh, *The Seven Valleys and the Four Valleys*, p. 24-25
85 Caldwell, Jenabe, *Reflections, Commentary on the Seven Valleys*, p. 72-73
86 Bahá'u'lláh, *The Seven Valleys and the Four Valleys*, p. 29
87 Ibid.
88 Ibid., p. 30
89 Ibid., p. 30-31
90 Caldwell, Jenabe, *The Seven Valleys and the Four Valleys*, p. 75
91 Taherzadeh, Adib, *The Revelation of Bahá'u'lláh* Vol. 1, p. 99
92 Ibid., p. 100
93 Bahá'u'lláh, *The Seven Valleys and the Four Valleys*, p. 31
94 Caldwell, Jenabe, *Reflections, Commentary on the Seven Valleys*, p. 76
95 Taherzadeh, Adib, *The Revelation of Bahá'u'lláh* Vol. 1, p. 101
96 Bahá'u'lláh, *The Seven Valleys and the Four Valleys*, p. 32
97 Caldwell, Jenabe, *Reflections, Commentary on the Seven Valleys*, p. 77
98 Ibid., p. 80
99 Ibid., p. 81
100 Bahá'u'lláh, *The Seven Valleys and the Four Valleys*, p. 34
101 Ibid.
102 Caldwell, Jenabe, *Reflections, Commentary on the Seven Valleys*, p. 82
103 Bahá'u'lláh, *The Seven Valleys and the Four Valleys*, p. 35
104 Caldwell, Jenabe, *Reflections, Commentary on the Seven Valleys*, p. 85
105 Bahá'u'lláh, *The Seven Valleys and the Four Valleys*, p. 36
106 Caldwell, Jenabe, *Reflections, Commentary on the Seven Valleys*, p. 85
107 Ibid., p. 91
108 Ibid., p. 87-92
109 Ibid., p. 92
110 Bahá'u'lláh, *The Seven Valleys and the Four Valleys*, p. 38
111 Ibid., p. 39

112 Ibid., p. 39-40
113 Caldwell, Jenabe, *Reflections, Commentary on the Seven Valleys*, p. 97
114 Gawain, Shakti, *Developing Intuition* (Novato, CA: Nataraj Publishing, 2000), p. 49-51
115 Harris, Russ, *ACT with Love, Stop Struggling, Reconcile Differences, and Strengthen Your Relationship with Acceptance and Commitment Therapy* (Oakland, CA: New Harbinger Publications, 2009), p. 106
116 Ibid., p. 102
117 Ibid.
118 Tolle, Eckhart, *The Power of Now* (Novato, Ca: New World Library, 2004), p. 63
119 Gawain, Shakti, *Developing Intuition*, p. 54-56
120 Sage, Carnelian, *The Greatest Manifestation Principle in the World* (Think-Outside-The- Book Publications, 2007)
121 Tolle, Eckhart, *The Power of Now*, p. 112-113; 125-126
122 Ibid., p. 94-95
123 Thich Nhat Hanh, *Peace is Every Step* (New York: Bantam Books, 1991), p. 8; 10
124 Grun, Anselm, *The Challenge of Silence* (Schuyler, Nebraska: Benedictine Mission House Publications, 1993), p. 69
125 Ibid., p. 40
126 Ibid., p. 69-70
127 Ibid., p. 42
128 Ibid., p. 31
129 Ibid., p. 59
130 Ibid., p. 61

Chapter 4
Observing the Fast

Chapter 4
Observing the Fast

Bahá'u'lláh has told mankind that *"obligatory prayer and fasting occupy an exalted station in the sight of God"*.[1] *"Fasting and obligatory prayer are as two wings to man's life. Blessed be the one who soareth with their aid in the heaven of the love of God, the Lord of all worlds."* [2] 'Abdu'l-Bahá refers to them as *"the two mightiest pillars of God's Holy Law"* [3] and states that they are *"among the most great ordinances of this holy Dispensation."* [4] Through them, Bahá'u'lláh tells us, we may *"draw nigh unto God."* [5]

In this chapter we will explore the Bahá'í Writings about the nineteen-day Fast. Every year between March 2nd and the 20th, it is an obligation for Bahá'ís to refrain from eating and drinking from sunrise to sunset. The Writings in this chapter refer specifically to the Bahá'í Fast but fasting is observed in all religious traditions. Buddhists practice periods of fasting as a method for purification and freeing their minds. Hindus commonly fast during the New Moon and certain festivals to enhance their concentration in worship and purify their systems. Yom Kippur, the Day of Atonement, is a day of fasting for those who follow the Jewish tradition as are six other fast days. And in various branches of Christianity, fasting is observed. Catholics abstain from meat on Ash Wednesday and Good Friday and also all Fridays during Lent. The purpose is the control of bodily desires, penance for their sins and also solidarity with poor people. In the Eastern Orthodox Church, Lent is also observed as well as other fast days and individuals generally do not eat meat, eggs and dairy products. In some Protestant churches fasts have become popular for individuals as an attempt to improve spiritually, to relate to the poor and to counterbalance our consumer world. The Mormons fast on the first Sunday of every month, having no food or drink for two meals and donating money or food to the needy. Muslims have a fasting period from sunrise to sunset for thirty days.[6]

Fasting is truly a spiritual experience. When carried out in the spirit for which it was intended I am not aware of any other spiritual practice we can engage in that has such potential to transform us. I am going to describe the experience of fasting in light of a statement by Bahá'u'lláh:

"There are various stages and stations for the Fast and innumerable effects and benefits are concealed therein. Well is it with those who have attained unto them." [7]

I can't pretend to really understand what this means but let's explore the concept of "stages" and "stations" further. On a superficial level, when I fast, there is generally a break in my daily routine. My schedule may not be as hectic. I may spend less time on food preparation and find that I have some quiet time, time to slow down so that my senses become more attuned and I become more thoughtful in questioning who I really am. I am also tested. My will and self-discipline is definitely put to the test as I go all day without food or drink. I don't believe that there is any other obligation or action in the Bahá'í Faith that teaches individuals to surrender their will to God as does fasting. Whereas before The Fast, they may feel strong and independent, hunger takes them down a peg and they realize that they are reliant on things in this life. Then they may progress to a deeper level, a different stage. Once they consciously adjust somewhat to not having food or drink during the day, they are practicing detachment – detachment from food, from the physical world and physical desires. The detachment may only be for one hour of the time that they fast but it is still detachment. They cannot help but think about why they are doing this and that they are spiritual beings. They begin to consider their actions, preferring to practice virtuous behavior rather than giving in to the urges of their lower natures. They take the time to listen to others and share in their lives, ignoring their rumbling stomachs and a desire to rush home for a nap. Moving to an even deeper level or stage, during the Fast they may find that their love for God increases as they have more time to pray and they say their prayers with more purity and significance. Bahá'ís have been blessed with special prayers for fasting, prayers that are filled with reminders of the proper attitude they should have when fasting (that of surrender to the will of God and detachment from the physical world) and that also recount the bounties they receive if they fast wholly for God and with detachment from all save Him. Ruhiyyih Khanum, the wife of Shoghi Effendi, writes of her experience in saying one of the long fasting prayers in the book, *Fasting, A Bahá'í Handbook* by Duane L. Herrmann, noting that *"the blessing of keeping the fast and the blessing of saying this prayer with it become one great annual bounty, one special privilege of life."* [8] The prayer she is referring to is the one with the repeating phrase, **" Thou seest me, O my God, holding to Thy Name, the Most Holy, the Most Luminous, the Most Mighty, the Most Great, the Most Exalted, the Most Glorious, and clinging to the hem of the robe to which have clung all in this world and in the world to come."** This particular prayer can be a powerful meditation.

On another level, or in another station, as individuals become more totally immersed in their prayers, they may feel God's presence in their lives more deeply and the influence of His love and they may begin to feel a longing desire to become stronger in their Faith and to consecrate themselves more deeply in service as their detachment from their selfish desires increases and they begin to recognize the power invested in these days. They may wish to dedicate more of their time and energy to such service and let go of the parts of their lives that have less meaning or spiritual significance. They may seek more balance, spending less time on work or work-related activities outside of the office, for example. With prayer, contemplation and meditation during the Fast, they may reach a station in which they really want to dedicate themselves to the service of Bahá'u'lláh in a new way, in a way they've never envisaged before, to reach a higher station, and thus receive the blessings and confirmations of God. These are only my thoughts about a process of transformation possible by means of fasting.

And so, having engaged in this exercise and perhaps having reached a higher station in our thinking, we will now explore the Writings about The Fast.

The Fast is a law, a commandment, ordained by Bahá'u'lláh for the spiritual regeneration of mankind. Shoghi Effendi explains: *"As regards fasting, it constitutes, together with the obligatory prayers, the two pillars that sustain the revealed Law of God."* [9]

But it is not just a law, as Bahá'u'lláh explains:

"Think not that We have revealed unto you a mere code of laws. Nay, rather, We have unsealed the choice Wine with the fingers of might and power. To this beareth witness that which the Pen of Revelation hath revealed. Meditate upon this, O men of insight!" [10]

'Abdu'l-Bahá tells us:

"Thou hast written about the Fast. This is a most weighty matter and thou shouldst exert thine utmost in its observance. It is a fundamental of the Divine law, and one of the pillars of the religion of God." [11]

These are the essential requirements laid down in Bahá'u'lláh's Kitab-i-Aqdas, The Most Holy Book, The Book of Laws.

"We have commanded you to pray and fast from the beginning of maturity; this is ordained by God, your Lord and the Lord of your forefathers. He has exempted from this those who are weak from illness or age, as a bounty from His Presence, and He is the Forgiving, the Generous." [12]

"...Abstinence from food and drink, from sunrise to sunset, is obligatory ...Fasting is binding on men and women on attaining the age of maturity, which is fixed at 15.

"Exemption from fasting is granted to travellers . . . those who are ill . . . those who are over 70 . . . women who are with child . . . women who are nursing . . . women in their courses . . . those who are engaged in heavy labour, who are advised to show respect for the law by using discretion and restraint when availing themselves of the exemption." [13]

And Bahá'ís are advised to follow the instructions as given in the *Kitab-i-Aqdas* and not to follow their own "idle imaginings" concerning the Fast:

"Praise be unto Him Who hath revealed laws in accordance with His good-pleasure. Verily, He is sovereign over whatsoever He wisheth. O My friends! Act ye in accordance with what ye have been commanded in the Book. Fasting hath been decreed for you in the month of 'Ala. Fast ye for the sake of your Lord, the Mighty, the Most High. Restrain yourselves from sunrise to sunset. Thus doth the Beloved of mankind instruct you as bidden by God, the All-Powerful, the Unconstrained. It is not for anyone to exceed the limits laid down by God and His law, nor should anyone follow his own idle imaginings. Well is it with the one who fulfilleth My decrees for the love of My Beauty, and woe to the one who neglecteth the Dayspring of Command in the days of his Lord, the Almighty, the Omnipotent." [14]

There are many Writings from the Pen of Bahá'u'lláh related to fasting and the obligatory prayers. Of course, Bahá'u'lláh is the Law-Maker and this is a Law of God. And Bahá'u'lláh attached great importance to The Fast. Fasting has been endowed with great importance by God throughout time and its importance is now reiterated by Bahá'u'lláh.

"Nothing, after prayer, will cause the development of the spirit, save fasting. The Primal Point, The Báb, ordained for all the people to fast until they should reach the age of forty-two, but the Blessed Perfection said: 'We love fasting! Unless the people become old and weak, they should fast.' . . . His Holiness, the Blessed Perfection, used to fast throughout the set time every year . . ." [15]

Bahá'u'lláh is quite adamant about the importance of keeping this Law of God:

"Be not neglectful of obligatory prayer and fasting. He who faileth to observe them hath not been nor will ever be acceptable in the sight of God. Follow ye wisdom under all conditions. He, verily, hath bidden all to observe that which hath been and will be of profit to them. He, in truth, is the All-Sufficing, the Most High." [16]

And 'Abdu'l-Bahá strongly urges us to keep the commandment of fasting:

"In the realm of worship, fasting and obligatory prayer constitute the two mightiest pillars of God's holy Law. Neglecting them is in no wise permitted, and falling short in their performance is of a certainty not acceptable. In the Tablet of Visitation He saith: 'I beseech God, by Thee and by them whose faces have been illumined with the splendors of the light of Thy countenance, and who, for love of Thee, have observed all whereunto they were bidden.' He declareth that observance of the commands of God deriveth from love for the beauty of the Best-Beloved. The seeker, when immersed in the ocean of the love of God, will be moved by intense longing and will arise to carry out the laws of God..." [17]

The laws of God regarding fasting and obligatory prayer are absolutely incumbent upon His servants. Therefore, they must turn their faces to the Point of Adoration of the celestial Concourse, hold fast to the most sublime Station, and pray and supplicate that they may be freed from the doubts of misinterpretation. This is the way of 'Abdu'l-Bahá. This is the religion of 'Abdu'l-Bahá. This is the path of 'Abdu'l-Bahá. Whoever cherisheth the love of Bahá, let him choose this straight path. Whoever abandoneth this path, verily, he is of them who are shut out as by a veil from Him ... [18]

"The laws of God, such as fasting, obligatory prayer and the like, as well as His counsels regarding virtues, good deeds and proper conduct, must be carried out everywhere to the extent possible, unless some insurmountable obstacle or some great danger presents itself or it runneth counter to the dictates of wisdom. For indolence and laxity hinder the outpourings of love from the clouds of divine mercy, and people will thus remain deprived." [19]

It is clear to me that 'Abdu'l-Bahá is telling the Bahá'ís that they have no excuses for not observing the commandments of God, including fasting. He warns them not to be lazy and negligent in carrying out this important law and that, if they do, they are deprived of spiritual progress.

And Bahá'u'lláh exhorts them to follow His laws for the love of His beauty:

"We, verily, have set forth all things in Our Book, as a token of grace unto those who have believed in God, the Almighty, the Protector, the Self-Subsisting. And We have ordained obligatory prayer and

fasting so that all may by these means draw nigh unto God, the Most Powerful, the Well-Beloved. We have written down these two laws and expounded every irrevocable decree. We have forbidden men from following whatsoever might cause them to stray from the Truth, and have commanded them to observe that which will draw them nearer unto Him Who is the Almighty, the All-Loving. Say: Observe ye the commandments of God for love of His beauty, and be not of those who follow in the ways of the abject and foolish." [20]

And observing the Fast is a bounty from God and our protection:

"This is one of the nights of the Fast, and during it the Tongue of Grandeur and Glory proclaimed: There is no God beside Me, the Omnipotent Protector, the Self-Subsisting. We, verily, have commanded all to observe the Fast in these days as a bounty on Our part, but the people remain unaware, except for those who have attained unto the purpose of God as revealed in His laws and have comprehended His wisdom that pervadeth all things visible and invisible. Say: By God! His Law is a fortress unto you, could ye but understand. Verily, He hath no purpose therein save to benefit the souls of His servants, but, alas, the generality of mankind remain heedless thereof. Cling ye to the cord of God's laws, and follow not those who have turned away from the Book, for verily they have opposed God, the Mighty, the Beloved." [21]

'Abdu'l-Bahá tells us about the "Divine Wisdom" of fasting. This is one wisdom:

The Divine wisdom in fasting is manifold. Among them is this: As during those days (i.e. the period of fasting which the followers afterward observe) the Manifestation of the Sun of Reality, through Divine inspiration, is engaged in the descent (revealing) of Verses, the instituting of Divine Law and the arrangement of teachings, through excessive occupation and intensive attraction, there remains no condition or time for eating and drinking. For example, when His Holiness Moses went to Mount Tur (Sinai) and there engaged in instituting the Law of God, He fasted forty days. For the purpose of awakening and admonishing the people of Israel, fasting was enjoined upon them. Likewise, His Holiness Christ, in the beginning of instituting the Spiritual Law, the systemizing of the teachings and the arrangement of counsels, for forty days abstained from eating and drinking. In the beginning the disciples and Christians fasted. Later the assemblages of the chief Christians changed fasting into lenten observances. Likewise the Qur'an [Koran] having descended in the month of Ramadan, fasting during that month became a duty. In like manner His Holiness the Supreme (The Báb), in the beginning of the Manifestation through the excessive effect of descending verses, passed days in which His nourishment was reduced to tea only. Likewise, the Blessed Beauty (Bahá'u'lláh), when busy with instituting the Divine Teachings and during the days when the Verses (The Word of God) descended continuously, through the great effect of the Verses and the throbbing of the heart, took no food except the least amount. The purpose is this: In order to follow the Divine Manifestation and for the purpose of admonition and the commemoration of their state, it became incumbent upon the people to fast during those days. For every sincere soul who has a beloved longs to experience that state in which his beloved is. If his beloved is in a state of sorrow, he desires sorrow; if in a state of joy, he desires joy; if in a state of rest, he desires rest; if in a state of trouble, he desires trouble. Now, since in this Millennial Day, His Holiness the Supreme (The Báb) fasted many days, and the Blessed Beauty (Bahá'u'lláh) took but little food or drink, it becomes necessary that the friends should follow that example. For thus saith He in the Tablet of Visitation: They, the believers, who, for love of Thee, have observed all whereunto they were bidden. [22]

Bahá'u'lláh discusses the importance of fasting:

"Cling firmly to obligatory prayer and fasting. Verily, the religion of God is like unto heaven; fasting is its sun, and obligatory prayer is its moon. In truth, they are the pillars of religion whereby the righteous are distinguished from those who transgress His commandments. We entreat God, exalted and glorified be He, that he may graciously enable all to observe that which He hath revealed in His Ancient Book." [23]

He explains the terminology of the "sun" and the "moon" in this passage:

In another sense, by the terms 'sun', 'moon', and 'stars' are meant such laws and teachings as have been established and proclaimed in every Dispensation, such as the laws of prayer and fasting. These have, according to the law of the Qur'án, been regarded, when the beauty of the Prophet Muhammad had passed beyond the veil, as the most fundamental and binding laws of His dispensation . . .

Moreover, in the traditions the terms sun and moon have been applied to prayer and fasting, even as it is said: Fasting is illumination, prayer is light. One day, a well-known divine came to visit Us. While We were conversing with him, he referred to the above-quoted tradition. He said:

Inasmuch as fasting causeth the heat of the body to increase, it hath therefore been likened unto the light of the sun; and as the prayer of the night-season refresheth man, it hath been compared unto the radiance of the moon. Thereupon We realized that that poor man had not been favoured with a single drop of the ocean of true understanding, and had strayed far from the burning Bush of divine wisdom. We then politely observed to him saying: The interpretation your honour hath given to this tradition is the one current amongst the people. Could it not be interpreted differently? He asked Us: What could it be? We made reply: Muhammad, the Seal of the Prophets, and the most distinguished of God's chosen Ones, hath likened the Dispensation of the Qur'án unto heaven, by reason of its loftiness, its paramount influence, its majesty, and the fact that it comprehendeth all religions. And as the sun and moon constitute the brightest and most prominent luminaries in the heavens, similarly in the heaven of the religion of God two shining orbs have been ordained -- fasting and prayer . . . [24]

And Bahá'u'lláh explains the purpose and the benefits of fasting:

"Even though outwardly the Fast is difficult and toilsome, yet inwardly it is bounty and tranquillity. Purification and training are conditioned and dependent only on such rigorous exercises as are in accord with the Book of God and sanctioned by Divine law, not those which the deluded have inflicted upon the people. Whatsoever God hath revealed is beloved of the soul. We beseech Him that He may graciously assist us to do that which is pleasing and acceptable unto Him." [25]

"These are the days of the Fast. Blessed is the one who through the heat generated by the Fast increaseth his love, and who, with joy and radiance, ariseth to perform worthy deeds. Verily, He guideth whomsoever He willeth to the straight path." [26]

"Verily, I say, fasting is the supreme remedy and the most great healing for the disease of self and passion". [27]

And from 'Abdu'l-Bahá:

"Fasting is the cause of awakening man. The heart becomes tender and the spirituality of man increases. This is produced by the fact that man's thoughts will be confined to the commemoration of God, and through this awakening and stimulation surely ideal advancements follow." [28]

". . . prayer and fasting is the cause of awakening and mindfulness and conducive to protection and preservation from tests . . ." [29]

And from Rumi:

"There's hidden sweetness in the stomach's emptiness.
We are lutes, no more, no less.
If the sound box is stuffed full of anything, no music.
If the brain and belly are burning clean with fasting,
every moment a new song comes out of the fire.
The fog clears, and new energy makes you run up the steps in front of you.
Be emptier and cry like reed instruments cry.
Emptier, write secrets with the reed pen.
When you're full of food and drink, Satan sits where your spirit should,
an ugly metal statue in place of the Kaaba.
When you fast, good habits gather like friends who want to help. Fasting
is Solomon's ring.
Don't give it to some illusion and lose your power, but even if you have,
if you've lost all will and control, they come back when you fast,
like soldiers appearing out of the ground, pennants flying above them.
A table descends to your tents, Jesus' table.
Expect to see it, when you fast, this table spread with other food,
better than the broth of cabbages." [30]

Bahá'u'lláh tells the Bahá'ís that they should be thankful to God for this amazing gift:

"All praise be to the one true God Who hath assisted His loved ones to observe the Fast and hath aided them to fulfill that which hath been decreed in the Book. In truth, ceaseless praise and gratitude are due unto Him for having graciously confirmed His loved ones to perform that which is the cause of the exaltation of His Word. If a man possessed ten thousand lives and offered them all to establish the truth of God's laws and commandments, he would still be beholden unto Him, since whatsoever proceedeth from His irresistible decree serveth solely to benefit His friends and loved ones." [31]

Bahá'u'lláh urges the Bahá'ís not to fast if they are ill:

"... obligatory prayer and fasting occupy an exalted station in the sight of God. It is, however, in a state of health that their virtue can be realized. In time of ill-health it is not permissible to observe these obligations; such hath been the bidding of the Lord, exalted be His glory, at all times. Blessed be such men and women as pay heed, and observe His precepts. All praise be unto God, He who hath sent down the verses and is the Revealer of undoubted proofs!" [32]

"In clear cases of weakness, illness, or injury the law of the Fast is not binding. This injunction is in conformity with the precepts of God, eternal in the past, eternal in the future. Well is it with them who act accordingly." [33]

"The law of the Fast is ordained for those who are sound and healthy; as to those who are ill or debilitated, this law hath never been nor is now applicable." [34]

Shoghi Effendi clarifies that fasting is good for health but that Bahá'ís should not fast if they are ill:

"Keeping the Fast is enjoined upon all Bahá'ís, regardless of nationality; it has a very salutary effect both physically and spiritually, and the friends should realize Bahá'u'lláh never would have instituted it if it were detrimental to the health." [35]

"As to your question regarding the Fast: if there is any doubt in the mind of a person as to whether it will really be bad for that person's health to keep it, the best doctor's advice should be obtained. But generally speaking most people can keep it, anywhere in the world, with no detriment to their health. It is very good for the health and, once one forms the habit, each year it becomes easier to keep, unless one is rundown. No one is obliged to keep it if it really harms them." [36]

Scientific research is also demonstrating that fasts like the Bahá'í Fast (which falls into the category of intermittent fasting) may have benefits to our physical health. We evolved from hunters and gatherers who often had to go without food if it was not available. It was either feast or famine. It seems that we evolved a genetic code to adapt to a cycle of feast and fasting. Many researchers attest to the benefits of emptying the digestive system and allowing it to cleanse and purify itself. Evidence indicates that intermittent fasting can reduce risk factors for chronic diseases in animals and humans and increase life span for animals. More studies on humans are needed but experiments to date are promising. Studies indicate that *"intermittent fasting acts in part as a form of mild stress that continually revs up cellular defenses against molecular damage."* [37]

But, as Duane Hermann, a Bahá'í writer, explains in his book on fasting, the material fast is only a symbol of the spiritual fast which lifts us to the heavenly realm and away from our selfish desires. Someone who has a medical condition and is unable to fast is therefore not denied spiritual development. *"Clearly the eating (or not eating of food) is not the most important aspect of observing the Fast."* [38] If medically it is not possible to physically fast or any of the other conditions for exemption apply, we should not fast. It is our motives, rather than our actions that receive the blessings of God. If our hearts and our motives are pure, God will accept our actions if we continue to pray and strive to make adjustments and reinvigorate our spiritual lives.[39]

'Abdu'l-Bahá explains this in his "third wisdom" of fasting:

". . . Fasting is of two kinds, material and spiritual. The material fasting is abstaining from food or drink, that is, from the appetites of the body. But spiritual, ideal fasting is this, that man abstain from selfish passions, from negligence, and from satanic animal traits. Therefore, material fasting is a token of the spiritual fasting. That is:

O Divine Providence! As I am abstaining from bodily desires and not occupied with eating and drinking, even so purify and sanctify my heart from the love of anyone save Thyself and shield and protect my soul from corrupt desires and satanic qualities so that my spirit may commune with the breaths of holiness and fast from the mention of all else besides Thee." [40]

"For this material fast is an outer token of the spiritual fast; it is a symbol of self-restraint, the withholding of oneself from all appetites of the self, taking on the characteristics of the spirit, being carried away by the breathings of heaven and catching fire from the love of God." [41]

Shoghi Effendi reiterates the words of 'Abdu'l-Bahá:

". . . the fasting period, which involves complete abstention from food and drink from sunrise till sunset, is . . . essentially a period of meditation and prayer, of spiritual recuperation, during which the believer must strive to make the necessary readjustments in his inner life, and to refresh and reinvigorate the spiritual forces latent in his soul. Its significance and purpose are, therefore, fundamentally spiritual in character. Fasting is symbolic, and a reminder of abstinence from selfish and carnal desires." [42]

Shoghi Effendi sympathizes with Bahá'ís in attempting to do something that may be foreign to them but He points out the benefits:

"It is often difficult for us to do things because they are so very different from what we are used to, not because the thing itself is particularly difficult. With you, and indeed most Bahá'ís, who are now, as adults, accepting this glorious Faith, no doubt some of the ordinances, like fasting and daily prayer, are hard to understand and obey at first. But we must always think that these things are given to all men for a thousand

years to come. For Bahá'í children who see these things practiced in the home, they will be as natural and necessary a thing as going to church on Sunday was to the more pious generation of Christians. Bahá'u'lláh would not have given us these things if they would not greatly benefit us, and, like children who are sensible enough to realize their father is wise and does what is good for them, we must accept to obey these ordinances even though at first we may not see any need for them. As we obey them we will gradually come to see in ourselves the benefits they confer." [43]

He also clarifies that it is really up to the individual to observe the Fast:

"Regarding the nineteen-day fast; its observance has been enjoined by Bahá'u'lláh upon all believers, once they attain the age of fifteen and until they reach seventy. Children of all countries, nationalities and classes, who are fifteen years old are under this obligation. It matters not whether they mature later in one country than in another. The command of Bahá'u'lláh is universal, irrespective of any variance in the age of maturity in different countries and among different peoples. In the Aqdas [The Book of Laws] *Bahá'u'lláh permits certain exceptions to this general obligation of fasting, among them are included those who do hard work, such as workers in heavy industries. But while a universal obligation, the observance of the nineteen day fast has been made by Bahá'u'lláh the sole responsibility of the individual believer. No Assembly has the right to enforce it on the friends, or to hold anybody responsible for not observing it. The believer is free, however, to ask the advice of his Assembly as to the circumstances that would justify him to conscientiously break such a fast. But he is by no means required to do so."* [44]

This is a reminder to me not to feel compelled to instruct or advice other Bahá'ís to fast or to judge those who are not fasting and I confess that in the past I have judged my fellow-believers who don't fast. I am trying to be compassionate and to understand that what constitutes illness can be quite subjective. I need to recognize and remember that we are all individuals with our own unique constitutions: physical weaknesses, mental barriers, and often emotional scars, and we are all on our own paths to God. And if it seems difficult for any of us to fast, we need only to look at the influence of our present-day society. Food has become important not just as sustenance but as an art form. New and complicated recipes arise out of the fascination and infatuation with food and the constant search for novelty. People may also put their energies into food in order to make up for something that is missing in their lives, not recognizing that it is their souls rather than their bodies that crave sustenance. They may overeat to stifle the lack of meaning in their lives and to deal with their emotions and their issues. And we only have to go down one aisle of a grocery store to be aware of the infinite varieties of a particular product or check the latest fast food menu to see the new items since we last visited. We're bombarded with food ads and told repeatedly how important food is. Surely this has an impact on the ability to fast. I know I find it easier to physically fast when I'm out of the city and away from all the restaurants and billboards advertising food. How wonderful it is to live in this age and to be blessed with such ordinances as the Fast, to be guided on a spiritual path away from the material pursuits of a frenzied society!

Fasting is truly a time of spirituality and there are so many benefits. But we are told not to fast if we are ill or have a medical condition that prevents it. And we know that even if someone can not fast he can still benefit from observing the fast by consecrating the time of the fast to prayer and meditation and strengthening his spiritual character. 'Abdu'l-Bahá tells us:

"Fasting is a symbol. Fasting signifies abstinence from lust. Physical fasting is a symbol of that abstinence, and is a reminder; that is, just as a person abstains from physical appetites, he is to abstain from self-appetites and self-desires. But mere abstention from food has no effect on the spirit. It is only a symbol, a reminder. Otherwise it is of no importance. Fasting for this purpose does not mean entire abstinence from food. The golden rule as to food is, do not take too much or too little. Moderation is necessary. . ." [45]

Hermann points out that if a person cannot do the physical fast prescribed in the Bahá'í Faith, he as a Bahá'í still has no excuse to ignore its reality.[46] The Fast needs to be observed with the heart. And that applies to all who are physically fasting or not fasting. It may present more of a challenge to those who cannot physically fast to continue their regular pattern of eating, maintain detachment and aim for spiritual readjustment in their lives.

Fasting is entirely up to the individual and his relationship to God. And the Bahá'ís are told:

"Shouldst thou observe any soul who is in doubt about this commandment or who misinterpreteth it, but hath no secret motive or defiance in what he doeth, be friendly towards him, and with the utmost cordiality and through kind speech, endeavor to turn him from the path of such interpretation towards the plain meaning of the verses of God." [47]

Bahá'ís are told to follow *"the plain meaning"* of the requirements of the Fast as written in the Kitab-i- Aqdas, the Book of Laws. And they have a role to assist other Bahá'ís to understand the Law.

Still, for those of us in the west, the idea of the nineteen -day Fast is probably the most difficult thing to consider even though we are assured of its benefits spiritually. I remember being so worried about being able to follow this law that I tried the Fast before I became a Bahá'í to see if I could do it. If I had been brought up as a Muslim before becoming a Bahá'í I would probably find it easier to fast. At least I would be accustomed to fasting as part of a religious culture. And having experienced a 30-day Fast, I would probably consider the nineteen-day fast a breeze in comparison! Having to deprive myself of food for the day is not comfortable physically, for sure; my stomach constantly reminds me that I've forgotten something. Of course many of us have gone without food when we've been busy with an activity or been working hard and at night we suddenly feel ravenous and realize we haven't eaten for a long time. Or we've survived on coffee all day until evening to get through a job. But the Bahá'í Fast requires more of individuals and in this day of instant gratification, self-denial is an alien concept. And if we begin to think about what the Bahá'í Fast means - Nothing to eat or drink all day? Not even water? What if I choke? What if I have a coughing fit? Or get the hiccups? Bahá'ís have probably all had similar thoughts, not just the first year of the Fast but every year as they rush out the door to an important meeting. Probably the most amazing experience of the Fast for me is that we are definitely assisted to get through it. I am tested. Perhaps I get sick, not sick enough to stop fasting, just some annoying little cough or sore throat and I'm not sure if I should keep fasting. I think to myself that it might get worse if I fast and I'll really get sick. Or maybe I should not fast today and I may feel better tomorrow and can continue my fast. But I may feel guilty if I stop fasting and later I feel fine. I may decide to try the Fast and rely on Bahá'u'lláh to guide me and let me know if I should continue. After I start fasting I may feel so ill that I know I can't possibly fast or perhaps Bahá'u'lláh may reward my effort and I will feel charged spiritually and able to carry on fasting. And that is the crux of the matter, I believe, to trust in Bahá'u'lláh and know that He will guide me. So, yes, my sincerity and desire to please God is tested, but I am assisted, too. And I have to fast *"one day at a time"*.[48] Some days are better than others; some days I feel quite spiritual, other days drag and all I can think about is food. Or I may feel spiritual during one part of the day, perhaps when I'm saying my prayers and at another part, I feel quite miserable and self- centered. The Fast gives individuals ample practice in becoming aware of their lower and higher natures and how they constantly have to struggle to follow a spiritual path. I usually find that by Day 10 (I do count the days off) I start to feel sorry that it's going to end soon – that's in between feeling like I won't make it that day because I'm so hungry and I should have had more food for breakfast, and other negative thoughts. If individuals can fast, I vouch for it being an amazing experience. There are probably so many things I don't do well that I'm asked to do as a Bahá'í. And who can say if I fast well? As Bahá'u'lláh says, it is our surrender to His will that is the criterion:

"In the Prayer of Fasting We have revealed: 'Should Thy Will decree that out of Thy mouth these words proceed and be addressed unto them, "Observe, for My Beauty's sake, the fast, O people, and set no limit to its duration," I swear by the majesty of Thy glory, that every one of them will faithfully observe it, will abstain from whatsoever will violate Thy law, and will continue to do so until they yield up their souls unto Thee.' In this consisteth the complete surrender of one's will to the Will of God. Meditate on this, that thou mayest drink in the waters of everlasting life which flow through the words of the Lord of all mankind, and mayest testify that the one true God hath ever been immeasurably exalted above His creatures. He, verily, is the Incomparable, the Ever-Abiding, the Omniscient, the All-Wise. The station of absolute self-surrender transcendeth, and will ever remain exalted above, every other station." [49]

If I fast between sunrise and sunset, I still don't know if I've obeyed the law of fasting. Only Bahá'u'lláh knows. In the prayer for Naw-Ruz, He states:

"Shouldst Thou regard him who hath broken the fast as one who hath observed it, such a man would be reckoned among them who from eternity had been keeping the fast. And shouldst Thou decree that he who hath observed the fast hath broken it, that person would be numbered with such as have caused the Robe of Thy Revelation to be stained with dust, and been far removed from the crystal waters of this living Fountain." [50]

But I have experienced fasting and I heartily recommend it. I am so grateful to the people who taught me about the Bahá'í Faith, because they were exceptional role models when it came to observing the Fast. And there are so many joys in fasting, so many bounties for our souls that if I neglect this law, my soul can be harmed because, after all, it is *"conducive to protection and preservation from tests"*, not to mention *"the cause of awakening and mindfulness"*. [51]

Many of the prayers for the Bahá'í Fast are very long and individuals may not always have the time or inclination to say them. In my research for this chapter, I found a few short prayers of Bahá'u'lláh for the Fast:

"Praise be unto Thee, O Lord my God! We have observed the Fast in conformity with Thy bidding and break it now through Thy love and Thy good-pleasure. Deign to accept, O my God, the deeds that we have performed in Thy path wholly for the sake of Thy beauty with our faces set towards Thy Cause, free from aught else but Thee. Bestow, then, Thy forgiveness upon us, upon our forefathers, and upon all such as have believed in Thee and in Thy mighty signs in this most great, this most glorious Revelation. Potent art Thou to do what Thou choosest. Thou art, verily, the Most Exalted, the Almighty, the Unconstrained." [52]

"Praised be Thou, O God, my God! These are the days whereon Thou hast enjoined Thy chosen ones, Thy loved ones and Thy servants to observe the Fast, which Thou hast made a light unto the people of Thy kingdom, even as Thou didst make obligatory prayer a ladder of ascent unto those who acknowledge Thy unity. I beg of Thee, O my God, by these two mighty pillars, which Thou hast ordained as a glory and honor for all mankind, to keep Thy religion safe from the mischief of the ungodly and the plotting of every wicked doer. O Lord, conceal not the light which Thou hast revealed through Thy strength and Thine omnipotence. Assist, then, those who truly believe in Thee with the hosts of the seen and the unseen by Thy command and Thy sovereignty. No God is there but Thee, the Almighty, the Most Powerful." [53]

"In the Name of Him Who hath been promised in the Books of God, the All-Knowing, the All-Informed! The days of fasting have arrived wherein those servants who circle round Thy throne and have attained Thy presence have fasted. Say: O God of names and creator of heaven and earth! I beg of Thee by Thy Name, the All-Glorious, to accept the fast of those who have fasted for love of Thee and for the sake of Thy good-pleasure and have carried out what Thou hast bidden them in Thy Books and Tablets. I beseech Thee by them to assist me in the promotion of Thy Cause and to make me steadfast in Thy love, that my footsteps may not slip on account of the clamor of Thy creatures. Verily, Thou art powerful over whatsoever Thou willest. No God is there but Thee, the Quickener, the All-Powerful, the Most Bountiful, the Ancient of Days." [54]

I'll close this chapter with a story about 'Abdu'l-Bahá and fasting:

The early believers in Akka not only observed the Bahá'í Fast, but also observed the Muslim 30-day Fast of Ramadan!

The following beautiful story illustrates how taxing that Fast was on the Master, 'Abdu'l-Bahá:

"The resident believers used to say that the phrase 'effulgences of the Prison' was a term which had been revealed by the Tongue of Glory [Bahá'u'lláh] to characterize the hardships and tribulations associated with life in Akka; it had endured among the friends through word of mouth.

At the beginning these hardships were numerous, but many of them disappeared little by little, mainly because of the changes to the environment. Others still persisted. The various deadly epidemics, which during the time of Bahá'u'lláh's imprisonment in the barracks had annihilated a large number of the inhabitants, had disappeared leaving no trace, as had the foul-smelling fumes which had caused and spread infectious diseases. Still, one of those 'effulgences of the Prison' which the passing of time and change in the climate had failed to overcome was the assault of the fleas, mosquitoes, flies and ants, which confirmed the expression, 'Blessed the one who is bitten by the insects of Akka'. Another was the thirty-day fast, which according to the command of Bahá'u'lláh was to be observed until the end of the period of incarceration to commemorate the Islamic holy month. Every sincere and devoted believer was expected to observe it gladly and of his own free will.

This thirty-day fast, which according to the Islamic calendar is observed in the month of Ramadan, continued to be kept until the end of the period of imprisonment in 1909 A.D. For the pilgrims and resident believers, who led relatively comfortable and peaceful lives, observing the thirty-day fast was not a difficult undertaking. But for the blessed person of the Centre of the Covenant, whose life was filled with numerous occupations and hardships. . . it can be imagined how arduous and exhausting such an observance was. This was especially true when in the month of Ramadan the Muslims of Akka, including all the government officials, switched their nights and days and conveniently slept during the daytime, while at night, after breaking the fast and observing the obligatory prayers, they crowded 'Abdu'l-Bahá's biruni [living room] to while away the night and disturb the Master until dawn.

But that spiritual and heavenly Being had to begin His many tasks before the rising of the sun . . . And so in the month of Ramadan no comfort was possible for 'Abdu'l-Bahá; at times even the opportunity to partake of the meals did not present itself, and therefore His fast began without any breakfast and ended without any dinner. Thus the 'effulgences of the Most Great Prison' sapped His strength and weakened His body. Many times during these days of fasting I saw the Master in such a state of exhaustion that I was deeply shaken.

On one such day He summoned me to His presence in the biruni area. As He spoke, signs of melancholy and weariness were apparent in His voice. He slowly paced the floor and then began to climb the stairs with difficulty. The symptoms of fatigue gave way to expressions of displeasure and weariness: 'I don't feel well. Yesterday I did not eat any breakfast and when the time came to break the fast I had no appetite. Now I need a bit of rest.' As He spoke, His face was so ashen that I became alarmed for His well-being. So I boldly exclaimed, 'It is better for the Master to break the fast.'

'No, it is not proper,' was 'Abdu'l-Bahá's reply.

I persisted. 'With the way the Master feels, fasting itself is not proper either.'

'It is not important, I will rest awhile,' responded 'Abdu'l-Bahá.

'The believers can not endure to see the Master in such a state of physical weakness and exhaustion,' I remained unyielding.

'Abdu'l-Bahá gave an effective and moving explanation in the hope of convincing me to relent. It did not work. In fact, it increased my ardour, and I continued to try to persuade Him to break the fast. As He would not yield, my words became mixed with tears and lamentations. But He would not let up.

Suddenly I realized that I had found a new quality in myself which did not allow me to give in, despite all the reasons that 'Abdu'l-Bahá had offered. And so, stubbornly holding my ground, I told myself, 'Regardless of what may come of this, I will continue to beg, plead and implore until I achieve my purpose, for I can no longer behold the Beloved of the world in such a condition.'

While begging and supplicating, strange thoughts crowded my mind. It was as if I wished to discover in what light my servitude and devotion to that Threshold was regarded in the sight of God. As such, I would consider success in this to be a good omen. And so from the very depths of my heart I entreated the Most Holy Shrine for assistance.

Spontaneously these words flowed from my lips, 'So may I make a suggestion?'

'What do you want me to do?' 'Abdu'l-Bahá replied.

Tears streaming from my eyes, I begged Him, 'Come and for this once break your fast, to bring happiness to the heart of a sinful servant of Bahá'u'lláh.'

God be praised, I know not where those words came from, but they brought such joy to the heart of that quintessence of kindness and love that quite loudly He exclaimed,' Of course, of course, of course.'

Immediately He called for Nasir and told him, 'Put some water in the pot and boil it and make a cup of tea for me.' And then He put His blessed hand on my shoulder and said, 'Are you pleased with me now? If you wish, you can go back to your tasks now and I will drink the tea and pray for you.'

Such feelings of joy and ecstasy flooded my being at that moment that I was rendered incapable of a reasonable response. Looking at me, 'Abdu'l-Bahá remarked, 'Do you want to be present to see with your own eyes when I break my fast? Very well, come and sit down.' He then withdrew to His small office, took up the pen and began to write, as I watched. Aqa Rida now came into the presence of the Master for some particular purpose. 'Abdu'l-Bahá remarked, 'Today I do not feel well and in response to the request of one of the loved ones of God I want to break my fast.'

As Aqa Rida left the room, the teapot with a single glass and a bowl of sugar were brought in. Addressing me, 'Abdu'l-Bahá said, 'Jinab-i-Khan, you have performed a praiseworthy service. May God bless you. If I had not broken the fast now, I would surely have fallen ill and would have been forced to break the fast.' And with every sip of the tea, He bestowed on me other kind and loving words. After that He arose and said, 'Now that I feel better, I will go after my work and will continue to pray for you.'

And then He started down the stairs. In the biruni reception room there was no one except the late Aqa Siyyid Ahmad-i-Afnan . . . Addressing him, 'Abdu'l-Bahá said, 'Jinab-i-Afnan, today I was not feeling well and intended to rest, but at the request of a beloved friend I have broken my fast. I am happy to have done so, for otherwise I would have fallen ill. But now I feel well and can continue the work of the Cause.' Having said this, He walked out of the room.

Jinab-i-Afnan, his eyes shining with the light of pure joy and delight, said, 'God Almighty, who was that "beloved friend", so that I can sacrifice my life for him?' And I, drunk with manifest victory, exclaimed, 'It was I, it was I.'

In brief, rather than any attempt at sacrifice of life, and filled with heavenly joy, we embraced each other as our spirits soared. As we did so, I placed in the storehouse of my memory the fact that the thirty-day fast truly was an 'effulgence of the Most Great Prison.'" [55]

REFERENCES

1 Bahá'u'lláh, *The Kitab-i-Aqdas, The Most Holy Book*, p. 134
2 Bahá'u'lláh, *The Importance of Obligatory Prayer and Fasting*, III
3 'Abdu'l-Bahá, Ibid., II
4 Ibid., I
5 Ibid., I
6   http://www.beliefnet.com/Faiths/2001/02/Fasting-Chart.aspx
7 Bahá'u'lláh, *The Importance of Obligatory Prayer and Fasting*, XIX
8 Hermann, Duane L., *Fasting, a Bahá'í Handbook* (Oxford: George Ronald, 1988), p. 44-45
9 Shoghi Effendi, *Principles of Bahá'í Administration*, p. 8
10 Bahá'u'lláh, The *Kitab-i-Aqdas*, [5], p. 21
11 'Abdu'l-Bahá, *The Importance of Obligatory Prayer and Fasting*, XXV
12 Bahá'u'lláh, The *Kitab-i-Aqdas*, [10], p. 22-23
13 Ibid., p. 148-149
14 Bahá'u'lláh, *The Importance of Obligatory Prayer and Fasting*, XIII
15 Hermann, Duane L. *Fasting, A Bahá'í Handbook*, p. 50
16 Bahá'u'lláh, *The Importance of Obligatory Prayer and Fasting*, VI
17 'Abdu'l-Bahá, Ibid., II
18 Ibid., III
19 Ibid., IV
20 Bahá'u'lláh, *The Importance of Obligatory Prayer and Fasting*, I
21 Ibid., XIV
22 Hermann, Duane L. *Fasting, A Bahá'í Handbook*, p. 16-17
23 Bahá'u'lláh, *The Importance of Obligatory Prayer and Fasting*, IV
24 Bahá'u'lláh, *The Kitab-i-Iqan*, p. 38-40
25 Bahá'u'lláh, *The Importance of Obligatory Prayer and Fasting*, XVI
26 Ibid., XV
27 Ibid., XVII
28 Hermann, Duane L. *Fasting, A Bahá'í Handbook*, p. 16
29 'Abdu'l-Bahá, *Bahá'í World Faith*, p. 368
30 Rumi, Jalal Al-Din, *The Essential Rumi* (New York: Castle Books, 1997), p. 51
31 Bahá'u'lláh, *The Importance of Obligatory Prayer and Fasting*, XVIII
32 Bahá'u'lláh, The *Kitab-i-Aqdas*, 93, p. 134
33 Bahá'u'lláh, *The Importance of Obligatory Prayer and Fasting*, XX
34 Ibid., XXI
35 Shoghi Effendi, *Lights of Guidance*, 777, p. 233
36 Ibid., 778, p. 233-234

37 Langness, David
http://bahaiteachings.org/the-benefits-of-intermittent-fasting
38 Hermann, Duane L. *Fasting, A Bahá'í Handbook*, p. 55
39 Ibid., p. 55-56
40 Ibid., p. 16-17
41 'Abdu'l-Bahá, *Selections from the Writings of 'Abdu'l-Bahá*, 35, p. 70
42 Bahá'u'lláh, The *Kitab-i-Aqdas*, 25, p. 176-177
43 Shoghi Effendi, *Lights of Guidance*, 1150, p. 342-343
44 Ibid., 776, p. 233
45 Esslemont, Dr. J.E., *Bahá'u'lláh and the New Era*, p. 184
46 Hermann, Duane, *Fasting, A Bahá'í Handbook*, p. 56
47 'Abdu'l-Bahá, *The Importance of Obligatory Prayer and Fasting*, III
48 Hermann, Duane, *Fasting, A Bahá'í Handbook*, p. 40
49 Bahá'u'lláh, *Gleanings from the Writings of Bahá'u'lláh*, CLX, p. 337-338
50 Bahá'u'lláh, *Prayers and Meditations by Bahá'u'lláh*, XLVI, p. 67-68
51 'Abdu'l-Bahá, *Bahá'í World Faith*, p. 368
52 Bahá'u'lláh, *The Importance of Obligatory Prayer and Fasting*, Prayers by Bahá'u'lláh, III
53 Ibid., V
54 Ibid., II
55 Afroukteh, Dr. Youness, *Memories of Nine Years in Akka* (Oxford: George Ronald), p. 294-297

Chapter 5
Detachment, Self-Surrender and Sacrifice

Chapter 5
Detachment, Self-Surrender and Sacrifice

The concepts of detachment, self-surrender and sacrifice are closely interwoven in the Bahá'í Revelation and when I began researching the concept of "detachment" in the Bahá'í Writings I discovered that detachment in its essence means to let go of self, or self-surrender, and to sacrifice self. Consequently I included all three concepts in this chapter. Again, I will be relying almost completely on the Bahá'í Writings to enhance our understanding of this important component of our spiritual growth.

You may wonder why this is the next topic of the book. In the words of Taherzadeh,*"In many of His Tablets Bahá'u'lláh has stated that the greatest achievement for man is detachment from all things save God. The soul can acquire faith and progress towards God to the degree of its detachment from this world."* [1]

"Perhaps it may be said that there are few, if any, among Bahá'u'lláh's exhortations which have been stressed so much as detachment from this world and from every selfish desire." [2]

Wikipedia defines detachment as a *"state in which a person overcomes his or her attachment to desire for things, people or concepts of the world and thus attains a heightened perspective."* [3] In the Bahá'í Faith, the ability to detach from the things of this world and the *"concepts of the world"*,[4] such as pride in our doings and our accomplishments, is a huge achievement that enables us to reach a lofty spiritual station.

Bahá'u'lláh has declared:

"At one time this sublime Word was heard from the Tongue of Him Who is the Possessor of all being and the Lord of the throne on high and of earth below–exalted is the glory of His utterance –: Piety and detachment are even as two most great luminaries of the heaven of teaching. Blessed the one who hath attained unto this supreme station, this habitation of transcendent holiness and sublimity." [5]

And 'Abdu'l-Bahá tells us that detachment is needed for our divine happiness:

"If thou art seeking after spiritual tranquility, turn thy face at all times toward the Kingdom of Abha. If thou art desiring divine joy, free thyself from the bands of attachment." [6]

He explains:

"Detachment does not consist in setting fire to one's house, or becoming bankrupt or throwing one's fortune out of the window, or even giving away all of one's possessions. Detachment consists in refraining from letting our possessions possess us. A prosperous merchant who is not absorbed in his business knows severance. A banker whose occupation does not prevent him from serving humanity is severed. A poor man can be attached to a small thing.

A rich man and a poor man lived in the same town. One day the poor man said to the rich man,' I want to go to the Holy Land.' The rich man replied, 'Very good, I will go also,' and they started from the town and began their pilgrimage. But night fell and the poor man said,' Let us return to our houses to pass the night.' The rich man replied,' We have started for the Holy Land and must not now return.' The poor man said,' The Holy Land is a long distance to travel on foot. I have a donkey, I will go and fetch it.' 'What?' replied the rich man,' are you not ashamed?' I leave all my possessions to go on this pilgrimage and you wish to return to get your donkey! I have abandoned with joy my whole fortune. Your whole wealth consists of a donkey and you cannot leave it!' You see that fortune is not necessarily an impediment. The rich man who is thus detached is near to reality. There are many rich people who are severed and many poor who are not." [7]

Taherzadeh summarizes the meaning of detachment. *"In a nutshell, detachment is to submit one's will to the will of God and to seek His good pleasure above one's own. Therefore, the challenge to every believer in this life is detachment from all else save God."* [8]

So being attached to the world refers to anything that gets in the way of the soul drawing near to God. Pride in our personal opinions, our accomplishments, our knowledge, our social status and our popularity are barriers to detachment.[9] All the veils and barriers mentioned in Chapter 1 keep us attached to this material world.

Detachment is the *"renunciation of attachment in order to achieve a greater realization of the meaning of creation and of the purpose of life."* [10] Possessing the things of this world is only one form of attachment, as 'Abdu'l-Bahá described, and Bahá'u'lláh writes of the dangers therein:

"Earthly treasures We have not bequeathed, nor have We added such cares as they entail. By God! In earthly riches fear is hidden and peril is concealed." [11]

"Busy not thyself with this world, for with fire We test the gold, and with gold We test Our servants!" [12]

Bahá'u'lláh teaches us that everything in the world is for man to possess and enjoy as long as he does not become attached to the pleasures and things of this world:

"Should a man wish to adorn himself with the ornaments of the earth, to wear its apparels, or partake of the benefits it can bestow, no harm can befall him, if he alloweth nothing whatever to intervene between him and God, for God hath ordained every good thing, whether created in the heavens or in the earth, for such of His servants as truly believe in Him. Eat ye, O people, of the good things which God hath allowed you, and deprive not yourselves from His wondrous bounties. Render thanks and praise unto Him, and be of them that are truly thankful." [13]

But He challenges us:

"He is not to be numbered with the people of Bahá [followers of Bahá'u'lláh] *who followeth his mundane desires, or fixeth his heart on things of the earth. He is My true follower who, if he come to a valley of pure gold, will pass straight through it aloof as a cloud, and will neither turn back, nor pause. Such a man is, assuredly, of Me. From his garment the Concourse on high can inhale the fragrance of sanctity. . . ."* [14]

The Concourse on high refers to holy souls who have gone on to the next world.

'Abdu'l-Bahá tells us:

". . . We can appreciate without attaching ourselves to the things of this world. It sometimes happens that if a man loses his fortune he is so disheartened that he dies or becomes insane. While enjoying the things of this world we must remember that one day we shall have to do without them." [15]

But it is often difficult to let these things go. As 'Abdu'l-Bahá notes:

"Material favors sometimes deprive us of spiritual favors and material rest of spiritual rest. A rich man said to Christ,' I would fain be thy

disciple.' 'Go and put into practice the Ten Commandments,' replied the Christ. 'But I know them by heart and have always practiced them.' 'Then sell what thou hast and take up thy cross and follow me.' The man returned to his home." [16]

Here is a story that 'Abdu'l-Bahá told in Denver about attachment to possessions:

"The Persian friends travel mostly on foot. They sleep whenever they get tired. They rest whenever they see a shady tree. Once a person came to an Amir. The Amir wished to present him with a gift and with insistence gave him a robe. Later, when he became tired, he lay down under a tree in the forest with the robe folded under his head. But he could not sleep as he repeatedly imagined that a thief was crouching nearby to take away the robe. At last he rose, threw the robe away and said,'As long as this robe is with me, I shall not find rest. To find rest, I must give it up.' [And 'Abdu'l-Bahá then said:] How long will you desire a robe for your body? Release your body that you may have no need for a robe." [17]

Bahá'u'lláh says:

"O Son of Passion!

Cleanse thyself from the defilement of riches and in perfect peace advance into the realm of poverty; that from the well-spring of detachment thou mayest quaff the wine of immortal life." [18]

A rich man detached from wealth attains such a station that his *"splendor... shall illuminate the dwellers of heaven even as the sun enlightens the people of the earth!"* [19]

But this description of detaching from our material things can be interpreted to mean renunciation from the world, such as living in a monastery. This is not what Bahá'u'lláh means:

"O people of the earth! Living in seclusion or practising asceticism is not acceptable in the presence of God. It behoveth them that are endued with insight and understanding to observe that which will cause joy and radiance. Such practices as are sprung from the loins of idle fancy and are begotten of the womb of superstition ill beseem men of knowledge. In former times and more recently some people have been taking up their abodes in the caves of the mountains while others have repaired to graveyards at night. Say, give

ear unto the counsels of this Wronged One . . . Deprive not yourselves of the bounties which have been created for your sake." [20]

We demonstrate our detachment from our possessions by giving them away, by being generous or even sacrificial in our giving. Taherzadeh discusses two stages of unity, referred to by Bahá'u'lláh in one of His Tablets.[21] One is characterized by generosity, the giving of some of the riches God has bestowed upon us to our fellow-men. It is the state of "musavat" or equality. The other is characterized by sacrifice. In this state of "muvasat" we sacrifice our own needs for others and give them preference, a state regarded by Bahá'u'lláh as the *"highest and noblest quality in man"*.[22] But this preference, He emphasizes, should only be exercised in relation to earthly possessions.

Taherzadeh reminds us that love for oneself is the greatest barrier between man and God.[23] But we have discussed how difficult it is to detach from self, from our lower nature, and to soar above it. We will always slip and fall. As 'Abdu'l-Bahá tells us: *". . . self-love is kneaded into the very clay of man, and it is not possible that, without any hope of a substantial reward, he should neglect his own present material good."* [24]

We live in a material world. We are involved in it and share in its joys and sorrows. We eke out a living, raise a family, contribute to its wellbeing and try to be of service to others and, beyond that, we strive to better it, ultimately helping to build a new world. That is the challenge: to live in the material world with our souls soaring in the heavenly realm.

As a graphic description of detachment Nabil, a great historian of the Bahá'í Faith, writes this description of the detachment of the Bahá'ís in Baghdad, those who subdued their ego and *"demonstrated their utter nothingness when they came face to face with their Lord."* [25]

"Many a night . . . no less than ten persons subsisted on no more than a pennyworth of dates. No one knew to whom actually belonged the shoes, the cloaks, or the robes that were found in their houses. Whoever went to the bazaar could claim that the shoes upon his feet were his own, and each one who entered the presence of Bahá'u'lláh could affirm that the cloak and robe he then wore belonged to him. Their own names they had forgotten, their hearts were emptied of aught else except adoration for their Beloved. . . . " [26]

We may at times feel frustrated because we want to attain a level of detachment from the things of this world but we find ourselves behaving at times in an "unspiritual" manner, an experience with which I'm very familiar. I have gained awareness of it over a period of years and by reading many books and I need to strive daily to make improvements in my behavior. But it is something commonly experienced. It can be a particular situation in which we respond negatively every time it occurs. Nothing seems to help and we feel stuck. I am talking about situations in which we are "triggered". Something happens to unsettle us or someone unsettles us and it takes us back to another time, to something that happened previously that was uncomfortable. If we have difficulty in a particular situation or with a particular person (the personality characteristics of that person), we will always be hindered in our attempts to respond in a spiritual manner. And we will certainly not be detached. We will be for a time period totally self-absorbed and attached to our emotions. It is not easy to deal with such a situation and it requires honest self-examination and courage to make the effort to change.

I feel very fortunate to have encountered a book that addresses this issue in a way that can be meaningful to those of us who are fighting this spiritual battle. The book is *Taking the Leap* by Pema Chodron, an American Buddhist nun. Chodron's method is taken from Buddhist teachings. There is much more in her book than I am describing here and what follows, I feel, may be rather a simplistic version of what she is teaching. But it serves to provide the basis of dealing with a very important issue that affects our lives. Chodron refers to attachment or being hooked as "shenpa". It works like this. For example, someone says something in a way that we perceive to be harsh and we tighten up – we're hooked. A slight, uneasy feeling or tightening of the stomach of jaw muscles can quickly evolve and demonstrate itself through "lashing out" with negative, possibly harsh words or gestures of dismissal (blaming the other person) or through withdrawal and silence as we belittle ourselves for our reaction.[27] It's personal. What someone said gets to us. It triggers us. It may not bother someone else but it touches us in a sore place. If we're criticized for what we believe in, our actions or our appearance, we may be triggered.[28] We feel lonely and "shenpa" is there.[29] We feel discomfort, or feel restless or bored – any insecurity – "shenpa" clicks in.[30] It's not necessary to figure out why we get trapped in a particular situation.[31] We just need to figure out how to get out of it so that it doesn't interfere with our ability to function and be the spiritual beings that we are. Generally we choose short-term gratification and stay stuck in the cycle.[32] And then we find a way to help cope with the discomfort, something that has become a habit such as overeating, escaping or looking for some pleasurable experience, something to ease the pain or numb us in some way. (I use overeating and escape as two possibilities because I know them both very well!) But if we can pause and breathe, we can see the consequences and stay in the uncomfortable feelings. We can be kind and patient with ourselves and remain open and curious about what will happen next.[33] As one of Chodron's masters points out, *"you may find a particular feeling intolerable, but instead of acting on that you could come to know intolerableness very, very well."* [34]

Chodron gives us three steps to follow to move out of our old pattern:

1. *"Acknowledge that you're hooked.*
2. *Pause, take three conscious breaths, and lean in . . . to the energy. Experience it fully . . . Get curious about it . . . What thoughts does it give birth to?. . . Keep breathing . . . Stay awake and compassionate, interrupting the momentum and refraining from causing harm. Just do not speak, do not act, and feel your energy . . . embrace it.*
3. *. . . Relax and move on. Just go on with your life so that the practice doesn't become a big deal . . ."* [35]

At first, we may only be able to abide the unpleasantness and pull ourselves out for brief moments before habit takes over.[36] We can begin practicing with small irritations, like being in traffic.[37] Eventually we'll be able to deal with more personal difficulties by keeping our sense of humour and persisting. Some things may keep coming back and triggering our same feelings. It is easy then to feel discouraged and upset with ourselves. But, as Chodron points out, we need to acknowledge our courage and respond with loving-kindness towards ourselves and eventually our insight will lead to humility as well as compassion for everyone else as we all deal with these same difficulties![38]

So we have something that may help us with "triggers". But our degree of detachment is tested on a daily basis. Here is a story told by 'Abdu'l-Bahá to illustrate this point:

"The King decided to go on a Royal Tour of his kingdom. Preparations started immediately and within a few days the magnificent procession was ready to leave. The ministers of the King's government, ambassadors and diplomats, courtiers and men of importance, soldiers and bandsmen, all splendid in their finery, set out to accompany the King. And, of course, the faithful Ios rode alongside his beloved master at the front of the throng.

Each evening the splendid party made camp and the wonderful imperial tent was erected for the King. This tent was the most beautiful and precious tent you have ever seen – woven from the finest silk, it was decorated with hundreds of jewels and precious stones, which so shone and sparkled . . . one day, as the King and his retinue were making their way through some especially beautiful countryside, the King remembered that he had passed this way before. It had been on this very stretch of road, years ago, that he had first glanced upon the adoring face of his faithful Ios.

In gratitude for that meeting the King, seized of a sudden impulse, took the box of jewels and cast them on the road.

As the procession went on its way the King looked back to see all his followers, all except Ios, forgetful of their duty, scrambling on the ground in great confusion trying to gather up the precious stones.

'Look at Ios,' they muttered to each other, 'see how proud he is, he even despises the King's jewels and makes no effort to pick them up.'

'How is it, Ios,' the King asked him, 'that you do not join the others to gather up the jewels? Are they not precious? Do you despise the very things that were mine?'

'O my King,' replied Ios, 'never in my life have I despised the least thing that is yours. But to be near you and gaze on your face has always been more than sufficient for me. Why should I leave your side to scramble for what you have thrown away?'

And the loyal and steadfast Ios rode on by the side of his grateful master, his gaze never for a moment leaving the face of his beloved King." [39]

How is it possible for us to become detached from our possessions, from titles, our educational level, our popularity, when everything and everyone in our society asks us to be the person who has the beautiful house by the ocean (as an example), to strive to be the manager of the company rather than a "lowly" (but happy) employee, to get a PhD to have the competitive edge, and to accumulate "friends" on Facebook! It may be difficult to sway us from our path as spiritual beings but we can still be influenced to follow these values because we cannot forget for one moment that we have an animal nature. It is always ready to goad us and remind us that we are fallible and prone to error. I remember having a conversation with a colleague who was attempting to establish his suitability to work with youth on a particular project by relating at some length his academic achievements for the job. Even as I was thinking that there were other important qualifications for the job, I found myself describing my own educational background, thereby justifying my ability to do the job! I, like him, was taking pride in my educational background! Yes, it is easy to fall into the mire of attachment.

At the end of the chapter I have given some suggestions that may be of assistance in practicing detachment and sacrifice. And I am reiterating the point that I've already discussed in this book that it is really important to be aware of the times we slip, to call ourselves to account and to try to do better next time, but being gentle and forgiving with ourselves, remembering that we have all of eternity to get it right! We just need to make a start and work at it a little at a time and we will make progress. As long as we are aware and we are striving to achieve our spiritual goals through prayer and meditation, we will become more detached from this world and attracted more and more to the spiritual realm. As Bahá'u'lláh says:

"The essence of detachment is for man to turn his face towards the courts of the Lord, to enter His Presence, behold His Countenance, and stand as witness before Him." [40]

"Say: Deliver your souls, O people, from the bondage of self, and purify them from all attachment to anything besides Me. Remembrance of Me cleanseth all things from defilement, could ye but perceive it." [41]

One way to detach from this world is to remember how quickly this life passes us by, as Bahá'u'lláh explains:

"Know ye that the world and its vanities and its embellishments shall pass away. Nothing will endure except God's Kingdom which pertaineth to none but Him, the Sovereign Lord of all . . . The days of your life shall roll away and all the things with which ye are occupied and of which ye boast yourselves shall perish. . ." [42]

And 'Abdu'l-Bahá reiterates:

"These brief days shall pass away, this present life shall vanish from our sight; the roses of this world shall be fresh and fair no more, the garden of this earth's triumphs and delights shall drop and fade . . . And therefore is none of this worth loving at all, and to this the wise will not anchor his heart." [43]

". . . Attach not thyself to anything unless in it thou seest the reality of God – this is the first step into the court of eternity. The earth life lasts but a short time, even its benefits are transitory; that which is temporary does not deserve our heart's attachment." [44]

God created the world and all that is therein for man's benefit. But he must be careful not to allow all the earth's resources and wealth and all its pleasures to become a barrier keeping him from drawing near to God. Taherzadeh [45] explains that man can be detached from worldly things if he lives according to the Teachings of God and makes them the centre of his life so that all other interests come secondary to his faith. In this case, because his faith is the prime motivating force of his life, everything he does in his daily life is in harmony with the Teachings. When he attains this station, the interests of his fellow- men supersede his own personal interests. He reaches the summit in his detachment when he is ready to meet any challenge in service for his faith. But the process of becoming detached from the material world can be painful, involving sacrifice. When a believer can sacrifice something important to him for the faith and in service for mankind, he makes progress spiritually.

And so we come to the concept of sacrifice. We detach from the material world and surrender ourselves to His Will. Bahá'u'lláh says:

"Say: Even should ye tear our bodies asunder, ye could not banish from our hearts the love of God. We were of a truth created for sacrifice, and in this do we take pride before all creation." [46]

We were created for sacrifice. To be truly who we are as noble beings we need to sacrifice.

We are asked to sacrifice our *"abilities, talents and possessions in the Path of God."* [47] We are asked to sacrifice everything.

"We must know the value of this and sacrifice ourselves entirely; nay, we must forget ourselves. We must wish for no rest and seek no joy. We must seek no name nor fame, no ease, amplitude nor convenience; nay, we must sacrifice everything in order that we may be clad in the kingdom of immortality." [48]

A synonym for "amplitude" is "abundance". We are asked to sacrifice our lives:

"The wish of 'Abdu'l-Bahá, that which attracts His good pleasure and, indeed, His binding command, is that Bahá'ís, in all matters, even in small daily transactions and dealings with others, should act in accordance with the divine Teachings. He has commanded us not to be content with lowliness, humility and meekness, but rather to become manifestations of selflessness and utter nothingness. Of old, all have been exhorted to loyalty and fidelity, compassion and love; in this supreme Dispensation, the people of Bahá are called upon to sacrifice their very lives. Notice the extent to which the friends

have been required in the Sacred Epistles and Tablets, as well as in our Beloved's Testament, to be righteous, well-wishing, forbearing, sanctified, pure, detached from all else save God, severed from the trappings of this world and adorned with the mantle of a goodly character and godly attributes. [49]

"The souls who sacrifice self, become detached from the imperfections of the realm of man and free from the shackles of this ephemeral world, assuredly the splendors of the rays of divine union shall shine in their hearts and in the eternal paradise they shall find ideal relationship, union and happiness." [50]

Taherzadeh explains further:

"To cite one example: some of the laws which govern the life of a tree are similar to those in the life of man. A tree thrusts its roots into the soil from which it receives its nourishment and upon which it depends for its existence. But the tree itself, its trunk, branches and leaves grow in the opposite direction. As if it dislikes the soil, the tree moves away from it. This is similar to the state of detachment from material things in the world of man when the soul aspires to spiritual things and away from earthly desires. By moving in the opposite direction the tree receives the rays of the sun and as a result it will blossom and bear fruit. Of course, the growth of a tree is involuntary; it is dictated by nature. But supposing the tree had a choice; what a difference it would have made if, feeling an attachment for the soil, it had inclined its branches and leaves towards the earth and buried itself in the ground! Then it would have rotted away and been deprived of the life-giving rays of the sun.

The same principle is true of man, for he has to live in this material world and is entirely dependent upon this earth for his existence. His soul, however, ought to become detached from the material world and turn instead towards spiritual things. But unlike the plant, which has no control over its growth and development, man has been given the power to determine his own destiny. He has been given free will and can choose the direction in which he wants to move. If he focuses his attention only on material things and becomes attached to this world and its vanities, pomp and glory, his soul will remain in relative darkness. But if like a tree, he does not direct all his affection towards material things, and reaches a state of detachment from this world and allows his soul to aspire towards heavenly qualities, he could then receive the rays of the sun of Truth – the Manifestation of God. Then and only then can his soul produce a fruit and give birth to the spirit of faith which is the ultimate purpose of creation." [51]

'Abdu'l-Bahá uses the analogy of a seed becoming a fruit to explain such detachment and sacrifice:

"... *If you plant a seed in the ground, a tree will become manifest from that seed. The seed sacrifices itself to the tree that will come from it. The seed is outwardly lost, destroyed; but the same seed which is sacrificed will be absorbed and embodied in the tree, its blossoms, fruits and branches. If the identity of that seed had not been sacrificed to the tree which became manifest from it, no branches, blossoms or fruits would have been forthcoming. ..."* [52]

The seed must completely disintegrate in the soil before a tree is produced. It is amazing to contemplate how a tiny insignificant seed can through complete sacrifice be transformed into a small sapling and eventually a tree with branches and flowers, and then fruit. 'Abdu'l-Bahá explains that Christ sacrificed Himself for the tree of Christianity. He disappeared like a seed disappears, but His qualities and perfections were manifest in the Christian community. He sacrificed Himself that the tree of Christianity would grow. [53]

He also explains:

"... *The moth is a sacrifice to the candle. The spring is a sacrifice to the thirsty one. The sincere lover is a sacrifice to the loved one and the longing one is a sacrifice to the beloved ... Man must become severed from the human world, be delivered from the contingent gloominess, the illumination of mercifulness must shine and radiate in him, the nether world become as non-existent and the Kingdom become manifest. He must become like unto the iron thrown within the furnace of fire. The qualities of iron, such as blackness, coldness and solidity which belong to the earth disappear and vanish while the characteristics of fire, such as redness, glowing and heat, which belong to the Kingdom become apparent and visible. Therefore, iron hath sacrificed its qualities and grades to the fire, acquiring the virtues of that element ..."* [54]

In a talk in North America, referring to the significance of sacrifice, 'Abdu'l-Bahá said:

"... *It is the principle that a reality sacrifices its own characteristics. Man must sever himself from the influences of the world of matter, from the world of nature and its laws; for the material world is the world of corruption and death. It is the world of evil and darkness, of animalism and ferocity, bloodthirstiness, ambition and avarice, of self-worship, egotism and passion; it is the world of nature. Man must strip himself of all these imperfections, must sacrifice these tendencies which are peculiar to the outer and material world of existence. On the other hand, man must acquire heavenly qualities and attain divine attributes. He must become the image and likeness of God. He must seek the bounty of the eternal, become the manifestor of the love of God, the light of guidance, the tree of life and the depository of the bounties of God. That is to say, man must sacrifice the qualities and attributes of the world of nature for the qualities and attributes of the world of God."* [55]

And so we return once more to the theme of this book – to "let go" of the insistent self and to live as spiritual beings. It seems to me that there are three aspects of self-sacrifice which 'Abdu'l-Bahá refers to in His Writings. One is to give up personal pleasures for the sake of Bahá'u'lláh. Another is to be detached from self, our animal nature. And the third is to sacrifice our will for God's will.

'Abdu'l-Bahá told the friends in Paris:

"Detachment does not imply lack of means; it is marked by the freedom of the heart. In Tihran, we possessed everything at a nightfall, and on the morrow we were shorn of it all, to the extent that we had no food to eat. I was hungry, but there was no bread to be had. My mother poured some flour into the palm of my hand and I ate that instead of bread. Yet, we were contented." [56]

So one of the secrets of detachment is being content:

"O Quintessence of Passion!

Put away all covetousness and seek contentment, for the covetous hath ever been deprived, and the contented hath ever been loved and praised." [57]

"Contentment is real wealth. If one develops within himself the quality of contentment he will become independent. Contentment is the creator of happiness. When one is contented he does not care either for riches or poverty. He lives above the influence of them and is indifferent to them." [58]

And in His Words of Wisdom, Bahá'u'lláh states," *The source of all glory is acceptance of whatsoever the Lord hath bestowed, and contentment with that which God hath ordained."* [59]

Bahá'u'lláh compares the soul to a bird:

"Know also that the soul is endowed with two wings: should it soar in the atmosphere of love and contentment, then it will be related to the All-Merciful. And should it fly in the atmosphere of self and desire, then it will pertain to the Evil One . . ." [our lower nature or insistent self] [60]

And remember that the traveller passes through the Valley of Contentment and becomes inwardly rich and endowed with spiritual strength. In the final station, the Valley of True Poverty and Utter Nothingness, he becomes totally detached and free from his captivity in this world.

Many of the Bábís, the followers of The Báb, were given the choice between sacrificing their lives for their beliefs and recanting their faith, thus demonstrating the ultimate detachment and sacrifice. And they had the fortitude and power of faith that may seem incomprehensible to us. Taherzadeh discusses the dilemma such a believer faces:

"If at that moment of decision he is unable to sever himself from the things of the world, from its delights and pleasures, or from the joys and contentment of life at home where he could continue to live among his loved ones, then such a person remains fully attached to this world and consequently severs his connection with Bahá'u'lláh. It is at this point under the threat of death that the individual becomes deprived of the sustaining power of Bahá'u'lláh, and as a result becomes filled with such fear that he will recant his faith in order to save his life. . .

This barrier [attachment to this world]. . . stops the flow of divine power to the human soul and denudes the individual of the mantle of courage and faith . . . if the believer at the hour of his gravest test decides not to barter the precious gift of his faith for this transitory life, such a person reaches the pinnacle of detachment. This is the absolute limit, for there can be no greater detachment than to give one's life . . . [By] becoming completely detached from this world, he becomes filled with such powers from on high as to become a spiritual giant. The confirmations of Bahá'u'lláh will instantly descend on him and will surround and strengthen him." [61]

I'm sure this passage will give us much to ponder as we think about the many believers who have given up their lives for their beloved faith. And perhaps we may have a glimmering of understanding about their ability to do so. It is probably very difficult for us to relate to martyrdom for the sake of one's religion. And in fact Bahá'u'lláh has exhorted His followers that they should teach the Bahá'í Faith rather than seeking martyrdom. He has exalted teaching to the level of martyrdom. Taherzadeh explains that in one of His Tablets Bahá'u'lláh has stated explicitly that in His Dispensation it is preferred that an individual should teach the Cause with wisdom to those who are interested rather than give up his life.[62]

I am now turning to a study of The Hidden Words as part of our discussion because so much of this work of Bahá'u'lláh's relates to our theme.

Bahá'u'lláh's chief aim in The Hidden Words *"is to detach man from this mortal world and to protect his soul from its greatest enemy, himself."* [63] 'Abdu'l-Bahá urged one of the believers in a Tablet addressed to him to *"peruse the verses of The Hidden Words by day and night, and to supplicate God to enable him to carry out the exhortations of the Blessed Beauty."* [64] So we would be wise to meditate upon His counsels in this treasury and use them as a guide for all our actions.

Bahá'u'lláh tells us that we need to cast out the "stranger", man's attachment to the world, and turn to God:

"O My Friend in Word!

Ponder awhile. Hast thou ever heard that friend and foe should abide in one heart? Cast out then the stranger, that the Friend may enter His home." [65]

And He says:

"O Son of Spirit!

There is no peace for thee save by renouncing thyself and turning unto Me; for it behooveth thee to glory in My name, not in thine own; to put thy trust in Me and not in thyself, since I desire to be loved alone and above all that is." [66]

'Abdu'l-Bahá explains:

"Regarding the statement in The Hidden Words, that man must renounce his own self, the meaning is that he must renounce his inordinate desires, his selfish purposes and the promptings of his human self, and seek out the holy breathings of the spirit, and follow the yearnings of his higher self, and immerse himself in the sea of sacrifice, with his heart fixed upon the beauty of the All-Glorious ... he should not seek out anything whatever for his own self in this swiftly-passing life, but that he should cut the self away, that is, he should yield up the self and all its concerns on the field of martyrdom, at the time of the coming of the Lord." [67]

"O Son of Earth!

Wouldst thou have Me, seek none other than Me; and wouldst thou gaze upon My beauty, close thine eyes to the world and all that is therein; for My will and the will of another than Me, even as fire and water, cannot dwell together in one heart." [68]

As Taherzadeh explains,[69] when we recognize Bahá'u'lláh as the Manifestation for this Day we become humble before Him. Humility is an important prerequisite so that we can drive the "stranger" gradually out of our hearts.

". . . Humble thyself before Me, that I may graciously visit thee," [70] Bahá'u'lláh admonishes us.

Taherzadeh recounts a Persian story to illustrate the degree of detachment needed in our lives and the heights of humility we can reach:

The story is about *"a drop of rain falling down from the clouds. The drop knows itself to be the water of life, the most precious element that God had created, and so it is proud of itself. Boasting all the way down, it suddenly sees that it is falling into an ocean, whereupon it recognizes its own insignificance and exclaims: 'If this exists then what am I?' When the ocean hears this expression of humility it attracts the drop to itself and, as a reward, makes it a companion of the pearl."* [71]

'Abdu'l-Bahá tells us:

"Our requirements of faithfulness is that thou mayest sacrifice thyself and, in the divine path, close thine eyes to every pleasure and strive with all thy soul that thou mayest disappear and be lost, like unto a drop, in the ocean of the love of God." [72]

Also in The Hidden Words Bahá'u'lláh says:

". . . Prefer not your will to Mine, never desire that which I have not desired for you, and approach Me not with lifeless hearts, defiled with worldly desires and cravings..." [73]

And He teaches us how we should relate to this mortal world:

"O Friends!

Abandon not the everlasting beauty for a beauty that must die, and set not your affections on this mortal world of dust." [74]

And to the "prison of self":

"O My Servant!

Free thyself from the fetters of this world, and loose thy soul from the prison of self. Seize thy chance, for it will come to thee no more." [75]

To achieve this detachment from everything save God we need to continually beseech Him in prayer:

"O Son of Light! Forget all save Me and commune with My spirit. This is of the essence of My command, therefore turn unto it." [76]

Bahá'u'lláh tells us in the closing words of the Persian Hidden Words:

"Let it now be seen what your endeavours in the path of detachment will reveal." [77]

The Hidden Words are truly a guide for detachment and self-surrender.

Bahá'u'lláh states that recognizing the truth depends on detachment from the world:

"No man shall attain the shores of the ocean of true understanding except he be detached from all that is in heaven and on earth . . .

The essence of these words is this: they that tread the path of faith, they that thirst for the wine of certitude, must cleanse themselves of all that is earthly – their ears from idle talk, their minds from vain imaginings, their hearts from worldly affections, their eyes from that which perisheth. They should put their trust in God, and, holding fast unto Him, follow in His way. They will then be made worthy of the effulgent glories of the sun of divine knowledge and understanding, and become the recipients of a grace that is infinite and unseen . . ." [78]

We need to surrender ourselves and put ourselves in God's hands. And Bahá'u'lláh tells us about the station of self-surrender:

"O Shaykh, O thou who hast surrendered thy will to God! By self-surrender and perpetual union with God is meant that men should merge their will wholly in the Will of God, and regard their desires as utter nothingness beside His Purpose. Whatsoever the Creator commandeth His creatures to observe, the same must they diligently, and with the

utmost joy and eagerness, arise and fulfil. They should in no wise allow their fancy to obscure their judgment, neither should they regard their own imaginings as the voice of the Eternal. In the Prayer of Fasting We have revealed: 'Should Thy Will decree that out of Thy mouth these words proceed and be addressed unto them, "Observe, for My Beauty's sake, the fast, O people, and set no limit to its duration," I swear by the majesty of Thy glory, that every one of them will faithfully observe it, will abstain from whatsoever will violate Thy law, and will continue to do so until they yield up their souls unto Thee.' In this consisteth the complete surrender of one's will to the Will of God. Meditate on this, that thou mayest drink in the waters of everlasting life which flow through the words of the Lord of all mankind, and mayest testify that the one true God hath ever been immeasurably exalted above His creatures. He, verily, is the Incomparable, the Ever-Abiding, the Omniscient, the All-Wise. The station of absolute self-surrender transcendeth, and wilt ever remain exalted above, every other station." [79]

Bahá'u'lláh then tells us that we need to consecrate ourselves:

"It behoveth thee to consecrate thyself to the Will of God. Whatsoever hath been revealed in His Tablets is but a reflection of His Will. So complete must be thy consecration, that every trace of worldly desire will be washed from thine heart." [80]

Consecration, according to the dictionary, means dedication to a goal or service and implies something sacred, involving sacrifice, something that may be more important than life or death. Until the sacrifice of self is made, an individual has no power against the force of inertia. 'Abdu'l-Bahá tells us:

"You must ever press forward, never standing still, avoid stagnation, the first step to a backward movement, to decay." [81]

And Shoghi Effendi refers to it as a natural phenomenon which we must fight:

". . . manfully struggle against the natural inertia that weighs him down in his effort to arise, shed heroically and irrevocably, the trivial and superfluous attachments which hold him back . . ." [82]

Bahá'u'lláh describes the qualities of a true seeker:

"But, O my brother, when a true seeker determines to take the step of search in the path leading to the knowledge of the Ancient of Days [God],

he must, before all else, cleanse and purify his heart, which is the seat of the revelation of the inner mysteries of God, from the obscuring dust of all acquired knowledge, and the allusion of the embodiments of satanic fancy. He must purge his breast, which is the sanctuary of the abiding love of the beloved, of every defilement, and sanctify his soul from all that pertaineth to water and clay, from all shadowy and ephemeral attachments. He must so cleanse his heart that no remnant of either love or hate may linger therein, lest that love blindly incline him to error, or that hate repel him away from the truth . . . That seeker must at all times put his trust in God, must renounce the peoples of the earth, detach himself from the world of dust, and cleave unto Him Who is the Lord of Lords." [83]

'Abdu'l-Bahá clarifies this passage:

". . . the seeker must be endowed with certain qualities. First of all, he must be just and severed from all else save God; his heart must be entirely turned to the supreme horizon; he must be free from the bondage of self and passion, for all these are obstacles. Furthermore, he must be able to endure all hardships. He must be absolutely pure and sanctified, and free from the love or the hatred of the inhabitants of the world. Why? Because the fact of his love for any person or thing might prevent him from recognizing the truth in another, and, in the same way, hatred for anything might be a hindrance in discerning truth. This is the condition of seeking, and the seeker must have these qualities and attributes. Until he reaches this condition, it is not possible for him to attain to the Sun of Reality.[God] [84]

Bahá'u'lláh exhorts humanity to *". . . conduct themselves in such a manner that the earth upon which they tread may never be allowed to address to them such words as these, 'I am to be preferred above you. For witness, how patient I am in bearing the burden which the husbandman layeth upon me. I am the instrument which continually imparteth unto all beings the blessings with which He Who is the Source of all grace hath entrusted me. Notwithstanding the honour conferred upon me, and the unnumbered evidences of my wealth- a wealth that supplieth the needs of all creation – behold the measure of my humility, witness with what absolute submissiveness I allow myself to be trodden beneath the feet of men. . ."* [85]

And 'Abdu'l-Bahá tells us how to reach that station:

"We must strive to attain to that condition by being separated from all things and from the people of the world and by turning to God alone.

It will take some effort on the part of man to attain to that condition, but he must work for it, strive for it. We can attain to it by thinking and caring less for material things and more for the spiritual. The further we go from the one, the nearer we are to the other. The choice is ours. Our spiritual perception, our inward sight must be opened, so that we can see the signs and traces of God's spirit in everything. Everything can reflect to us the light of the Spirit." [86]

And again:

"If thou seekest to be intoxicated with the cup of the Most Mighty Gift, cut thyself from the world and be quit of self and desire. Exert thyself night and day until spiritual powers may penetrate thy heart and soul. Abandon the body and the material, until the merciful powers may become manifest, because not until the soil is become pure will it develop through the heavenly bounty; not until the heart is purified, will the radiance of the Sun of Truth shine therein. I beg of God that thou wilt day by day increase the purity of thy heart, the cheerfulness of thy soul, the light of thy insight and the search for Truth." [87]

But it is definitely not an easy task to detach ourselves and it is a mighty challenge, as Bahá'u'lláh points out:

"This is not a Cause which may be made a plaything for your idle fancies, nor is it a field for the foolish and faint of heart. By God, this is the arena of insight and detachment, of vision and upliftment, where none may spur on their chargers save the valiant horsemen of the Merciful, who have severed all attachment to the world of being." [88]

Every word, every look, every action of 'Abdu'l-Bahá was the epitome of selflessness and sacrifice. By studying His life, we can be inspired to emulate in some small measure the selflessness He epitomized.

"The first person singular seldom crept into the Master's speech. He once told a group of New York friends that in the future the words 'I' and 'Me' and 'Mine' would be regarded as profane." [89]

"...He disliked photographs of Himself, permitting them only to satisfy His friends. 'But to have a picture of oneself,' He said, 'is to emphasize the personality, which is merely the lamp, and is quite unimportant. The light

burning within the lamp has the only real significance.'" [90]
"... He desired no name or title except that of 'Abdu'l-Bahá – the Servant of God. He forbade pilgrims to fall at His feet. In the early days in Akka, He cooked for His fellow prisoners, and later, when entertaining visitors at His table, He sometimes served His guests Himself..." [91]

"When Bahá'u'lláh lived at Bahji – and 'Abdu'l-Bahá at Akka – the Master would visit His Father once a week. He liked to do this on foot and when asked why He did not ride to Bahji He responded by asking, ..'who am I that I should ride where the Lord Christ walked?' However, His Father requested Him to ride, so in order to comply the Master rode out of Akka, but when He sighted Bahá'u'lláh's Mansion, He dismounted." [92]

"... Once, wealthy visitors from the West planned an elaborate pre-meal, hand-washing scene for Him – it included a page boy, a clean bowl with 'crystal water' and even a scented towel! When the Master saw the group walking across the lawn, He knew their purpose. He hurried to a small water-trough, washed as usual and then wiped His hands on the cloth of the gardener. ..." [93]

We also have the example of Shoghi Effendi:

"Shoghi Effendi's selflessness was not only outstanding but exemplary. He never placed his personal interests or desires ahead of his functions as Guardian. Those who were near to him inevitably felt that his life was something to be fully expended in the service of God and humanity, in a dedication unlike that of any other human being. When close to him I always felt the powerful process of his sublimation to the reality of the unseen world, while his body was there, near to me, like a visible, finely-tuned musical instrument whose melodies, imperceptible to the human ear, vibrated unseen through the ether.

He was always ready to give comfort, verbally or in writing, to encourage, to praise and to stimulate to such a degree that one felt the urge to place at his disposal life, time and possessions within the range of one's capacity and emotional exaltation. This was the essence of his detachment from worldly things. The less he thought of himself, the higher he soared in the sphere of spiritual authority and prestige. This was perhaps the secret of his tremendous attraction and influence upon those who came close to him." [94]

Let us now continue our discussion of sacrifice.

We have already discussed the need to sacrifice everything for God. The Bahá'í Writings state this clearly:

"That individual, however, who puts his faith in God and believes in the words of God – because he is promised and certain of a plentiful reward in the next life, and because worldly benefits as compared to the abiding joy and glory of future planes of existence are nothing to him – will for the sake of God abandon his own peace and profit and will freely consecrate his heart and soul to the common good. 'A man, too, there is who selleth his very self out of desire to please God.'" [95]

"The essence of all exhortation is that thou shouldst abandon thyself and sacrifice life, body and heart for the Beloved One of the world." [96]

"O my brother! A pure heart is like unto a mirror; polish it with the purity of love and severance from all else save God, until the ideal sun may reflect therein, and the eternal morn may dawn. Then wilt thou find clear and manifest the meaning of: 'Neither doth My earth nor My heaven occupy Me, but the heart of My faithful servant occupieth Me' – and wilt take thy life in thy hands and sacrifice it, with a thousand longings, to the new Beloved." [97]

And we sacrifice for our fellow humans:

"Sacrifice thyself for the well-being of the people and be thou a kind comforter to all the inhabitants of the world." [98]

"... we also must strive in this pathway of love and service, sacrificing life and possessions, passing our days in devotion, consecrating our efforts wholly to the cause of God, so that, God willing, the ensign of universal religion may be uplifted in the world of mankind and the oneness of the world of humanity be established." [99]

And here is the prescription, what it means to sacrifice:

"Man must become evanescent in God, . . . must forget his own selfish conditions that he may thus arise to the station of sacrifice. It should be to such a degree that if he sleep, it should not be for pleasure, but to rest the body in order to do better, to speak better, to explain more beautifully, to serve the servants of God and to prove the truths. When he remains awake, he should seek to be attentive, serve the Cause of God

and sacrifice his own stations for those of God. When he attains to this station, the confirmations of the Holy Spirit will surely reach him, and man with this power can withstand all who inhabit the earth." [100]

"O maid-servant of God! It is incumbent upon thee, since thou hast attained the knowledge of God and His love, to sacrifice thy spirit and all thy conditions for the life of the world, bearing every difficulty for the comfort of the souls, sinking to the depth of the sea of ordeals for the sake of the love of faithfulness and burning with the fire of torture and regret like unto a lamp while the light is shining from thee unto the surroundings.

O maid-servant of God! The mystery of sacrifice is that man should sacrifice all his conditions for the divine station of God. The station of God is mercy, kindness, forgiveness, sacrifice, favor, grace and giving life to the spirits and lighting the fire of His love in the hearts and arteries. I ask God to make thee a sign of mercy, the banner of kindness among His maid-servants." [101]

We cannot be near to God without self-sacrifice.:

"Divine nearness is dependent upon attainment to the knowledge of God, upon severance from all else save God. It is contingent upon self-sacrifice and to be found only through forfeiting wealth and worldly possessions. . . . . All the Prophets have drawn near to God through severance. We must emulate those Holy Souls and renounce our own wishes and desires. . . . nearness to God is possible through devotion to Him, through entrance into the Kingdom and service to humanity . . . In a word, nearness to God necessitates sacrifice of self, severance and the giving up of all to Him. Nearness is likeness." [102]

And the condition of self-sacrifice is love:

"In the world of existence there is indeed no greater power than the power of love. When the heart of man is aglow with the flame of love, he is ready to sacrifice all – even his life." [103]

'Abdu'l-Bahá tells us:

"Until a being setteth his foot in the plane of sacrifice, he is bereft of every favor and grace; and this place of sacrifice is the realm of dying to the self, that the radiance of the living God may then shine forth. Do all ye can to become wholly weary of self, and bind yourselves to that Countenance of Splendors; and once ye have reached such heights

of servitude, ye will find, gathered within your shadow, all created things. This is boundless grace; this is the highest sovereignty; this is the life that dieth not. All else save this is at the last but manifest perdition and great loss." [104]

And so it seems that when we are able to cut our attachments to this world and die to our selves, it evokes such power in our hearts that is beyond comprehension.[105] We eagerly forge ahead, sacrificing our rest and comfort, and we are able to change ourselves into spiritual beings.

But we are told not to overdo the extent of our sacrifice, so that we are unable to serve. 'Abdu'l-Bahá cautions . . ."*not that he should allow his physical health to deteriorate and his body become infirm."* [106]

Shoghi Effendi also stated in a letter to believer that *"he was very glad that . . . a visit will give you a chance to rest . . . There should always be a limit to self-sacrifice."* [107] After all we are only human. 'Abdu'l-Bahá describes the level of sacrifice the Manifestations of God achieve:

". . . All Divine Manifestations give up all personal conditions, considerations and grades in the Cause of God to such an extent that there is nothing judged of their personality; that is, they sacrifice their personality entirely in the world; their life is only the life of God, their thought is the thought of God and their grades are those chosen by God. They have nothing. They sacrifice everything in the way of God. They suffer every sort of affliction and calamity in the world – that is, the afflictions and calamities in addition to those suffered spiritually – in order to show that the spiritual equals the material in consecration and sacrifice. They sacrifice spiritually in the way of God, and so they sacrifice all apparent and outward conditions in order to show the perfection and completeness of the truth of their manifestation.

This is the station of simple radiance which shines forth and makes them separate from all worldly things, and this leads them to such a condition that while they are walking on the earth, they are moving in the supreme Horizon. They have cut themselves off entirely from worldly conditions, and while they are on the earth they never see it, but look to the Horizon. They close their eyes to their material ease and to all else, and hasten with all joy and fragrance to martyrdom in the Cause of God. [108]

The Báb sacrificed His life for the redemption and purification of mankind. Bahá'u'lláh was intimately acquainted with sacrifice:

". . . Bahá'u'lláh . . . declared that imprisonment was no obstacle to Him. He said, 'This imprisonment will prove to be the means of the promotion of My Cause. This imprisonment shall be the incentive for the spreading of My teachings. No harm shall come to Me because I have sacrificed My life, I have sacrificed My blood, I have sacrificed My possessions, I have sacrificed all and for Me this imprisonment is no loss.'" [109]

'Abdu'l-Bahá lived the station of self-sacrifice and selflessness and told the friends:

"Know ye that 'Abdu'l-Bahá dwelleth in continual delight. To have been lodged in this faraway prison is for me exceeding joy. By the life of Bahá! This prison is my supernal paradise; it is my cherished goal, the comfort of my bosom, the bliss of my heart; it is my refuge, my shelter, my asylum, my safe haven, and within it do I exult amid the hosts of heaven and the Company on high.

Rejoice in My bondage, O ye friends of God, for it soweth the seeds of freedom; rejoice at my imprisonment, for it is the well-spring of salvation; be ye glad on account of my travail, for it leadeth to eternal ease. By the Lord God! I would not exchange this prison for the throne of the whole world, nor give up this confinement for pleasures and pastimes in all the fair gardens on earth. My hope is that out of the Lord's abundant grace, His munificence and loving-kindness, I may in His pathway, be hanged against the sky, that my heart may become the target of a thousand bullets, or that I may be cast into the depths of the sea, or be left to perish on desert sands. This is what I long for most; this is my supreme desire; it refresheth my soul, it is balm for my breast, it is the very solace of mine eyes." [110]

And 'Abdu'l-Bahá gives us another example of sacrifice: *"It is related that once in the days of the Apostle of God* [Muhammad] *He signified the desire that an army should advance in a certain direction, and leave was granted unto the faithful to raise contributions for the holy war. Among many was one man who gave a thousand camels, each laden with corn, another who gave half his substance, and still another who offered all that he had. But a woman stricken in years, whose sole possession was a handful of dates, came to the Apostle and laid at His feet her humble contribution. Thereupon the Prophet of God – may my life be offered up as a sacrifice unto Him – bade that this handful of dates be placed over and above all the contributions that had been gathered, thus asserting the merit and superiority thereof over all the rest. This was done because that elderly woman had no other earthly possessions but these."* [111]

This concludes our discussion on sacrifice. But what does the concept of sacrifice mean to us and for our lives? It is very difficult for us living in this material world to really understand the mystery of sacrifice. Because we are attracted to this world and attached to our animal nature, it can be painful to detach ourselves. When we sacrifice something in the material world which involves suffering or depriving ourselves of worldly benefits, we can attain to a higher station spiritually according to the measure of our sacrifice. Taherzadeh points out that if we arise eagerly and with devotion to serve our faith, if we are ready to give up our interests, our time and our possessions for this service, we are truly experiencing sacrifice and we receive God's good-pleasure.[112]

For me, sacrifice occurs in the little things we do in our everyday lives in which we put others and God and our faith before ourselves. We often make jokes about sacrificing sleep to make breakfast for our family or sacrificing a TV show to attend a spiritual gathering, but when we act joyfully and with sincerity and consciously make a choice in our lives to put others before ourselves we are practicing the act of sacrifice. At times we are pushed into a corner and given the choice between our wants or letting go of them and giving of ourselves. And we are tested to see how we will respond in situations that require sacrifice. Being sacrificial in our lives is a bounty and an essential component in our path of spiritual growth. When we are not conscious of making a decision about whether or not we should sacrifice, and instead we just do something that others would label sacrificial, it may be an important milestone in our spiritual development. And it may be that in our lives we may do some things consciously as a sacrifice and others are done without awareness that they could be labelled as "sacrifice". I feel that I am only now beginning to understand the concept of sacrifice. I am learning that I am always rewarded when I choose to sacrifice and I always gain so much more than I lose (the loss quickly fades away!). There is no doubt in my mind that the mystery of sacrifice is that there really is no sacrifice; we always gain so much more when we make a sacrifice. The link between love and sacrifice is particularly strong, I feel. We sacrifice for love, for the love of others and for the love of God. We will always be tested when we are given the choice. I've found that concern about my health has often interfered with my desire to do something for others and I am left to weigh the consequences. I am reminded about the many times while 'Abdu'l-Bahá was in North America that He would go visit someone who was sick and could not attend a meeting. He certainly wasn't concerned for his own health! We are so attached to our fragile bodies and our desires and needs that it is a constant battle to keep moving in the direction of sacrifice. We need to depend on God's help. Reading about people who have been sacrificial in their lives such as the martyrs in the Bahá'í Faith can serve as inspiration for us.

To close this chapter, I have two passages from the Writings of 'Abdu'l-Bahá to share:

"... look at Me, follow Me, be as I am; take no thought for yourselves or your lives, whether ye eat or whether ye sleep, whether ye are comfortable , whether ye are well or ill, whether ye are with friends or foes, whether ye receive praise or blame; for all of these things ye must care not at all. Look at Me and be as I am; ye must die to yourselves and to the world, so shall ye be born again and enter the Kingdom of Heaven. Behold a candle how it gives its light. It weeps its life away drop by drop in order to give forth its flame of light." [113]

"Let us put aside all thoughts of self; let us close our eyes to all on earth, let us neither make known our sufferings nor complain of our wrongs. Rather let us become oblivious of our own selves, and drinking down the wine of heavenly grace, let us cry out our joy, and lose ourselves in the beauty of the All-Glorious." [114]

Practical Suggestions:

    1. Simplify your life. 'Abdu'l-Bahá practiced simplicity in His life. He *"... kept little clothing – one coat at a time was ample. He ate little food. He was known to begin his day with tea, goat's milk cheese and wheat bread. And at the evening meal a cup of milk and a piece of bread might suffice.* [115] *'Abdu'l-Bahá's family was taught to dress in such a way that they would be 'an example to the rich and an encouragement to the poor.' Available money was stretched to cover more than the Master's family needs. One of his daughters wore no bridal gown when she married- a clean dress sufficed..."* [116] Practice "voluntary simplicity" if you wish. Simplifying can mean eliminating things that drain your energy and your soul and don't bring contentment and peace. I appreciate the voluntary simplicity movement because its proponents advocate caring for the earth and resetting our priorities – focusing less on materialism and more on our relationships with God and people in our lives. There are many valuable ideas on the website – www.choosingvoluntarysimplicity.com

    2. Get out into nature. See God's creation and feel a closeness

to it and to its Creator. It's a humbling experience to be in the presence of crashing waves or gazing at a mountaintop. Appreciate the miracle of life. Looking at the evening sky makes any trouble we have seem very small and it makes us feel very small in comparison with the infinity of the universe!

3. Depend on God. Turn your lives over to Him and ask for His guidance. In the words of Rumi:

"Do you think I know what I'm doing?
That for one breath or half-breath I belong to myself?
As much as a pen knows what it's writing,
or the ball can guess where it's going next." [117]

4. Challenge yourself to live one full day without thinking of yourself. You will not be offended, feel unappreciated or upset or not treated fairly. You will just observe the world and notice what people do, without making comparisons to yourself, you will just give without expectations.

5. Take notice of the number of times you use the words "I", "me" or "mine" in a day to attribute merit to yourself and make efforts to eliminate some.[118] Of course we use those words in everyday conversation for clarity, but I think that we can note when we are using them and if we are speaking from our lower natures.

6. Repeat the phrase (or a similar one from the Writings) in your mind as you go through the day,

"Give me the chalice of selflessness".

7. Increase your awareness when you begin the Long Obligatory Prayer that you are asking God for detachment.

8. Take on more "difficult" jobs in becoming detached. Bring yourself to account and notice the changes, the improvements and set the bar higher for yourself. Just as we build muscles by picking up heavier and heavier weights, we set ourselves more and more difficult tasks to build our spiritual muscles.

9. Be patient. There is no doubt in my mind that patience is a key to increased spiritual perception and the ability to detach from all save God. Rather than pushing ourselves to get to the next step, know that God will reveal the next steps. Remember

that God doesn't operate within the constraints of time.

"He, verily, rewardeth beyond measure them that endure with patience." [119]

10.   Be conscious of your life – how much of it you devote to your own pursuits, how much you devote to others, how many times you sacrifice comforts to help your fellowman or to serve the Cause. Practice "sacrifice" – don't tell anyone that you're doing it. It may be a small thing or a big leap in your life. If you begrudge the time spent in sacrifice, it's not sacrifice. Then start smaller. Be aware when you have done something you consider a sacrifice and your feelings about it, your closeness to the person you've sacrificed for, your nearness to God. Resolve to continue in the path of sacrifice and ask God to help you.

This is my favourite prayer of detachment:

"I give praise to Thee, O my God, that the fragrance of Thy lovingkindness hath enraptured me, and the gentle winds of Thy mercy have inclined me in the direction of Thy bountiful favors. Make me to quaff, O my Lord, from the fingers of Thy bounteousness the living waters which have enabled every one that hath partaken of them to rid himself of all attachment to any one save Thee, and to soar into the atmosphere of detachment from all Thy creatures, and to fix his gaze upon Thy loving providence and Thy manifold gifts.

Make me ready, in all circumstances, O my Lord, to serve Thee and to set myself towards the adored sanctuary of Thy Revelation and of Thy Beauty. If it be Thy pleasure, make me to grow as a tender herb in the meadows of Thy grace, that the gentle winds of Thy will may stir me up and bend me into conformity with Thy pleasure, in such wise that my movement and my stillness may be wholly directed by Thee.

Thou art He, by Whose name the Hidden Secret was divulged, and the Well-Guarded Name was revealed, and the seals of the sealed-up Goblet were opened, shedding thereby its fragrance over all creation, whether of the past or of the future. He who was athirst, O my Lord, hath hasted to attain the living waters of Thy grace, and the wretched creature hath yearned to immerse himself beneath the ocean of Thy riches.

I swear by Thy glory, O Lord the Beloved of the world and the Desire of all them that have recognized Thee! I am sore afflicted by the grief of my separation from Thee, in the days when the Day-Star of Thy presence hath shed its radiance upon Thy people. Write down, then, for me the recompense decreed for such as have gazed on Thy face, and have, by Thy leave, gained admittance into the court of Thy throne, and have, at Thy bidding, met Thee face to face.

I implore Thee, O my Lord, by Thy name the splendors of which have encompassed the earth and the heavens, to enable me so to surrender my will to what Thou hast decreed in Thy Tablets, that I may cease to discover within me any desire except what Thou didst desire through the power of Thy sovereignty, and any will save what Thou didst destine for me by Thy will.

Whither shall I turn, O my God, powerless as I am to discover any other way except the way Thou didst set before Thy chosen Ones? All the atoms of the earth proclaim Thee to be God, and testify that there is none other God besides Thee. Thou hast from eternity been powerful to do what Thou hast willed, and to ordain what Thou hast pleased.

Do Thou destine for me, O my God, what will set me, at all times, towards Thee, and enable me to cleave continually to the cord of Thy grace, and to proclaim Thy name, and to look for whatsoever may flow down from Thy pen. I am poor and desolate, O my Lord, and Thou art the All-Possessing, the Most High. Have pity, then, upon me through the wonders of Thy mercy, and send down upon me, every moment of my life, the things wherewith Thou hast recreated the hearts of all Thy creatures who have recognized Thy unity, and of all Thy people who are wholly devoted to Thee.

Thou, verily, art the Almighty, the Most Exalted, the All-Knowing, the All-Wise." [120]

REFERENCES

1 Taherzadeh, Adib, *The Revelation of Bahá'u'lláh* Vol. 2, p. 34-35
2 Ibid., p. 214
3 Ghadirian, Abdu'l-Missagh, M.D. *Materialism, Moral and Social Consequences*, p. 139-140
4 Ibid., p. 140
5 Bahá'u'lláh, *Tablets of Bahá'u'lláh*, p. 253
6 'Abdu'l-Bahá, *Tablets of 'Abdu'l-Bahá Abbas* Vol. III, p. 557
7 'Abdu'l-Bahá, *Divine Philosophy*, p. 135-136
8 Taherzadeh, Adib, *The Revelation of Bahá'u'lláh* Vol. 3, p. 212
9 Taherzadeh, Adib, *The Revelation of Bahá'u'lláh*, Vol. 1, p. 77
10 Ghadirian, Abdu'l-Missagh, M.D. *Materialism, Moral and Social Consequences*, p. 141
11 Bahá'u'lláh, *Tablets of Bahá'u'lláh*, p. 219
12 Bahá'u'lláh, *The Hidden Words*, Arabic no. 55, p. 16
13 Bahá'u'lláh, *Gleanings from the Writings of Bahá'u'lláh*, CXXVIII, p. 276
14 Ibid., LX, p. 118
15 'Abdu'l-Bahá, *Divine Philosophy*, p.134
16 Ibid., p. 135-137
17 Redman, Earl, *'Abdu'l-Bahá in their Midst*, p. 206
18 Bahá'u'lláh, *The Hidden Words*, Persian no. 55, p. 41-42
19 Ibid., Persian no. 53, p. 41
20 Bahá'u'lláh, *Tablets of Bahá'u'lláh*, p. 71
21 Taherzadeh, Adib, *The Revelation of Bahá'u'lláh* Vol. 4 (Oxford: George Ronald, 1988), p. 195
22 Ibid.
23 Taherzadeh, Adib, *The Revelation of Bahá'u'lláh* Vol. 1, p. 77
24 'Abdu'l-Bahá, *The Secret of Divine Civilization*, p. 96-97
25 Taherzadeh, Adib, *The Revelation of Bahá'u'lláh* Vol. 2, p. 215
26 Shoghi Effendi, *God Passes By*, (Wilmette, IL: Bahá'í Publishing Trust), p. 137
27 Chodron, Pema, *Taking the Leap*, p. 22
28 Ibid., p. 27
29 Ibid., p. 37
30 Ibid., p. 25
31 Ibid., p. 24
32 Ibid., p. 16
33 Ibid., p. 38-39
34 Ibid., p. 39
35 Ibid., p. 40-41
36 Ibid., p. 41

37 Ibid., p. 42
38 Ibid., p. 57-58
39 Ghadirian, Abdu'l-Missagh, M.D. *Materialism, Moral and Social Consequences*, p. 141-142
40 Bahá'u'lláh, *Tablets of Bahá'u'lláh*, p. 155
41 Bahá'u'lláh, *Gleanings from the Writings of Bahá'u'lláh*, CXXXVI, p. 294-295
42 Ibid., LXV, p. 125
43 'Abdu'l-Bahá, *Selections from the Writings of 'Abdu'l-Bahá*, 188, p. 220-221
44 'Abdu'l-Bahá, *Divine Philosophy*, p. 135
45 Taherzadeh, Adib, *The Covenant of Bahá'u'lláh* (Oxford: George Ronald, 1992), p.22-23
46 Bahá'u'lláh, *The Summons of the Lord of Hosts* (Australia: Bahá'í Publications, 2002), [27], p. 152
47 'Abdu'l-Bahá, *Tablets of 'Abdu'l-Bahá 'Abbás* Vol. III, p. 557
48 Ibid, p. 663
49 Shoghi Effendi, *The Compilation of Compilations* Vol. II, 1267, 19 December 1923, p. 1
50 'Abdu'l-Bahá, *Bahá'í World Faith*, p. 373
51 Taherzadeh, Adib, *The Revelation of Bahá'u'lláh* Vol. 3, p. 287-288
52 'Abdu'l-Bahá, *The Promulgation of Universal Peace*, 29 November 1912, [8], p. 451
53 Ibid.
54 'Abdu'l-Bahá, *Tablets of 'Abdu'l-Bahá 'Abbás* Vol. II, p. 354
55 'Abdu'l-Bahá, *The Promulgation of Universal Peace*, 29 November 1912, [9-10], p. 451-452
56 Afshin, Mahnaz, *The Beloved Master* (Klang, Malaysia: Bahá'í Publishing Trust Committee, 1986), p. 76
57 Bahá'u'lláh, *The Hidden Words*, Persian no. 50, p.39
58 'Abdu'l-Bahá, *Wisdom of the Master* (Los Angeles: Kalimat Press, 2002), p. 66
59 Bahá'u'lláh, *Tablets of Bahá'u'lláh*, p. 155
60 Bahá'u'lláh, *The Summons of the Lord of Hosts*, [34], p. 154
61 Taherzadeh, Adib, *The Revelation of Bahá'u'lláh* Vol. 3. p. 193
62 Taherzadeh, Adib, *The Revelation of Bahá'u'lláh* Vol. 2, p. 97 63 Taherzadeh, Adib, *The Revelation of Bahá'u'lláh* Vol.1, p. 75
64 Ibid., p. 77
65 Bahá'u'lláh, *The Hidden Words*, Persian no. 26, p. 31
66 Ibid., Arabic no. 8, p. 5
67 'Abdu'l-Bahá, *Selections from the Writings of 'Abdu'l-Bahá*, 181, p. 207
68 Bahá'u'lláh, *The Hidden Words*, Persian no. 31, p.33
69 Taherzadeh, Adib, *The Revelation of Bahá'u'lláh*, Vol. 4, p. 65

70 Bahá'u'lláh, *The Hidden Words*, Arabic no. 42, p. 13
71 Taherzadeh, Adib, *The Child of the Covenant, A Study Guide to the Will and Testament of 'Abdu'l-Bahá* (Oxford: George Ronald, 2000), p. 406
72 'Abdu'l-Bahá, *Tablets of 'Abdu'l-Bahá 'Abbás* Vol.III, p. 552
73 Bahá'u'lláh, *The Hidden Words*, Persian no. 19, p. 28
74 Ibid., Persian no. 14, p. 26
75 Ibid., Persian no. 40, p. 36
76 Ibid., Arabic no. 16, p. 8
77 Bahá'u'lláh, *The Hidden Words*, p. 52
78 Bahá'u'lláh, *The Kitab-i-Iqan*, p. 3
79 Bahá'u'lláh, *Gleanings from the Writings of Bahá'u'lláh*, CLX, p. 337-338
80 Ibid., CLX, p.338
81 'Abdu'l-Bahá, *Paris Talks*, The Evolution of the Spirit, [11], p. 90
82 Shoghi Effendi, , *The Compilation of Compilations* Vol. II, 1336, 19 July 1956, p. 25
83 Bahá'u'lláh, *The Kitab-i-Iqan*, p. 192-193
84 'Abdu'l-Bahá, *Some Answered Questions*, p. 38-39
85 Bahá'u'lláh, *Gleanings from the Writings of Bahá'u'lláh*, V, p. 7-8
86 'Abdu'l-Bahá, *Bahá'u'lláh and the New Era*, p. 89
87 'Abdu'l-Bahá, *Bahá'í World Faith*, p. 362
88 Bahá'u'lláh, The *Kitab-i-Aqdas*, [178], p. 84
89 Honnold, Annamarie, *Vignettes from the Life of 'Abdu'l-Bahá*, 6, p. 11
90 Ibid., 10, p. 13
91 Ibid., 15, p. 15
92 Ibid.,16, p. 16
93 Ibid., 18, p. 17-18
94 Giachery, Ugo, *Shoghi Effendi – Recollections* (Oxford: George Ronald, 1973), p. 19
95 'Abdu'l-Bahá, *The Secret of Divine Civilization*, p. 97
96 'Abdu'l-Bahá, *Tablets of 'Abdu'l-Bahá 'Abbás* Vol. III, p. 545
97 Bahá'u'lláh, *Bahá'í Scriptures*, 171, p. 165
98 'Abdu'l-Bahá, *Tablets of 'Abdu'l-Bahá 'Abbás* Vol. III, p. 546
99 'Abdu'l-Bahá, *Bahá'í World Faith*, p. 231
100 Ibid., p. 384
101 'Abdu'l-Bahá, *Tablets of 'Abdu'l-Bahá 'Abbás* Vol. I, p. 65
102 'Abdu'l-Bahá, *The Promulgation of Universal Peace*, 26 May 1912, [1-2], p. 147-148
103 'Abdu'l-Bahá, *Paris Talks*, The Four Kinds of Love, [3], p. 179-180
104 'Abdu'l-Bahá, *Selections from the Writings of 'Abdu'l-Bahá*, 36, p. 76-77
105 Taherzadeh, Adib, *The Revelation of Bahá'u'lláh*, Vol. 2, p. 233
106 'Abdu'l-Bahá, *Selections from the Writings of 'Abdu'l-Bahá* , 153, p. 180
107 Shoghi Effendi in *Japan Will Turn Ablaze*, Tablets of 'Abdu'l-Bahá, Letters of Shoghi Effendi and the Universal House of Justice, and

Historical Notes About Japan (Japan: Bahá'í Publishing Trust, 1992), p. 62
108 'Abdu'l-Bahá, *Bahá'í Scriptures*, 958, p. 497-498
109 'Abdu'l-Bahá, *The Promulgation of Universal Peace*, 5 July 1912, [12], p. 224
110 'Abdu'l-Bahá, *Selections from the Writings of 'Abdu'l-Bahá*, 199, p. 241-242
111 Ibid., 63, p. 98-99
112 Taherzadeh, Adib, *The Revelation of Bahá'u'lláh*, Vol. 2, p. 96
113 Honnold, Annamarie, *Vignettes from the Life of 'Abdu'l-Bahá*, 9, p. 12
114 'Abdu'l-Bahá, *Selections from the Writings of 'Abdu'l-Bahá*, 195, p. 236
115 Honnold, Annamarie, *Vignettes from the Life of 'Abdu'l-Bahá*, 26, p. 21
116 Ibid., 31, p. 24
117 Dyer, Dr. Wayne W., *Your Sacred Self*, p. 77
118 Ibid., p. 74
119 Bahá'u'lláh, *Gems of Divine Mysteries* (Bahá'í World Centre, 2002), p. 71
120 Bahá'u'lláh, *Prayers and Meditations by Bahá'u'lláh*, CL, p. 240-242

Chapter 6
Trials for our Perfecting

Chapter 6
Trials for our Perfecting

Human life is one of adversity. Life is meant to be difficult. It is not meant to run smoothly, but is meant to be fraught with problems. The process of facing problems and solving them is painful. They evoke frustration, guilt, anger, regret, anxiety, sadness and other very uncomfortable emotions and can be as painful as physical pain, which is also another adversity we have to face. It is in dealing with these problems that we grow spiritually. The realm of problems, difficulties, pain, suffering and trials are referred to as "tests" in the Bahá'í Faith. We find ourselves dealing with a variety of tests in our lives, some of our own creating such as tests that arise from the desires and passions of a lower nature and tests that come from our difficulties in relating to others in a spiritual manner. Sometimes God gives us tests for our own improvement. Tests help us on our own spiritual journey and teach us to become more selfless. So in this chapter we will study the purpose of tests, the types of tests we encounter and how we can learn to deal with tests in our life, using the Bahá'í Writings as our source.

Tests are really God's gifts to us.

"Verily I say: Whatever befalleth in the path of God is the beloved of the soul and the desire of the heart. Deadly poison in His path is pure honey, and every tribulation a draught of crystal water. In the Tablet to His Majesty the Shah it is written: 'By Him Who is the Truth! I fear no tribulation in His path, nor any affliction in My love for Him. Verily God hath made adversity as a morning dew upon His green pasture, and a wick for His lamp which lighteth earth and heaven.'" [1]

"O Son of Man!

My calamity is My providence, outwardly it is fire and vengeance, but inwardly it is light and mercy. Hasten thereunto that thou mayest become an eternal light and an immortal spirit. This is My command unto thee, do thou observe it." [2]

Adversity is part of anything we want to accomplish in the world. And we grow primarily through our ability to overcome adversity and solve difficult problems. Our adversities and difficulties transform us into new spiritual beings, reflecting the qualities of God.

"Thou hast written concerning the tests that have come upon thee. To the sincere ones, tests are as a gift from God, the Exalted, for a heroic person hasteneth, with the utmost joy and gladness, to the tests of a violent battlefield, but the coward is afraid and trembles and utters moaning and lamentation. Likewise, an expert student prepareth and memorizeth his lessons and exercises with the utmost effort, and in the day of examination he appeareth with infinite joy before the master. Likewise, the pure gold shineth radiantly in the fire of test. Consequently, it is made clear that for holy souls, trials are as the gift of God, the Exalted; but for weak souls they are an unexpected calamity. This test is just as thou hast written: it removeth the rust of egotism from the mirror of the heart until the Sun of Truth may shine therein. For, no veil is greater than egotism and no matter how thin that covering may be, yet it will finally veil man entirely and prevent him from receiving a portion from the eternal bounty." [3]

It is human nature to avoid problems, to ignore them or to pretend they don't exist and hope they go away. We may try to skirt around them rather than dealing with them directly. I did not learn to deal with problems at a young age so later in life I procrastinated in dealing with something, hoping it would resolve itself. I did not know how to cope and neglected my responsibility in solving problems for myself. And fear intensified my avoidance behavior. If we have grown up ill-prepared to cope with the trials of life, we are surprised when they happen and treat them as dire calamities and misfortunes. We need to have faith and trust in God and know that in painful situations we can survive. If we learn to accept tests and turn to God for His guidance we will become more spiritually attuned and realize that suffering is a gift and for our benefit.

Bahá'u'lláh writes:

". . . the Almighty hath tried, and will continue to try, his servants, so that light may be distinguished from darkness, truth from falsehood, right from wrong, guidance from error, happiness from misery, and roses from thorns. Even as He hath revealed: 'Do men think when they say "We believe" they shall be let alone and not be put to proof?' [4]

The Universal House of Justice clarifies Bahá'u'lláh's Words:

". . . Every believer needs to remember that an essential characteristic of this physical world is that we are constantly faced with trials, tribulations, hardships and sufferings and that by overcoming them we achieve our moral and spiritual development; that we must seek to accomplish in the future what we may have failed to do in the past; that this is the way God

tests His servants and we should look upon every failure and shortcoming as an opportunity to try again and to acquire a fuller consciousness of the Divine Will and purpose." [5]

And Shoghi Effendi tells us:

"Suffering is both a reminder and a guide. It stimulates us better to adapt ourselves to our environmental conditions, and thus leads the way to self improvement. In every suffering one can find a meaning and a wisdom. But it is not always easy to find the secret of that wisdom. It is sometimes only when all our suffering has passed that we become aware of its usefulness. What a man considers to be evil turns often to be a cause of infinite blessings. [6]

"Suffering, of one kind or another, seems to be the portion of man in this world. Even the Beloved ones, the Prophets of God, have never been exempt from the ills that are to be found in our world; poverty, disease, bereavement, -they seem to be part of the polish God employs to make us finer, and enable us to reflect more of His attributes!" [7]

Justice St. Rain, a Bahá'í author, notes that with spiritual maturity and wisdom, we can look forward to tests, knowing that they will assist us on our spiritual path.[8] If we don't understand the purpose of tests, we become angry and rebel when something goes "wrong" or we feel that we're being punished and we try to avoid a test. Or we just accept the test and do nothing. Justice St. Rain, in his book, *Why Me, A Spiritual Guide to Growing through Tests*,[9] uses the analogy of four bushes to illustrate this point. The four rose bushes in the garden did their best all summer to grow long and produce many blossoms, only to be shocked when the gardener chopped off their branches at season's end. The first rose bush was angry and yelled at the gardener about the injustice of being cut down after trying to please him. It decided to rebel and concentrated on its root system in the spring, so that eventually it had only a few leaves and began to die. The second rose bush thought it was being punished for blossoming and so decided in the spring not to grow or blossom, but to do nothing so it looked as if it was dead. The third rose bush thought that things happened in life quite haphazardly and didn't have to be fair so in the spring it did the same thing it had done before, growing long branches with blossoms. Knowing that the gardener might just chop it down again at the end of the summer, it did not resist when the aphids began munching on leaves and petals. But the fourth bush trusted the gardener and wondered what he wanted it to do or learn from the experience. In the spring it noticed that it had many nodes on each branch and could branch out in many directions and blossom. And so with effort it could become a better rose bush with more blossoms rather than a leggy bush with only one blossom at the end of each stalk. Just like the fourth rose bush, we need to trust God (the Gardener) and know we can cope with any situation as long as we have faith in His love. We need to learn about ourselves in order to grow and explore our potential. And we have to make the effort to grow. We cannot control everything that happens but we can control our willingness and our capacity to respond to situations.

Taherzadeh [10] explains that Bahá'u'lláh warned people about the tests they would experience when they became believers. He also explains that because Bahá'u'lláh has released into the world incredible spiritual energies, the tests accompanying this Revelation are also great. As 'Abdu'l-Bahá says:

"The tests of every dispensation are in direct proportion to the greatness of the Cause, and as heretofore such a manifest Covenant, written by the Supreme Pen, hath not been entered upon, the tests are proportionately more severe. These trials cause the feeble souls to waver while those who are firm are not affected." [11]

And we are warned in the West about the kinds of tests we must endure:

"And yet, how often we seem to forget the clear and repeated warning of our beloved Master, ['Abdu'l-Bahá] *who in particular during the concluding years of His Mission on earth, laid stress on the severe mental tests that would inevitably sweep over His loved ones of the West . . . tests that would purge, purify and prepare them for their noble mission in life."* [12]

But we are promised that *"the tests and trials of God take place in this world, not in the world of the Kingdom."* [13]

In His Mercy, God gives us tests in order that we might remember Him because in His wisdom He knows that we can be easily distracted by this material world and are always in danger of being submerged in our selfish desires:

"If adversity befall thee not in My path, how canst thou walk in the ways of them that are content with My pleasure? If trials afflict thee not in thy longing to meet Me, how wilt thou attain the light in thy love for My beauty?" [14]

"While a man is happy he may forget his God; but when grief comes and sorrows overwhelm him, then will he remember his Father Who is in Heaven, and who is able to deliver him from his humiliations." [15]

"These tests, even as thou didst write, do but cleanse the spotting of self from off the mirror of the heart, till the Sun of Truth can cast its rays

thereon, for there is no veil more obstructive than the self, and however tenuous that veil may be, at the last it will completely shut a person out, and deprive him of his portion of eternal grace." [16]

If we don't experience tests, how can we experience the grace of God? St. Rain, in his book *Falling from Grace,* states that we live *"in a state of grace"* [17] when we are constantly aware of God's love and blessings.

"The portals of grace are wide open before the face of all men." [18]

But we don't experience that feeling of living in a state of grace until we fail and feel His hand picking us up and carrying us to grace.

". . . Unasked, I have showered upon thee My grace. Unpetitioned, I have fulfilled thy wish. In spite of thy undeserving, I have singled thee out for My richest, My incalculable favors. . . . " [19]

"My claim on thee is great, it cannot be forgotten. My grace to thee is plenteous, it cannot be veiled. My love has made in thee its home, it cannot be concealed. My light is manifest to thee, it cannot be obscured." [20]

Every time we slip and fall, St. Rain explains, we experience God's presence and unconditional support and we know that He will always be there for us.[21] We lose our fear that we may fall and with increased confidence we slip less. We are confirmed that God will continue to be there for us and that it's okay to make mistakes.

". . . do not look upon thy capacity, nay, rather, look upon the infinite grace of the Bounty of Abha whose grace is comprehending and whose bounty is perfect." [22]

"Not for a moment hath His grace been withheld, nor have the showers of His loving-kindness ceased to rain upon mankind." [23]

If we do not get the spiritual value from a test we may experience the same test again with more severity.

"Tests are a means by which a soul is measured as to its fitness and proven out by its own acts. God knows its fitness beforehand, and also its unpreparedness, but man, with an ego, would not believe himself unfit unless proof were given him." [24]

God wants us to master our tests and progress. 'Abdu'l-Bahá said to one of the Bahá'ís visiting him in Israel:

"The same test comes again in greater degree, until it is shown that a former weakness has become a strength and the power to overcome evil has been established." [25]

'Abdu'l-Bahá explains that every test contains a lesson from God for our perfection:

"Tests are benefits from God, for which we should thank Him. Grief and sorrow do not come to us by chance, they are sent to us by the Divine Mercy for our own perfecting." [26]

"Men who suffer not, attain no perfection. The plant most pruned by the gardeners is that one which, when summer comes, will have the most beautiful blossoms and the most abundant fruit . . . The labourer cuts up the earth with his plough, and from that earth comes the rich and plentiful harvest. The more a man is chastened, the greater is the harvest of spiritual virtues shown forth by him." [27]

And 'Abdu'l-Bahá wants us to experience suffering and tribulation because He knows how it benefits us:

"The more difficulties one sees in the world the more perfect one becomes. The more you plough and dig the ground the more fertile it becomes. The more you cut the branches of a tree the higher and stronger it grows. The more you put the gold in the fire the purer it becomes. The more you sharpen the steel by grinding the better it cuts. Therefore, the more sorrows one sees the more perfect one becomes. That is why, in all times, the Prophets of God have had tribulations and difficulties to withstand. The more often the captain of a ship is in the tempest and difficult sailing the greater his knowledge becomes. Therefore I am happy that you have had great tribulations and difficulties . . . Strange it is that I love you and still I am happy that you have sorrows." [28]

Here is a story that 'Abdu'l-Bahá told related to suffering:

"A certain ruler wished to appoint one of his subjects to a high office: so, in order to train him, the ruler cast him into prison and caused him to suffer much. The man was surprised at this, for he expected great favours. The ruler had him taken from prison and beaten with sticks. This greatly astonished the man, for he thought the ruler loved him. After this he was hanged on the gallows until he was nearly dead. After he recovered he asked the ruler, 'If you love me, why did you do these things?' The ruler replied: 'I wish to make you prime minister. By having gone through

these ordeals you are better fitted for that office. I wish you to know how it is yourself. When you are obliged to punish, you will know how it feels to endure these things. I love you so I wish you to become perfect.' Even so with you. After this ordeal you will reach maturity. God sometimes causes us to suffer much and to have many misfortunes that we may become strong in His Cause. You will soon recover and be spiritually stronger than ever before. You will work for God and carry the Message to many of your people." [29]

In order to benefit from the test given to us, we need to pray for assistance and also to read and understand Bahá'u'lláh's Teachings, as Shoghi Effendi explains:

"Naturally there will be periods of distress and difficulty, and even severe test; but if that person turns firmly towards the Divine Manifestation, studies carefully His Spiritual teachings and receives the blessings of the Holy Spirit, he will find that in reality these tests and difficulties have been the gifts of God to enable him to grow and develop." [30]

We need to follow the Bahá'í laws in meeting the difficulties in life:

"In considering the effect of obedience to the laws on individual lives, one must remember that the purpose of this life is to prepare the soul for the next. Here one must learn to control and direct one's animal impulses, not to be a slave to them. Life in this world is a succession of tests and achievements, of falling short and of making new spiritual advances. Sometimes the course may seem very hard, but one can witness, again and again, that the soul who steadfastly obeys the Law of Bahá'u'lláh, however hard it may seem, grows spiritually, while the one who compromises with the law for the sake of his own apparent happiness is seen to have been following a chimera: he does not attain the happiness he sought, he retards his spiritual advance and often brings new problems upon himself." [31]

'Abdu'l-Bahá tells us:

"Unless one accepts dire vicissitudes, he will not attain. To me prison is Freedom, troubles rest me, death is life, and to be despised is honour. Therefore, I was happy all that time in prison. When one is released from the prison of self, that is indeed release, for that is the greater prison. When this release takes place, then one cannot be outwardly imprisoned. When they put my feet in stocks, I would say to the guard, 'You cannot imprison me, for here I have light and air and bread and water. There will come a time when my body will be in the ground, and I shall have

neither light nor air nor food nor water, but even then I shall not be imprisoned.' The afflictions which come to humanity sometimes tend to centre the consciousness upon the limitations, and this is a veritable prison. Release comes by making of the will a Door through which the confirmations of the Spirit come." [32]

Let's take a few minutes to understand the meaning of this passage. First of all, we are told that we need to accept "dire vicissitudes" to attain. What is a vicissitude? According to various definitions on Google, it is a change of circumstance or fortune, typically one that is unwelcome and unpleasant that occurs by chance. It is a hardship that affects a way of life, a course of action usually beyond one's control. "Dire" means causing or involving great fear or suffering; having dreadful or terrible consequences; calamitous. So dire vicissitudes are extreme changes of circumstances. 'Abdu'l-Bahá experienced dire vicissitudes all his life. He lived his early years in a mansion, then He and His family lost everything overnight and lived in exile the rest of their lives before being banished to the Most Great Prison. 'Abdu'l-Bahá tells us that unless we accept such dreadful hardships, we cannot grow spiritually. We need to let go of our "self", our selfish nature in order to be able to cope with the hardships and progress. When we are experiencing afflictions, we tend to think about our limitations and feel we cannot cope. But if we centre our will on the will of God, we will receive confirmations. When 'Abdu'l- Bahá said this to his audience in London, someone asked him what the confirmations of the Spirit were. He replied, *"The confirmations of the Spirit are all those powers and gifts which some are born with (and which men sometimes call genius), but for which others have to strive with infinite pains. They come to that man or woman who accepts his life with radiant acquiescence."* [33] And so we learn that by accepting our tribulations, detaching from self and our limitations, and accepting our lot with faces beaming with joy, we will realize our spiritual destiny and receive the confirmations of God.

"Anybody can be happy in the state of comfort, ease, health, success, pleasure and joy; but if one will be happy and contented in the time of trouble, hardship and prevailing disease, it is the proof of nobility." [34]

We must experience affliction to be ready for the next world.

"Man's physical existence on this earth is a period during which the moral exercise of his free will is tried and tested in order to prepare his

soul for the other worlds of God, and we must welcome affliction and tribulations as opportunities for improvement in our eternal selves." [35]

Tests assist us to acquire virtues in preparation for the next world and provide opportunities to practice them. St. Rain[36] discusses the need to become more aware of the tests confronting us by asking ourselves questions – "Is the test from God or as a result of my own behavior? What is my attitude to a test – do I perceive it as an opportunity to grow and learn or a punishment to be avoided? What is the virtue needed in this situation? By doing this exercise, we can identify what areas require growth and we are in a better position to nurture our development. We just need to have confidence in our capacity and be receptive to tribulations.[37]

Some tests, as St. Rain points out, motivate us because we discover in certain situations the advantages of developing our virtues.[38] We can become careless and forget who we really are and our spiritual destiny. So we need reminders to polish our virtues. We are always given opportunities to practice qualities and each time we try to demonstrate a virtue we get closer to our potential. We may "fail" a test in that we fail to demonstrate a quality, but we will still learn something new about ourselves. And we become more of our true selves and reflect more of God's light. The test helps us to grow, whether or not it is "passed". Our capacity is known only to God and it is infinite so we have talents and qualities unknown to ourselves until we are suddenly in a situation that requires them.

St. Rain feels that many problems could be solved more readily if we applied simple virtues like love, patience and generosity.[39] We are meant to reflect God's qualities.[40] If we are not doing well spiritually, God will test us to point out where we need to grow and of course invite us to make the effort. We are given many opportunities to develop a virtue and He is quick to forgive us for our mistakes and give us another opportunity to learn; we, on the other hand are much harder on ourselves and experience guilt or shame and are quite unforgiving of ourselves. We have to repeat the practice of virtues many times so that they become habits and we need to be kind to ourselves when we slide backwards. We need to become proficient in order for a virtue to become part of our being and therefore be applied in service to others.[41]

The Bahá'í Writings assure us that God will not test us beyond our capacity:

"He will never deal unjustly with any one, neither will He task a soul beyond its power. He, verily, is the Compassionate, the All-Merciful." [42]

"Whatever hath befallen you, hath been for the sake of God. This is the truth, and in this there is no doubt. You should, therefore, leave all your affairs in His Hands, place your trust in Him, and rely upon Him. He will assuredly not forsake you. In this, likewise, there is no doubt. No father will surrender his sons to devouring beasts; no shepherd will leave his flock to ravening wolves. He will most certainly do his utmost to protect his own." [43]

"There is no need to fear opposition from without if the life within be sound and vigorous. Our Heavenly Father will always give us the strength to meet and overcome tests if we turn with all our hearts to Him, and difficulties if they are met in the right spirit only make us rely on God more firmly and completely." [44]

"Obedience to the Laws of Bahá'u'lláh will necessarily impose hardships in individual cases. No one should expect, upon becoming a Bahá'í, that faith will not be tested, and to our finite understanding of such matters these tests may occasionally seem unbearable. But we are aware of the assurance which Bahá'u'lláh Himself has given the believers that they will never be called upon to meet a test greater than their capacity to endure." [45]

As we have stated, we are not given a test impossible for us to pass. But, as St. Rain points out, we may refuse a test. God will continue to provide opportunities for us to grow, even though He knows we will refuse and this behavior will cause deep pain. But it is His duty to give us opportunities to grow because this is the one thing of value to us in this world – the capacity to reflect God's qualities in our hearts - and this is our true reality.[46]

Tests help us to become detached from this world. 'Abdu'l-Bahá explains:

"O thou servant of God! Do not grieve at the afflictions and calamities that have befallen thee. All calamities and afflictions have been created for man so that he may spurn this mortal world – a world to which he is much attached. When he experienceth severe trials and hardships, then his nature will recoil and he will desire the eternal realm – a realm which is sanctified form all afflictions and calamities. Such is the case with the man who is wise. He shall never drink from a cup which is at the end distasteful, but, on the contrary, he will seek the cup of pure and limpid water. He will not taste of the honey that is mixed with poison.

Praise thou God, that thou hast been tried and hast experienced such a test. Be patient and grateful. Turn thy face to the divine Kingdom and strive that thou mayest acquire merciful characteristics, mayest become illumined and acquire the attributes of the Kingdom and of the Lord. Endeavour to become indifferent to the pleasures of this world and to its comfort, to remain firm and steadfast in the Covenant and to promulgate the Cause of God.

This is the cause of the exaltation of man, the cause of his glory and of his salvation." [47]

". . . so suffering and tribulation free man from the petty affairs of this worldly life until he arrives at a state of complete detachment. His attitude in this world will be that of divine happiness. Man is, so to speak, unripe: the heat of the fire of suffering will mature him. Look back to the times past and you will find that the greatest men have suffered most." [48]

And Shoghi Effendi reiterates:

"Whenever you see tremendous personal problems in your private lives . . . you must remember that these afflictions are part of human life; and, according to our teachings one of their wisdoms is to teach us the impermanence of this world and the permanence of the spiritual bonds that we establish with God, His Prophet, and those who are alive in the faith of God." [49]

We have discussed the tests that God gives us for our own perfecting. But there are tests that we create for ourselves, as 'Abdu'l-Bahá explains:

"God alone ordereth all things and is all-powerful. Why then does He send trials to His servants?

The trials of man are of two kinds. (a) The consequences of his own actions. If a man eats too much, he ruins his digestion; if he takes poison he becomes ill or dies. If a person gambles he will lose his money; if he drinks too much he will lose his equilibrium. All these sufferings are caused by the man himself, it is quite clear therefore that certain sorrows are the result of our own deeds. (b) Other sufferings there are, which come upon the Faithful of God. Consider the great sorrows endured by Christ and by His apostles!

Those who suffer most, attain to the greatest perfection." [50]

If a test is the consequence of our own actions, it is within our power to avoid it, as St. Rain points out. We must of course look at our behaviors and make the decision to change those that are not in harmony with our spiritual life.[51]

"O Son of Spirit!

Noble have I created thee, yet thou hast abased thyself. Rise then unto that for which thou wast created." [52]

St. Rain states that we can abase or debase ourselves by abusing our bodies through neglect, underactivity, overeating; we can debase our spirits through lying, gambling, wasting time, neglecting education, and blaming others for failures; we can debase our relationships through gossiping, backbiting, judging, isolating ourselves, and being prone to fits of temper.[53] It requires a lot of effort and spiritual guidance in our lives to act differently but it's the only way to avoid these types of tests. We can't ask God to protect us from tests unless we're asking for help to change our behaviors. The tests of our own consequences are the majority of tests we face every day and we end up torturing ourselves by not following spiritual laws.[54]

Shoghi Effendi writes:

"He was very sorry to hear that you have had so many tests in your Bahá'í life. There is no doubt that many of them are due to our own nature. In other words, if we are very sensitive, or if we are in some way brought up in a different environment from the Bahá'ís amongst whom we live, we naturally see things differently and may feel them more acutely; and the other side of it is that the imperfections of our fellow-Bahá'ís can be a great trial to us.

We must always remember that in the cesspool of materialism, which is what modern civilization has to a certain extent become, Bahá'ís -- that is some of them -- are still to a certain extent affected by the society from which they have sprung. In other words, they have recognized the Manifestation of God, but they have not been believers long enough, or perhaps not tried hard enough, to become 'a new Creation'. He feels that, if you close your eyes to the failings of others, and fix your love and prayers upon Bahá'u'lláh, you will have the strength to weather this storm, and will be much better for it in the end, spiritually. Although you suffer, you will gain a maturity that will enable you to be of greater help to both your fellow-Bahá'ís and your children." [55]

Taherzadeh[56] explains that tests for Bahá'ís are mainly from the world we live in and from their fellow- Bahá'ís. It is very difficult to live the Bahá'í way of life in a world that is becoming increasingly more corrupt and spiritually bankrupt. As this world heads towards its destruction, Bahá'ís need to be confident in their vision of the society of the future and be happy and sincere in their Bahá'í lives, trying to live according to Bahá'u'lláh's teachings while surrounded by the evils of a decadent materialistic society. Within the Bahá'í community individuals experience tests working within their administrative institutions. Bahá'ís may not fully understand the nature of these institutions because their religious traditions taught them that such institutions were man-made bodies, rather than part of God's religion and because man-made institutions in society are so often the focus of strife and contention. And the requisites for consultation in the Assembly meeting and in general are lofty standards difficult to meet. When these standards are compromised, one's faith may be tested. The requisites for Bahá'ís consultation are discussed in the next chapter.

Bahá'ís are challenged by their fellow-believers because, on the one hand, they have the glorious vision of the Faith in front of their eyes and, on the other hand, they are the pitiful creatures of God falling short in their attempts to rise to that vision. Shoghi Effendi gives guidance in this respect:

"You have complained of the unsatisfactory conditions prevailing in the . . . Bahá'í Community; the Guardian is well aware of the situation of the Cause there, but is confident that whatever the nature of the obstacles that confront the Faith they will be eventually overcome. You should, under no circumstances, feel discouraged, and allow such difficulties, even though they may have resulted from the misconduct, or the lack of capacity and vision of certain members of the Community, to make you waver in your faith and basic loyalty to the Cause. Surely, the believers, no matter how qualified they may be, whether as teachers or administrators, and however high their intellectual and spiritual merits, should never be looked upon as a standard whereby to evaluate and measure the divine authority and mission of the Faith. It is to the Teachings themselves, and to the lives of the Founders of the Cause that the believers should look for their guidance and inspiration, and only by keeping strictly to such [a] true attitude can they hope to establish their loyalty to Bahá'u'lláh upon an enduring and unassailable basis. You should take heart, therefore, and with unrelaxing vigilance and unremitting effort endeavour to play your full share in the gradual unfoldment of this Divine World Order." [57]

It takes great spiritual maturity to focus on the Teachings rather than having one's faith dependent on the behavior of individual Bahá'ís or institutions. Shoghi Effendi addresses the tests Bahá'ís may experience in dealing with each other as Bahá'ís and he provides assurance:

"Often these trials and tests which all Bahá'í Communities inevitably pass through seem terrible, at the moment, but in retrospect we understand that

they were due to the frailty of Human nature, to misunderstanding, and to the growing pains which every Bahá'í community must experience." [58]

St. Rain suggests that there is a way to be proactive in dealing with tests and becoming more spiritual beings. We can decide to pick a virtue that needs developing and practice it.[59] This is possible with such virtues as generosity, knowledge and kindness but more difficult with those such as forgiveness and patience that depend on outside forces to be activated. But as St. Rain points out, there are enough spontaneous opportunities to practice those virtues in a safe environment where it doesn't matter if we succeed or fail. Then having practiced a virtue, we will have a better chance of succeeding when we need to use the virtue at a later time.[60]

St. Rain also discusses tests of choice such as volunteering in a difficult situation, choosing a lower-paid but humanitarian field of work and adopting children. Some choices may involve doing the right thing in a situation regardless of the possibility of negative consequences to our well-being, such as standing up for justice, answering someone's cry for help or offering services in a war-torn country. These choices clearly require faith and a great deal of courage. And they can be avoided if we so choose. But if we make the choice to follow such a path, our spiritual development is greatly enhanced.[61]

St. Rain asks us to consider why we would choose to experience tests. He feels that because we can't progress spiritually and become closer to God without experiencing tests, we might as well embrace them with eyes wide open rather than blindly tripping over them or being paralyzed with fear or running away like a coward.[62] And understanding our tests can be very helpful.[63] Awareness can make any tests – even those you failed years ago – a current success. This discussion puts me in mind of an experience I had in Siberia. I had volunteered to work at a children's camp. In Communist Russia there had been pioneer camps for children to learn to be good citizens of the state and parents had sent their children every summer. With the dissolution of communism, the camps were abandoned. The Bahá'ís were asked if they would like to run some camps and the Russian Bahá'ís put out the call for assistance from other Bahá'ís in the world. On the second day at the camp, just before the children arrived, I went down some stairs and twisted my ankle (or so I thought), but I really broke a bone in my foot and the doctor put a cast on it. A search went on to find crutches I could use because it was not possible to walk on the cast. One crutch was found and I could manage to lean on the crutch and hop on the other foot. But the camp was very hilly and the buildings were spread out over some distance and therefore presented a challenge for someone with one good leg. I could not help to patrol the grounds at night and supervise our unruly teenagers. And I started out trying to help a class on protecting the environment, led by one of the Russian-speaking Bahá'ís, but I couldn't physically participate in the activities and I eventually stopped going. I also helped with a singing group at first, and dropped it, too, not feeling that I was contributing much. I felt defeated by my physical limitations, even though a lack of mobility had little to do with my ability to lead a singing group! I was like the second rose bush, perhaps, trying to figure out why this had to happen to me, treating it like a punishment, feeling sorry for myself and giving up, rather than accepting my limitations and finding a solution. And it took me many years to see how I had failed this test. I think I was being tested to see how I could manage without mobility – how I could adjust and be of service anyway. Perhaps I was being asked to accept my situation and trust the Gardener to help me figure out what He wanted me to do.I could not see that Bahá'u'lláh may have been leading me to take on a different role. I was even given a few opportunities to demonstrate that I could serve in a different role with my listening skills and empathy for others. I remember one of the English-speaking Bahá'ís venting to me about the difficulties experienced with the youth and the language barrier. And I did have some positive experiences in relating to the youth. I needed to go home just after my leg healed and could not stay for the second camp. I left with a great deal of regret because I thought I could contribute more with two good legs. I was still focusing on the importance of having mobility to be of any use.

Years later when it suddenly occurred to me that I had been tested, I came to some conclusions about the nature of the test that I had "failed" and I learned a great deal just from reliving the experience in my mind and determining what I could have done differently. St. Rain notes that understanding why we experience specific tests and learning from them results in more control, allowing us to take responsibility for things we are able to control and leaving to God the things we cannot.[64] Later when we are in the middle of a test, we do not become consumed by fear, anger, sadness, guilt or resentment at a time when we need to think in a clear manner to find a solution.

The concept of awareness can be extended further. It's important for us to know why we respond the way we do. We may think that we're standing in a long line at the checkout counter because we need to practice patience. St. Rain explains that maybe we're not experiencing impatience; maybe we feel really agitated or feel stupid or feel angry at God for "picking on" us.[65] Our feelings may be much stronger that the situation warrants. What are our perceptions of the situation? What underlying beliefs are they bringing up? Or what triggers? You will remember our discussion of triggers in the last chapter. If we can identify what is really happening in the situation, we can then recognize what the test is really about and the specific qualities we're being asked to develop. Strong feelings in a situation often point to similar unresolved tests from the past. Perhaps God gives us the test again because He knows that we now have the maturity and resources to pass it.

Of course in all this discussion I am assuming that we want to develop virtues, that we recognize it as the purpose of our lives and that through tests we can acquire them. We need to acquire a thirst for spirituality. 'Abdu'l-Bahá gives us the formula:

"The first thing to do is to acquire a thirst for Spirituality, then Live the Life! Live the Life! Live the Life! The way to acquire this thirst is to meditate upon the future life. Study the Holy Words, read your Bible, read the Holy Books, especially study the Holy Utterances of Bahá'u'lláh; Prayer and Meditation, take much time for these two. Then will you know this Great Thirst, and then only can you begin to Live the Life!" [66]

To live the life we must practice the virtues. 'Abdu'l-Bahá gives us four tools to develop our thirst, which will transform our beliefs and perceptions – meditating upon the future life, studying the lives of the Prophets, studying the Holy Words, and also prayer and meditation. And Shoghi Effendi reminds us:

". . . as we suffer these misfortunes we must remember that the Prophets of God Themselves were not immune from these things which men suffer. They knew sorrow, illness and pain too. They rose above these things through Their spirits, and that is what we must try and do too, when afflicted. The troubles of this world pass, and what we have left is what we have made of our souls, so it is to this we must look to becoming more spiritual, drawing nearer to God, no matter what our human minds and bodies go through." [67]

It is definitely not easy to deal with the tests that assail us but when we turn to the Bahá'í Writings we glean assistance in how to pass the test.

In one of His Tablets discussed by Taherzadeh,[68] Bahá'u'lláh described the qualities of *"contentment and radiant acquiescence."* He stated that one must be resigned to God's Will to walk the path of contentment and accept with radiance whatever is part of his destiny. He must be content with himself. This is an impossible task if one is attached to this world as he will always be striving for perfection in this world and will resent hardships that interfere with his progress. So he must be detached from this world and accept with radiant acquiescence the trials and tests sent to him by God. As 'Abdu'l-Bahá states:

"Grieve not at the divine trials. Be not troubled because of hardships and ordeals; turn unto God, bowing in humbleness and praying to Him, while bearing every ordeal, contented under all conditions and thankful in every difficulty. Verily thy Lord loveth His maidservants who are patient, believing and firm. He draws them nigh unto Him through these ordeals and trials." [69]

Our prescription for bearing every difficulty is patience and thankfulness. Trusting God and turning humbly to Him in prayer are also essential.

"No matter what happens, nothing is as important as our feeling of trust in God, our inner peacefulness and faith that all, in the end, in spite of the severity of the ordeals we may pass through will come out as Bahá'u'lláh has promised." [70]

We need to be firm and steadfast.

"Today, the greatest of all titles and praises are firmness and steadfastness, for the tests and trials are of the utmost intensity. I ask God that day by day thou mayest increase in steadfastness, so like unto a solid rock thou mayest withstand the tempestuous sea of test." [71]

We need to be happy and more "ignited":

"O thou maid-servant of God! Become thou not extinguished by the winds of tests, but rather become ignited and be more happy, for then thou wilt become a tried believer." [72]

We need to be composed and confident in God's grace:

"When calamity striketh, be ye patient and composed. However afflictive your sufferings may be, stay ye undisturbed, and with perfect confidence in the abounding grace of God, brave ye the tempest of tribulations and fiery ordeals." [73]

And if we remember how Bahá'u'lláh suffered, our tests may not seem too formidable:

"Remember My days during thy days, and My distress and banishment in this remote prison." [74]

"Wrongly accused, imprisoned, beaten, chained, banished from country to country, betrayed, poisoned, stripped of material possessions, and at every moment tormented with a fresh torment . . . For two score years, until the end of His earthly days, He remained a prisoner and exile -- persecuted unceasingly by the rulers of Persia and the Ottoman Empire, opposed relentlessly by a vicious and scheming clergy, neglected abjectly by other sovereigns to whom He addressed potent letters. . .

The voice halts for shame from continuing so deplorable a recitation, the heart is torn by mere thought of the Divine Target of such grief -- grief no ordinary mortal could endure. But lest we give way to feelings of gloom and distress, we take recourse in the tranquil calm He induces with such meaningful words as these: 'We have borne it all with the utmost willingness and resignation, so that the souls of men may be edified, and the Word of God be exalted.' " [75]

'Abdu'l-Bahá tells us to join in His suffering to "some slight degree":

"Now ye, as well, must certainly become my partners to some slight degree, and accept your share of tests and sorrows. But these episodes shall pass away, while that abiding glory and eternal life shall remain unchanged forever. Moreover, these afflictions shall be the cause of great advancement." [76]

We are promised in *The Hidden Words* that we may at times have prosperity and at other times adversity, and so we must remain detached:

"Be not troubled in poverty nor confident in riches, for poverty is followed by riches, and riches are followed by poverty." [77]

"Should prosperity befall thee, rejoice not, and should abasement come upon thee, grieve not, for both shall pass away and be no more." [78]

But Bahá'u'lláh promises us *"days of blissful joy"*:

". . . Sorrow not if, in these days and on this earthly plane, things contrary to your wishes have been ordained and manifested by God, for days of blissful joy, of heavenly delight, are assuredly in store for you. Worlds, holy and spiritually glorious, will be unveiled to your eyes. You are destined by Him, in this world and hereafter, to partake of their benefits, to share in their joys, and to obtain a portion of their sustaining grace. To each and every one of them you will, no doubt, attain." [79]

So we know what our attitude towards tests should be, according to the Bahá'í Writings:

"O Thou Whose tests are a healing medicine to such as are nigh unto Thee, Whose sword is the ardent desire of all them that love Thee, Whose dart is the dearest wish of those hearts that yearn after Thee, Whose decree is the sole hope of them that have recognized Thy truth! I implore Thee, by Thy divine sweetness and by the splendors of the glory of Thy face, to send down upon us from Thy retreats on high that which will enable us to draw nigh unto Thee. Set, then, our feet firm, O my God, in Thy Cause, and enlighten our hearts with the effulgence of Thy knowledge, and illumine our breasts with the brightness of Thy names." [80]

"The more one is severed from this world, from desires, from human affairs, and conditions, the more impervious does one become to the tests of God." [81]

We all know people who have suffered a great deal in their lives. They seem to exude warmth, empathy and a depth of character we would espouse to.

If we don't go through troubled times it is very difficult for us to relate to others and their difficulties. As we grow spiritually through our adversities and God comforts us in times of troubles, we are then prepared to reach out to comfort others and become close to them. Our world desperately needs relationships based on love and understanding and the ability to reach out to others when they need help. As Shoghi Effendi said:

"Indeed the believers have not yet fully learned to draw on each other's love for strength and consolation in time of need. The Cause of God is endowed with tremendous powers, and the reason the believers do not gain more from it is because they have not learned to draw fully on these mighty forces of love and strength and harmony generated by the Faith." [82]

And when we suffer we join forces with all of mankind, ready to forget ourselves and our own problems in our desire to reach out to them:

"Our willingness to suffer is part of our demonstration of love for all mankind. Along with it, however, we must also be able to develop the spiritual muse not to dwell on our suffering but to turn our attention away to the great and many sources of our joy. For it is in God that we place our confidence, it is the life processes which the Faith has set in motion which we trust, knowing that it takes time and includes many setbacks." [83]

Our way through all tests and difficulties is service to our faith, as Shoghi Effendi points out:

"We must always look ahead and seek to accomplish in the future what we may have failed to do in the past. Failures, tests, and trials, if we use them correctly, can become the means of purifying our spirit, strengthening our characters, and enable us to rise to greater heights of service." [84]

"Thus you might look upon your own difficulties in the path of service. They are the means of your spirit growing and developing. You will suddenly find that you have conquered many of the problems which upset you, and then you will wonder why they should have troubled you at all. An individual must centre his whole heart and mind on service to the Cause, in accordance with the high standards set by Bahá'u'lláh. When this is done, the Hosts of the Supreme Concourse will come to the assistance of the individual, and every difficulty and trial will gradually be overcome." [85]

Here's a story that befittingly explains the process by which we are tried in our perfecting:

A couple vacationing in Europe went strolling down a little street and saw a quaint little gift shop with a beautiful teacup in the window. The lady collected teacups and she wanted this one for her collection so she went inside to pick up the teacup, and as the story goes the teacup spoke and said:

'I want you to know that I have not always looked like this. It took the process of pain to bring me to this point. You see, there was a time when I was just clay and the master came and he pounded me and he squeezed me and he kneaded me and I screamed: 'STOP THAT'. But he just smiled and he said, 'Not yet'.

Then he took me and put me on the wheel and I went round and round and round and round . . . and while I was spinning and getting dizzier and dizzier I screamed again and I said, 'Please get me off this thing . . . please get me off!!!' And the master was looking at me and he was smiling, as he said, 'Not yet'.

Then he took me and walked toward the oven and he shut the door and turned up the heat and I could see him through the window of the oven and it was getting hotter and hotter and I thought, 'He's going to burn me to death'. And I started pounding on the inside of the oven and I said 'Master, let me out, let me out, let me out', and I could see that he was smiling as he said 'Not yet'.

Then he opened the door and I was fresh and free and he took me out of the oven and he put me on the table and then he got some paint and a paintbrush. And he started dabbing me and making swirls all over me and I started to gag and I said: 'Master, stop it . . . stop it . . . stop it please . . . you're making me gag' and he just smiled as he said 'Not yet'.

Then very gently he picked me up again and he started walking toward the oven and I said, 'Master, NO! Not again, pleeeeease'. He opened the oven door and he slipped me inside and he shut the door and this time he turned the heat up twice as hot as before and I thought, 'He's going to kill me', and I looked through the window of the oven and I started to pound saying, 'Master . . . Master, please let me out ... please let me out . . . let me out . . . let me out'. And I could see that he was smiling, but I also noticed a tear trickle down his cheek as I watched him mouth the words, 'Not yet!'

Just as I thought I was about to die, the door opened and he reached in ever so gently and took me out, fresh and free and he went and placed me on a high shelf and he said: 'There, I have created what I intended. Would you like to see yourself?' I said 'Yes', so he handed me a mirror and I looked and I looked and I looked again and I said, 'That's not me, I'm just a lump of clay'. And he said: 'Yes, that IS you, but it took the process of pain to bring you to this place. You see, had I not worked you when you were clay, then you would have dried up. If I had not subjected you to the stress of the wheel, you would have crumbled. If I had not put you into the heat of the oven you would have cracked. If I had not painted you there would be no color in your life. But, it was the second oven that gave you the strength to endure. And now you are everything that I intended you to be – from the beginning.'

And I, the tea cup, heard myself saying something I never thought I would hear myself saying: 'Master, forgive me, I did not trust you, I thought you were going to harm me, I did not know you had a glorious future and a hope for me. I was too short-sighted, but I want to thank you. I want to thank you for suffering. I want to thank you for the process of pain. Here I am! I give you myself - fill me, pour from me, use me as you see fit. I really want to be a vessel that brings you glory within my life.'" [86]

REFERENCES

1 Bahá'u'lláh, *Epistle to the Son of the Wolf*, p. 17
2 Bahá'u'lláh, *The Hidden Words*, Arabic no.51, p. 15
3 'Abdu'l-Bahá, *Bahá'í World Faith*, p. 371-372
4 Bahá'u'lláh, *The Kitab-i-Iqan*, p. 8-9
5 The Universal House of Justice, *Lights of Guidance*, 1226, p. 366
6 Shoghi Effendi, *Lights of Guidance*, 944, p. 280
7 Ibid., 2049, p. 603-604
8 St. Rain, Justice, *Why Me? A Spiritual Guide to Growing Through Tests* (Hiltonville, IN: Special Ideas, 2003). P. 8
9 Ibid., p. 1-4
10 Taherzadeh, Adib, *The Revelation of Bahá'u'lláh*, Vol. 1, p. 129
11 'Abdu'l-Bahá, *Selections from the Writings of 'Abdu'l-Bahá*, 185, p. 210
12 Shoghi Effendi, *Lights of Guidance*, 450, p. 135
13 'Abdu'l-Bahá, *Selections from the Writings of 'Abdu'l-Bahá*, 163, p. 194
14 Bahá'u'lláh, *The Hidden Words*, Arabic no. 50, p. 15
15 'Abdu'l-Bahá, *Paris Talks*, The Benefits of God to Man, [8], p. 50-51
16 'Abdu'l-Bahá, *Selections from the Writings of 'Abdu'l-Bahá*, 155, p. 182
17 St. Rain, Justice, *Falling into Grace* (Hiltonville, IN: Special Ideas, 2006), p. 1
18 Bahá'u'lláh, *Gleanings from the Writings of Bahá'u'lláh*, CXXVI, p. 271
19 Ibid, CLII, p. 322
20 Bahá'u'lláh, *The Hidden Words*, Arabic no. 20, p. 8-9
21 St. Rain, Justice, *Falling into Grace*, p. 2
22 'Abdu'l-Bahá, *Bahá'í World Faith*, p. 361
23 Bahá'u'lláh, *Gleanings from the Writings of Bahá'u'lláh*, XIII, p. 18
24 'Abdu'l-Bahá, *Star of the West* Vol. 6, no. 6, p. 45
25 Hellaby, William and Madeline, *Prayer, A Bahá'í Approach*, p. 79
26 'Abdu'l-Bahá, *Paris Talks*, The Benefits of God to Man, [7], p. 50
27 Ibid., [9-10], p. 51
28 'Abdu'l-Bahá, *Star of the West* Vol. 14, no. 2, p. 41
29 'Abdu'l-Bahá, *Lights of Guidance*, 2040, p. 601-602
30 Shoghi Effendi, Ibid., 247, p. 70
31 The Universal House of Justice, Ibid., 1209, p. 359-360
32 'Abdu'l-Bahá, *'Abdu'l-Bahá in London*, p. 120
33 Ibid., p. 121
34 'Abdu'l-Bahá, *Bahá'í World Faith*, p. 363
35 The Universal House of Justice, *Lights of Guidance*, 1228, p. 367
36 St. Rain, Justice, *Why Me? A Spiritual Guide to Growing Through Tests*, p. 22
37 Ibid., p. 26
38 Ibid., p. 27

39 Ibid., p. 28
40 Ibid., p. 30
41 Ibid., p. 31
42 Bahá'u'lláh, *Gleanings from the Writings of Bahá'u'lláh*, LII, p. 106
43 Bahá'u'lláh, *The Compilation of Compilations* Vol. 1, 334, p. 171
44 Shoghi Effendi, *Lights of Guidance*, 1378, p. 417
45 The Universal House of Justice, Ibid., 1144, p. 341
46 St. Rain, Justice, *Why Me? A Spiritual Guide to Growing Through Tests*, p. 34
47 'Abdu'l-Bahá, *Selections from the Writings of 'Abdu'l-Bahá*, 197, p. 239
48 'Abdu'l-Bahá, *Paris Talks*, The Progress of the Soul, [1], p. 178
49 Shoghi Effendi, *The Unfolding Destiny of the British Bahá'í Community: Messages from the Guardian of the Bahá'í Faith to the Bahá'ís of the British Isles*, 10 February 1951, p. 459-460
50 'Abdu'l-Bahá, *Paris Talks*, The Benefits of God to Mankind, [1-4], p. 49-50
51 St. Rain, Justice, *Why Me? A Spiritual Guide to Growing Through Tests*, p. 41
52 Bahá'u'lláh, *The Hidden Words*, Arabic no. 22, p. 9
53 St. Rain, Justice, *Why Me? A Spiritual Guide to Growing Through Tests*, p. 41
54 Ibid., p. 42
55 Shoghi Effendi, *Lights of Guidance*, 2047, p. 603
56 Taherzadeh, Adib, *The Revelation of Bahá'u'lláh*, Vol.3, p. 48-51
57 Shoghi Effendi, *The Compilation of Compilations* Vol. II, 1292, 23 August, 1939, p. 10
58 Shoghi Effendi, *Lights of Guidance*, 2038, p. 601
59 St. Rain, Justice, *Why Me? A Spiritual Guide to Growing Through Tests*, p. 44
60 Ibid., p. 45
61 Ibid., p. 45-46
62 Ibid., p. 48
63 Ibid., p. 50
64 Ibid.
65 Ibid., p. 58-60
66 'Abdu'l-Bahá, *The Compilation of Compilations* Vol. I, 425, p. 204
67 Shoghi Effendi, *Lights of Guidance*, 1014, p. 297
68 Taherzadeh, Adib, *The Revelation of Bahá'u'lláh*, Vol. 1, p. 108
69 'Abdu'l-Bahá, *Tablets of 'Abdu'l-Bahá 'Abbás* Vol. I, p. 51
70 Shoghi Effendi, *Lights of Guidance*, 791, p. 237
71 'Abdu'l-Bahá, *Tablets of 'Abdu'l-Bahá 'Abbás* Vol. III, p. 683
72 Ibid., p. 591
73 'Abdu'l-Bahá, *Selections from the Writings of 'Abdu'l-Bahá*, 35, p. 74
74 Bahá'u'lláh, *Bahá'í Prayers*, p. 309
75 The Universal House of Justice, *A Wider Horizon: Selected Messages of the Universal House of Justice 1983-1992* (Riviera Beach, FL: Palabra Publications, 1992), p. 239-240
76 'Abdu'l-Bahá, *Selections from the Writings of 'Abdu'l-Bahá*, 196, p. 238-239

77 Bahá'u'lláh, *The Hidden Words*, Persian, no. 51, p. 40
78 Ibid., Arabic no. 52, p. 16
79 Bahá'u'lláh, *Gleanings from the Writings of Bahá'u'lláh*, CLIII, p. 329
80 Bahá'u'lláh, *Prayers and Meditations by Bahá'u'lláh*, CXXXIII, p. 220-221
81 'Abdu'l-Bahá, *Star of the West* Vol. 6, no. 6, p. 45
82 Shoghi Effendi, *Lights of Guidance*, 321, p. 93
83 The Universal House of Justice, *Quickeners of Mankind- Pioneering in a World Community* (National Spiritual Assembly of the Bahá'ís of Canada, 1980), p. 121
84 Shoghi Effendi, *Lights of Guidance*, 2039, p. 601
85 Ibid., 2042, p. 602
86 Unknown author. Variation submitted to local Bahá'í calendar by Daryush Yazdani; the story can be found on several websites, including http://www.turnbacktogod.com/story-teacup-speaks-%20%20about-its-potter.

Chapter 7
Ignite a Candle of Love

Chapter 7
Ignite a Candle of Love

"Act in accordance with the counsels of the Lord . . . So far as ye are able, ignite a candle of love in every meeting, and with tenderness rejoice and cheer ye every heart. Care for the stranger as for one of your own; show to alien souls the same loving kindness ye bestow upon your faithful friends. Should any come to blows with you, seek to be friends with him; should any stab you to the heart, be ye a healing salve unto his sores; should any taunt and mock at you, meet him with love. . ." [1]

The Bahá'í Writings give us the formula for living our lives and contributing to the well-being of humanity. How do we relate to others and serve mankind? By practicing the virtues of love and kindness and on every occasion seeing all as members of our family, loving and serving all regardless of how they behave towards us. If this seems like a tall order, it is still the high standard we are called to:

"I desire distinction for you. The Bahá'ís must be distinguished from others of humanity. But this distinction must not depend upon wealth -- that they should become more affluent than other people. I do not desire for you financial distinction. It is not an ordinary distinction I desire; not scientific, commercial, industrial distinction. For you I desire spiritual distinction -- that is, you must become eminent and distinguished in morals. In the love of God you must become distinguished from all else. You must become distinguished for loving humanity, for unity and accord, for love and justice. In brief, you must become distinguished in all the virtues of the human world -- for faithfulness and sincerity, for justice and fidelity, for firmness and steadfastness, for philanthropic deeds and service to the human world, for love toward every human being, for unity and accord with all people, for removing prejudices and promoting international peace. Finally, you must become distinguished for heavenly illumination and for acquiring the bestowals of God. I desire this distinction for you. This must be the point of distinction among you." [2]

"They should not content themselves merely with relative distinction and excellence. Rather they should fix their gaze upon nobler heights by setting the counsels and exhortations of the Pen of Glory as their supreme goal." [3]

In this chapter we will investigate how to behave in a spiritual manner with others, according to the Bahá'í Writings: the importance of love and forgiveness, establishing relationships "that nothing can shake" [4], reflecting spiritual qualities, dealing with our negative emotions, the significance of our words and the importance of deeds over words. Perhaps through this study, we can imbue our lives with an increased sense of our purpose. Let us keep in our minds and hearts the words of the opening quotation, which are now reiterated in the instructions we are now going to study, 'Abdu'l-Bahá's description of a Bahá'í. First, here is the full passage:

"You must manifest complete love and affection toward all mankind. Do not exalt yourselves above others, but consider all as your equals, recognizing them as the servants of one God. Know that God is compassionate toward all; therefore, love all from the depths of your hearts, prefer all religionists before yourselves, be filled with love for every race, and be kind toward the people of all nationalities.

Never speak disparagingly of others, but praise without distinction. Pollute not your tongues by speaking evil of another. Recognize your enemies as friends, and consider those who wish you evil as the wishers of good. You must not see evil as evil and then compromise with your opinion, for to treat in a smooth, kindly way one whom you consider evil or an enemy is hypocrisy, and this is not worthy or allowable. You must consider your enemies as your friends, look upon your evil-wishers as your well-wishers and treat them accordingly. Act in such a way that your heart may be free from hatred. Let not your heart be offended with anyone. If some one commits an error and wrong toward you, you must instantly forgive him. Do not complain of others. Refrain from reprimanding them, and if you wish to give admonition or advice, let it be offered in such a way that it will not burden the bearer. Turn all your thoughts toward bringing joy to hearts. Beware! Beware! lest ye offend any heart. Assist the world of humanity as much as possible. Be the source of consolation to every sad one, assist every weak one, be helpful to every indigent one, care for every sick one, be the cause of glorification to every lowly one, and shelter those who are overshadowed by fear.

In brief, let each one of you be as a lamp shining forth with the light of the virtues of the world of humanity. Be trustworthy, sincere, affectionate and replete with chastity. Be illumined, be spiritual, be divine, be glorious, be quickened of God, be a Bahá'í." [5]

Let's study the passage section by section.

"You must manifest complete love and affection toward all mankind."

We are to demonstrate complete love to all – not "some" love to "some" people but complete love- fully loving everyone.

'Abdu'l-Bahá explains:

"God is the Father of all. He educates, provides for and loves all; for they are His servants and His creation. Surely the Creator loves His creatures. It would be impossible to find an artist who does not love his own production. Have you ever seen a man who did not love his own actions? Even though they be bad actions, he loves them. How ignorant, therefore, the thought that God, Who created man, educated and nurtured him, surrounded him with all blessings, made the sun and all phenomenal existence for his benefit, bestowed upon him tenderness and kindness and then did not love him. This is palpable ignorance, for no matter to what religion a man belongs, even though he be an atheist or materialist, nevertheless, God nurtures him, bestows His kindness and sheds upon him His light. How then can we believe God is wrathful and unloving? How can we even imagine this, when as a matter of fact we are witnesses of the tenderness and mercy of God upon every hand? All about us we behold manifestations of the love of God. If, therefore, God be loving, what should we do? We have nothing else to do but to emulate Him. Just as God loves all and is kind to all, so must we really love and be kind to everybody". ⁶

"Bahá'u'lláh ... founded the oneness of the world of humanity, proclaimed that all are servants of the loving and merciful God who has created, nourished and provided for all; therefore why should men be unjust and unkind to each other, showing forth that which is contrary to God? As He loves us, why should we entertain animosity and hate? If God did not love all, He would not have created, trained and provided for all. Loving-kindness is the divine policy. Shall we consider human policy and attitude superior to the wisdom and policy of God? This would be inconceivable, impossible. Therefore, we must emulate and follow the divine policy, dealing with each other in the utmost love and tenderness." ⁷

We continue the passage.

"Do not exalt yourselves above others, but consider all as your equals, recognizing them as the servants of one God."

We are asked not to exalt ourselves above others. As Bahá'u'lláh tells us:

"O CHILDREN OF MEN!

Know ye not why We created you all from the same dust? That no one should exalt himself over the other. Ponder at all times in your hearts how ye were created. Since We have created you all from one same substance it is incumbent on you to be even as one soul, to walk with the same feet, eat with the same mouth and dwell in the same land, that from your inmost being, by your deeds and actions, the signs of oneness and the essence of detachment may be made manifest." [8]

We are created from the same dust. We are all equal in His eyes and in the eyes of each other. Through our actions we demonstrate that we see all men as equals and we are detached from ourselves and our accomplishments, but ever mindful of serving others.

Continuing our discussion on the passage, 'Abdu'l-Bahá advices:

"Know that God is compassionate toward all; therefore, love all from the depths of your hearts, prefer all religionists before yourselves, be filled with love for every race, and be kind toward the people of all nationalities."

Just as God demonstrates compassion to us all, we also love all, from every religion, race and nationality.

And again He says:

"Consort with all the peoples, kindreds and religions of the world with the utmost truthfulness, uprightness, faithfulness, kindliness, good-will and friendliness; that all the world of being may be filled with the holy ecstasy of the grace of Bahá [God's grace], *that ignorance, enmity, hate and rancor may vanish from the world and the darkness of estrangement amidst the peoples and kindreds of the world may give way to the Light of Unity."* [9]

In this Dispensation we are called to reach out to everyone from all walks of life:

"In every dispensation, there hath been the commandment of fellowship and love, but it was a commandment limited to the community of those in mutual agreement, not to the dissident foe. In this wondrous age, however, praised be God, the commandments of God are not delimited, not restricted to any one group of people, rather have all the friends been commanded to show forth fellowship and love, consideration and generosity and loving-kindness to every community on earth. Now must the lovers of God arise to carry out these instructions of His: let them be kindly fathers to

the children of the human race, and compassionate brothers to the youth, and self-denying offspring to those bent with years." [10]

Once again, our directive is to accept all men and love them from the depths of our hearts.

"But some souls are weak; we must endeavor to strengthen them. Some are ignorant, uninformed of the bounties of God; we must strive to make them knowing. Some are ailing; we must seek to restore them to health. Some are immature as children; they must be trained and assisted to attain maturity. We nurse the sick in tenderness and the kindly spirit of love; we do not despise them because they are ill. Therefore, we must exercise extreme patience, sympathy and love toward all mankind, considering no soul as rejected. If we look upon a soul as rejected, we have disobeyed the teachings of God. God is loving to all. Shall we be unjust or unkind to anyone? Is this allowable in the sight of God? God provides for all. Is it befitting for us to prevent the flow of His merciful provisions for mankind? God has created all in His image and likeness. Shall we manifest hatred for His creatures and servants? This would be contrary to the will of God . . ." [11]

'Abdu'l-Bahá demonstrates how deep our love should be for our fellow creatures as we continue our study of the passage:

"Never speak disparagingly of others, but praise without distinction. Pollute not your tongues by speaking evil of another. Recognize your enemies as friends, and consider those who wish you evil as the wishers of good. You must not see evil as evil and then compromise with your opinion, for to treat in a smooth, kindly way one whom you consider evil or an enemy is hypocrisy, and this is not worthy or allowable. You must consider your enemies as your friends, look upon your evil-wishers as your well-wishers and treat them accordingly. Act in such a way that your heart may be free from hatred."

We need to pour out lavish amounts of encouragement and praise on everyone, as did 'Abdu'l-Bahá. For example, while in America, He praised the black and the white races for their close association with each other at a time when the black Bahá'ís and the white Bahá'ís had separate Feasts. He praised and exalted it into being! And we sincerely perceive enemies as friends, not pretending that they are friends but making them friends, loving them all because we do not see them as different – we do not see their "otherness". 'Abdu'l-Bahá clarifies this in the following Writing:

"O ye lovers of this wronged one! Cleanse ye your eyes, so that ye behold no man as different from yourselves. See ye no strangers; rather see all men as friends, for love and unity come hard when ye fix your gaze on otherness. And in this new and wondrous age, the Holy Writings say that we must be at one with every people; that we must see neither harshness nor injustice, neither malevolence, nor hostility, nor hate, but rather turn our eyes toward the heaven of ancient glory. For each of the creatures is a sign of God, and it was by the grace of the Lord and His power that each did step into the world; therefore they are not strangers, but in the family; not aliens, but friends, and to be treated as such." [12]

'Abdu'l-Bahá reinforces the need to see all men as friends and family:

"So intense must be the spirit of love and loving-kindness, that the stranger may find himself a friend, the enemy a true brother, no difference whatsoever existing between them . . ." [13]

Back to our passage:

"Let not your heart be offended with anyone. If some one commits an error and wrong toward you, you must instantly forgive him."

We do not become offended and forgive anyone who tries to hurt us.

The Báb states:

"There is no paradise, in the estimation of the believers in the Divine Unity, more exalted than to obey God's commandments, and there is no fire in the eyes of those who have known God and His signs, fiercer than to transgress His laws and to oppress another soul, even to the extent of a mustard seed. . ." [14]

'Abdu'l-Bahá tells us:

". . . he must return good for evil, and not only forgive, but also, if possible, be of service to his oppressor." [15]

And this is from a note of one of the Bahá'ís attributed to 'Abdu'l-Bahá:

"In truth nothing is sweeter in man's taste than to do good toward those who have done him ill. For, whenever one remembers such kindness to one's enemies, one feels highly rejoiced." [16]

But we need to clarify when forgiveness should be the remedy and when justice needs to be upheld:

"... the constitution of the communities depends upon justice, not upon forgiveness. Then what Christ meant by forgiveness and pardon is not that, when nations attack you, burn your homes, plunder your goods, assault your wives, children and relatives, and violate your honor, you should be submissive in the presence of these tyrannical foes and allow them to perform all their cruelties and oppressions. No, the words of Christ refer to the conduct of two individuals toward each other: if one person assaults another, the injured one should forgive him." [17]

It is clear from this Writing of 'Abdu'l-Bahá that when two individuals are dealing with each other, forgiveness is the correct behavior. It does not apply to abhorrent behavior in a community that is unjust.

"To forgive him will not be easy, and this is not something to which either you or the members of your family can force yourselves. Nevertheless, you should know that forgiveness is the standard which individual Bahá'ís are called upon to attain. It is an essential part of the spiritual growth of a person who has been wronged. To nurse a grievance or hatred against another soul is spiritually poisonous to the soul which nurses it, but to strive to see another person as a child of God and, however heinous his deed, to attempt to overlook his sins for the sake of God, removes bitterness from the soul and both ennobles and strengthens it." [18]

And again, referring to bettering the conditions of the poor, 'Abdu'l-Bahá says:

"Do not be satisfied until each one with whom you are concerned is to you as a member of your family. Regard each one either as a father, or as a brother, or as a sister, or as a mother, or as a child. If you can attain to this, your difficulties will vanish, you will know what to do. This is the teaching of Bahá'u'lláh." [19]

'Abdu'l-Bahá demonstrated this in His own life:

"'Abdu'l-Bahá looked at everyone whom He met as a member of His own family. One day when He was sitting with two ladies in England, one of them said to Him, 'Master, are You not longing to get back to Haifa and be with Your beloved family?'

'Abdu'l-Bahá smiled and said, 'I want you to understand that both of you are my daughters, and you are just as dear to me as my own daughters in Haifa.'

The ladies could hardly believe their ears and they wondered how they could be worthy of so high and honour, but it made them realize what

Bahá'u'lláh meant by the Oneness of Mankind and that all men are part of one family." [20]

Now we continue our study of the passage:

"Do not complain of others. Refrain from reprimanding them, and if you wish to give admonition or advice, let it be offered in such a way that it will not burden the bearer. Turn all your thoughts toward bringing joy to hearts. Beware! Beware! lest ye offend any heart. Assist the world of humanity as much as possible. Be the source of consolation to every sad one, assist every weak one, be helpful to every indigent one, care for every sick one, be the cause of glorification to every lowly one, and shelter those who are overshadowed by fear."

We don't offend others. We don't complain about them or reprimand them, only giving a little advice *"with words as mild as milk"*.[21] Our only thought is to make everyone happy. We try to help everyone by consoling sad ones, helping the poor and weak, caring for the sick, raising up the lowly ones and sheltering the fearful. And we do it for the sake of God, following His divine example and demonstrating our gratitude for His mercies and blessings.

"Be in perfect unity. Never become angry with one another. Let your eyes be directed toward the kingdom of truth and not toward the world of creation. Love the creatures for the sake of God and not for themselves. You will never become angry or impatient if you love them for the sake of God. Humanity is not perfect. There are imperfections in every human being, and you will always become unhappy if you look toward the people themselves. But if you look toward God, you will love them and be kind to them, for the world of God is the world of perfection and complete mercy. Therefore, do not look at the shortcomings of anybody; see with the sight of forgiveness. The imperfect eye beholds imperfections. The eye that covers faults looks toward the Creator of souls. He created them, trains and provides for them, endows them with capacity and life, sight and hearing; therefore, they are the signs of His grandeur. You must love and be kind to everybody, care for the poor, protect the weak, heal the sick, teach and educate the ignorant." [22]

Shoghi Effendi reiterates this:

"We must love God, and in this state, a general love for all men becomes possible. We cannot love each human being for himself but our feeling towards humanity should be motivated by our love for the Father who created all men." [23]

". . . we must reach a spiritual plane where God comes first and great human passions are unable to turn us away from Him. All the time we see people who either through the force of hate or the passionate attachment they have to another person, sacrifice principle or bar themselves from the path of God." [24]

To what extent are we to love our fellow-man? 'Abdu'l-Bahá tells us:

"O ye friends of God! Show ye an endeavor that all the nations and communities of the world, even the enemies, put their trust, assurance and hope in you; that if a person falls into errors for a hundred-thousand times he may yet turn his face to you, hopeful that you will forgive his sins; for he must not become hopeless, neither grieved nor despondent. This is the conduct and the manner of the people of Bahá. This is the foundation of the most high pathway! Ye should conform your conduct and manners with the advices of 'Abdu'l-Bahá." [25]

"First of all, be ready to sacrifice your lives for one another, to prefer the general well-being to your personal well-being. Create relationships that nothing can shake; form an assembly that nothing can break up; have a mind that never ceases acquiring riches that nothing can destroy. If love did not exist, what of reality would remain? It is the fire of the love of God which renders man superior to the animal. Strengthen this superior force through which is attained all the progress in the world." [26]

As we continue our discussion of this theme, we will look at more Writings that help us to learn how to be like this. And step by step, day by day, we learn to be more spiritually attuned as we continue our journey here and through eternity.

Dorothy Baker said that she had two rules to guide her life. *"One is this: Look not to the creatures. Let your heart be supremely attached to our Beloved; then you can serve all of His children with detachment and joy, and never fail any of them, no matter what they do. When people make mistakes, you are only witnessing moments that are hook-ups between states of consciousness. It doesn't matter. The second rule is this: Make a joyous thing of the little services because you can never tell which is little and which is big in God's sight."* [27]

Bahá'u'lláh said:

"Shouldst thou step a little way into the worlds of severance, thou wilt testify that no day greater than this Day and no resurrection mightier than this Resurrection can be imagined, and that one deed in this Day

is equivalent to deeds performed during a hundred thousand years -- nay, I ask pardon of God for this limitation, because deeds done in this Day are sanctified beyond any limited reward." [28] *"One righteous act is endowed with a potency that can so elevate the dust as to cause it to pass beyond the heaven of heavens. It can tear every bond asunder, and hath the power to restore the force that hath spent itself and vanished. . . ."* [29]

One simple act of unselfish love can make a difference, as Anita Moorjani noticed when she had her near-death experience described in her book, *Dying to be Me*.[30] When she "reviewed" her life on the other side, it was the small things, the tiniest acts of kindness which were most significant.

K.Sri Dhammananda says:

"We are potentially storehouses of love. The spirit of love is more important than good work." *'All good works whatever are not worth an iota of love which sets free the heart. Love which sets free the heart comprises good work. It shines, gives light and radiance.'"* (Buddha)[31]

Marianne Williamson explains that we are capable of doing what God is asking us to do. It is arrogance not humility if we think we can't do it.[32] Who are we to think we know ourselves better than God who created us? *"Whatever it is you are guided to do, don't be concerned about your own readiness; just be consistently aware of His."*[33] She also says that when we see negative behavior in someone we may have difficulty seeing God reflected in a person but we need to believe in their basic goodness. We can try imagining someone as they were as a child to have more empathy.[34] Recognizing that someone may come into our lives to teach us something, to test us, to force us to learn a difficult lesson or virtue may help us, also. Every encounter is a learning experience and an opportunity to demonstrate love.[35] We need to love all – even those who hurt us – after all, they are learning, as we are. When we come to the realization that we are alike, and pass beyond that stage to realize that we *"actually are each other, then we will begin to find life outside the realm of love no longer acceptable."* [36] We learn to love the way God does – to love everyone, an impersonal love, unconditional, not based on what they do but who they are in essence.[37] Our purpose is to invoke each other's greatness and work a miracle in each other's lives.[38]

At this point, you might be wondering what happened to our discussion of 'Abdu'l-Bahá's passage about being a Bahá'í. Let's go back to it:

"In brief, let each one of you be as a lamp shining forth with the light of the virtues of the world of humanity. Be trustworthy, sincere, affectionate

and replete with chastity. Be illumined, be spiritual, be divine, be glorious, be quickened of God, be a Bahá'í."

Let us look at the importance of virtues. 'Abdu'l-Bahá says:

"Verily, it is better a thousand times for a man to die than to continue living without virtue. ... The All-loving God created man to radiate the Divine light and to illumine the world by his words, action and life." [39]

Shoghi Effendi espouses the importance of virtues on men's souls:

"First and foremost, one should use every possible means to purge one's heart and motives, otherwise, engaging in any form of enterprise would be futile. It is also essential to abstain from hypocrisy and blind imitation, inasmuch as their foul odour is soon detected by every man of understanding and wisdom. Moreover, the friends must observe the specific times for the remembrance of God, meditation, devotion and prayer, as it is highly unlikely, nay impossible, for any enterprise to prosper and develop when deprived of divine bestowals and confirmation. One can hardly imagine what a great influence genuine love, truthfulness and purity of motives exert on the souls of men. But these traits cannot be acquired by any believer unless he makes a daily effort to gain them ..." [40]

And these are the virtues mentioned by Bahá'u'lláh:

"The virtues and attributes pertaining unto God are all evident and manifest, and have been mentioned and described in all the heavenly Books. Among them are trustworthiness, truthfulness, purity of heart while communing with God, forbearance, resignation to whatever the Almighty hath decreed, contentment with the things His Will hath provided, patience, nay, thankfulness in the midst of tribulation, and complete reliance, in all circumstances, upon Him. These rank, according to the estimate of God, among the highest and most laudable of all acts. All other acts are, and will ever remain, secondary and subordinate unto them ..." [41]

We will discuss a few of the virtues here that relate specifically to our study passage. Although purity of heart is not mentioned in the passage, it is listed in the quotation above – "purity of heart while communing with God". And in the study passage 'Abdu'l-Bahá asks us to be "replete with chastity".

"O SON OF SPIRIT!

My first counsel is this: Possess a pure, kindly and radiant heart, that thine may be a sovereignty ancient, imperishable and everlasting." [42]

'Abdu'l-Bahá tells us:

"O Friends of the Pure and Omnipotent God! To be pure and holy in all things is an attribute of the consecrated soul and a necessary characteristic of the unenslaved mind. The best of perfections is immaculacy and the freeing of oneself from every defect. Once the individual is, in every respect, cleansed and purified, then will he become a focal centre reflecting the Manifest Light.

First in a human being's way of life must be purity, then freshness, cleanliness, and independence of spirit. First must the stream bed be cleansed, then may the sweet river waters be led into it. Chaste eyes enjoy the beatific vision of the Lord and know what this encounter meaneth; a pure sense inhaleth the fragrances that blow from the rose gardens of His grace; a burnished heart will mirror forth the comely face of truth." [43]

"Blessed thou art and more blessed thou shalt be if thy feet be firm, thy heart tranquil through the fragrance of His Holy Spirit and thy secret and hidden thoughts pure before the Lord of Hosts!" [44]

Bahá'u'lláh tells us:

"Let your eye be chaste, your hand faithful, your tongue truthful and your heart enlightened." [45]

Shoghi Effendi discussed the importance of chastity as a spiritual requisite in his book *The Advent of Divine Justice*. *"A chaste and holy life must be made the controlling principle in the behavior and conduct of all Bahá'ís, both in their social relations with the members of their own community, and in their contact with the world at large."* [46]

"Such a chaste and holy life, with its implications of modesty, purity, temperance, decency, and clean- mindedness, involves no less than the exercise of moderation in all that pertains to dress, language, amusements, and all artistic and literary avocations. It demands daily vigilance in the control of one's carnal desires and corrupt inclinations. It calls for the abandonment of a frivolous conduct, with its excessive attachment to trivial and often misdirected pleasures". [47]

Truthfulness was specifically mentioned in Bahá'u'lláh's list of virtues "pertaining unto God". And in our study passage, 'Abdu'l-Bahá mentioned that we should be sincere. There are differences in the meanings of truthfulness and sincerity because sincerity seems to be more all-encompassing, including being honest and genuine, earnest, frank, genuine and without pretense. But we need truthfulness to be sincere. 'Abdu'l-Bahá said: *"Sincerity is to be admired, whilst lying is despicable."* [48] Lying is definitely the opposite of truthfulness. And we know how important truthfulness is: *"Truthfulness is the foundation of all the virtues of the world of humanity. Without truthfulness, progress and success in all of the worlds of God are impossible for a soul. When this holy attribute is established in man, all the divine qualities will also become realized."* [49]

Shoghi Effendi clarifies:

"As to the question whether it is right to tell an untruth in order to save another, he feels that under no condition should we tell an untruth but at the same time try and help the person in a more legitimate manner. Of course it is not necessary to be too outspoken until the question is directly put to us." [50]

And 'Abdu'l-Bahá said: *"... if a doctor consoles a sick man by saying: 'Thank God you are better, and there is hope of your recovery', though these words are contrary to the truth, yet they may become the consolation of the patient and the turning-point of the illness. This is not blameworthy."* [51]

Juliet Thompson, a New York Bahá'í and successful painter, tells a story about truthfulness in her diary. As we pick up the threads of the story, note that 'Abdu'l-Bahá had already praised Juliet for her truthfulness:

"He spoke again of my 'truthfulness'.

'Oh,' I prayed, 'may I some day have all the virtues so that in every way I can make you happy.'

'But he who possesses truthfulness possesses all the virtues,' said the Master. Then He went on to tell us a story.

There was once a disciple of Muhammad who asked of another disciple, 'What shall I do to please God?' And the other disciple replied: 'Do not kill. Do not steal. Do not covet, 'etc., etc., etc. A great many 'do nots'. the Master laughed. He asked still another, 'What shall I do to become nearer to God?' And this one said: 'You must supplicate and pray. You must be generous. You must be courageous,' etc., etc., etc. Then the disciple went to 'Ali. 'What do you say I should do in order to please God and to become nearer to Him?' 'One thing only: be truthful.'

'For,' continued the Master, 'if you are truthful, you cannot commit murder. You would have to confess it! Neither can you steal. You would have to confess it. So, if one is truthful, he possesses all the virtues.'

'I may tell you this,' He said to me, and He told me a thing so wonderful that, even to keep and cherish His words and read them over in the time to come, I cannot repeat it here.

'My Lord,' I said, 'if ever I have told You an untruth it was because I deceived myself.'

'There are degrees of truth,' He answered, 'but that word of yours which has so pleased Me was absolute, perfect, extraordinary truth.'" 52

I have always thought of myself as a truthful person. I don't go out of my way to tell someone the truth if it would hurt their feelings, but I don't like exaggeration and have been criticized for being a stickler for details when someone is relating events. So, imagine me in this situation and the way I responded. I was attending a week-long summer school and was excited on the first evening when a man and a few others with instruments got up to perform and asked if anyone knew the words to "Daniel" by Elton John and would like to come up and sing with them. I jumped up eagerly because I liked the song and liked to sing. It was clear in a few short moments that I did not know the words to the song and I stood there, singing the words I did know (mainly the chorus). I remember the look of surprise, confusion and yes, disdain on the face of the man who was leading the sing-along. I enjoyed my week, not really giving the incident much thought, but knowing that I was out of favour with that man! I even got involved teaching a song to the school's participants. We practiced every morning until everyone knew all the words and actions. So the incident didn't really stop me from participating and even doing something musical. And I have thought about it now and again since that time, wondering why I did it but recognizing the impulsiveness and enthusiasm that precipitated my behavior and lack of truthfulness. Imagine that man's perplexity! Why would I deliberately lie? I'm sure that he was aware that I really didn't know the words of the song, that it wasn't just nervousness or shyness that had interfered. He may still be trying to figure out why someone would do such a thing. I was certainly a test for him – the lying Bahá'í- and it was another lesson in humility for one who prided herself in being truthful!

'Abdu'l-Bahá exhorts us to be trustworthy in our study quote. Taherzadeh explains that Bahá'u'lláh *"placed a special emphasis on trustworthiness"* 53 out of all the qualities.

Bahá'u'lláh states: *"The most precious of all things in the estimation of Him Who is the Sovereign Truth is trustworthiness: thus hath it been recorded in the sacred Scroll of God. Entreat ye the one true God to enable all mankind to attain to this most noble and lofty station."* [54]

He deemed it more meritorious that someone be trustworthy than to attain His presence:

"Were a man in this day to adorn himself with the raiment of trustworthiness it were better for him in the sight of God than that he should journey on foot towards the holy court and be blessed with meeting the Adored One and standing before His Seat of Glory. Trustworthiness is as a stronghold to the city of humanity, and as eyes to the human temple. Whosoever remaineth deprived thereof shall, before His Throne, be reckoned as one bereft of vision." [55]

And He states, *". . . trustworthiness . . . is the door of security for all that dwell on earth and a token of glory on the part of the All-Merciful. He who partaketh thereof hath indeed partaken of the treasures of wealth and prosperity. Trustworthiness is the greatest portal leading unto the tranquillity and security of the people. In truth the stability of every affair hath depended and doth depend upon it. All the domains of power, of grandeur and of wealth are illumined by its light."* [56]

In one of 'Abdu'l-Bahá's Tablets to a devoted Bahá'í, He indicated that a believer could carry out many good deeds but if he were not trustworthy his good deeds would come to naught:

"If a man were to perform every good work, yet fail in the least scruple to be entirely trustworthy and honest, his good works would become as dry tinder and his failure as a soul-consuming fire. If, on the other hand, he should fall short in all his affairs, yet act with trustworthiness and honesty, all his defects would ultimately be righted, all injuries remedied, and all infirmities healed. Our meaning is that, in the sight of God, trustworthiness is the bedrock of His Faith and the foundation of all virtues and perfections. A man deprived of this quality is destitute of everything. What shall faith and piety avail if trustworthiness be lacking? Of what consequence can they be? What benefit or advantage can they confer? " [57]

And again He reiterates its importance:

"You have written on the question of how the friends should proceed in their business dealings with one another. This is a question of the greatest

importance and a matter that deserveth the liveliest concern. In relations of this kind, the friends of God should act with the utmost trustworthiness and integrity. To be remiss in this area would be to turn one's face away from the counsels of the Blessed Beauty [Bahá'u'lláh] *and the holy precepts of God. If a man in his own home doth not treat his relations and friends with entire trustworthiness and integrity, his dealings with the outside world -- no matter how much trustworthiness and honesty he may bring to them -- will prove barren and unproductive. First one should order one's own domestic affairs, then attend to one's business with the public. One should certainly not argue that the friends need not be treated with undue care, or that it is unnecessary for them to attach too great importance to the practice of trustworthiness in their dealings with one another, but that it is in their relations with strangers that correct behaviour is essential. Talk like this is sheer fantasy and will lead to detriment and loss. Blessed be the soul that shineth with the light of trustworthiness among the people and becometh a sign of perfection amidst all men."* [58]

We have completed our study of 'Abdu'l-Bahá's passage on being a Bahá'í. I thought it would be fitting to finish this section of the chapter with examples of 'Abdu'l-Bahá's love for others:

"[This was] *Abdu'l-Bahá's answer to one who asked Him why it was that those who came from His presence possessed a shining face. He said, with that sublime smile and humble gesture of the hands which once seen may never be forgotten, that if it were so it must be because He saw in every face the face of His Heavenly Father."* [59]

And again Howard Colby Ives (a Unitarian minister who became a Bahá'í as a result of his meetings with Abdu'l-Bahá): "*I have mentioned several times the impression He always made upon me of an all-embracing love. How rarely we receive such an impression from those around us, even from our nearest and dearest, we all know. All our human love seems based upon self, and even its highest expression is limited to one or to a very few. Not so was the love which radiated from 'Abdu'l-Bahá. Like the sun it poured upon all alike and, like it, also warmed and gave new life to all it touched.*" [60]

We have examined many of the Bahá'í Writings that teach us to **"ignite a candle of love in every meeting."** And we do it out of obedience and by following the requisites for spiritual growth. But how do we overlook the faults of others and not take offence? How do we learn not to take offense, get angry, feel jealous or envious and complain about others? The Bahá'í Writings provide guidance to help us.

Buddha identified four kinds of wrong speech, which provide a framework for the Bahá'í teachings on this topic.[61] The first wrong speech is lying. We have already discussed the importance of truthfulness. The second is backbiting. Bahá'u'lláh tells us:

"O SON OF MAN!

Breathe not the sins of others so long as thou art thyself a sinner. Shouldst thou transgress this command, accursed wouldst thou be, and to this I bear witness." [62]

And 'Abdu'l-Bahá states:

"The worst human quality and the most great sin is backbiting, more especially when it emanates from the tongues of the believers of God. If some means were devised so that the doors of backbiting were shut eternally and each one of the believers unsealed his lips in praise of others, then the Teachings of His Holiness Bahá'u'lláh would spread, the hearts be illumined, the spirits glorified, and the human world would attain to everlasting felicity." [63]

"I hope that the believers of God will shun completely backbiting, each one praising the other cordially and believe that backbiting is the cause of Divine Wrath, to such an extent that if a person backbites to the extent of one word, he may become dishonored among all the people, because the most hateful characteristic of man is fault-finding. One must expose the praiseworthy qualities of the souls and not their evil attributes. The friends must overlook their shortcomings and faults and speak only of their virtues and not their defects.

It is related that His Holiness Christ -- May my life be a sacrifice to Him! -- one day, accompanied by His apostles, passed by the corpse of a dead animal. One of them said: 'How putrid has this animal become!' The other exclaimed: 'How it is deformed!' A third cried out: 'What a stench! How cadaverous looking!' but His Holiness Christ said: 'Look at its teeth! how white they are!' Consider, that He did not look at all at the defects of that animal; nay, rather, He searched well until He found the beautiful white teeth. He observed only the whiteness of the teeth and overlooked entirely the deformity of the body, the dissolution of its organs and the bad odour.

This is the attribute of the children of the Kingdom. This is the conduct and the manner of the real Bahá'ís. I hope that all the believers will attain to this lofty station." [64]

And Shoghi Effendi adds:

"The condemnation of backbiting could hardly be couched in stronger language than in these passages, and it is obviously one of the foremost obligations for Bahá'ís to set their faces against this practice. Even if what is said against another person be true, the mentioning of his faults to others still comes under the category of backbiting, and is forbidden." [65]

And so backbiting is the *"worst human quality and the most great sin"* and fault-finding is *"the most hateful characteristic of man."* Strong and persuasive words to motivate us to behave in the opposite way. Bahá'u'lláh addresses the issue of fault-finding in *The Hidden Words*. Since *The Hidden Words* contain the gems of guidance for our lives, it is significant to me that this specific issue is addressed several times:

"O SON OF BEING!

How couldst thou forget thine own faults and busy thyself with the faults of others? Whoso doeth this is accursed of Me." [66]

"O COMPANION OF MY THRONE!

Hear no evil, and see no evil, abase not thyself, neither sigh and weep. Speak no evil, that thou mayest not hear it spoken unto thee, and magnify not the faults of others that thine own faults may not appear great; and wish not the abasement of anyone, that thine own abasement be not exposed. Live then the days of thy life, that are less than a fleeting moment, with thy mind stainless, thy heart unsullied, thy thoughts pure, and thy nature sanctified, so that, free and content, thou mayest put away this mortal frame, and repair unto the mystic paradise and abide in the eternal kingdom for evermore." [67]

Shoghi Effendi said:

"If we Bahá'ís cannot attain to cordial unity among ourselves, then we fail to realize the main purpose for which the Báb, Bahá'u'lláh and the Beloved Master lived and suffered.

In order to achieve this cordial unity one of the first essentials insisted on by Bahá'u'lláh and 'Abdu'l-Bahá is that we resist the natural tendency to let our attention dwell on the faults and failings of others rather than on our own. Each of us is responsible for one life only, and that is our own. Each of us is immeasurably far from being perfect as our heavenly father is perfect and the task of perfecting our own life and character is one that requires all our attention, our will-power and energy. If we allow our attention and energy to be taken up in efforts to keep others right and remedy their faults, we are wasting precious time. We are like ploughmen each of whom has his team to manage and his plough to direct, and in order to keep his furrow straight he must keep his eye on his goal and concentrate on his own task. If he looks to this side and that to see how Tom and Harry are getting on and to criticize their ploughing, then his own furrow will assuredly become crooked.

On no subject are the Bahá'í teachings more emphatic than on the necessity to abstain from faultfinding and backbiting while being ever eager to discover and root out our own faults and overcome our own failings.

If we profess loyalty to Bahá'u'lláh, to our Beloved Master and our dear Guardian, then we must show our love by obedience to these explicit teachings. Deeds not words are what they demand, and no amount of fervour in the use of expressions of loyalty and adulation will compensate for failure to live in the spirit of the teachings." [68]

Bahá'u'lláh gives us the prescription for this "disease":

"If any differences arise amongst you, behold Me standing before your face, and overlook the faults of one another for My name's sake and as a token of your love for My manifest and resplendent Cause."[69]

'Abdu'l-Bahá also assists us in combating a tendency to backbite:

"If any soul speak ill of an absent one, the only result will clearly be this: he will dampen the zeal of the friends and tend to make them indifferent. For backbiting is divisive, it is the leading cause among the friends of a disposition to withdraw. If any individual should speak ill of one who is absent, it is incumbent on his hearers, in a spiritual and friendly manner, to stop him, and say in effect: would this detraction serve any useful purpose? Would it please the Blessed Beauty, contribute to the lasting honour of the friends, promote the holy Faith, support the Covenant, or be of any possible benefit to any soul? No, never! On the contrary, it would make the dust to settle so thickly on the heart that the ears would hear no more, and the eyes would no longer behold the light of truth.

If, however, a person setteth about speaking well of another, opening his lips to praise another, he will touch an answering chord in his hearers and they will be stirred up by the breathings of God. Their hearts and souls will rejoice to know that, God be thanked, here is a soul in the Faith who is a focus of human perfections, a very embodiment of the bounties of the Lord, one whose tongue is eloquent, and whose face shineth, in whatever gathering he may be, one who hath victory upon his brow, and who is a being sustained by the sweet savours of God.

Now which is the better way? I swear this by the beauty of the Lord: whensoever I hear good of the friends, my heart filleth up with joy; but whensoever I find even a hint that they are on bad terms one with another, I am overwhelmed by grief. Such is the condition of 'Abdu'l-Bahá. Then judge from this where your duty lieth." [70]

Because of His grief after the ascension of Bahá'u'lláh and His dismay concerning the misdeeds of faithless family members, 'Abdu'l-Bahá withdrew to Tiberias. While He was away, Munirih Khanum, His wife, was used as a scapegoat. 'Abdu'l-Bahá advised her that if something was related about a person, *"the hearer should observe complete silence, engage in communion with the True One and say that the remembrance of God is best."* [71]

And He said:

"Remember, above all, the teaching of Bahá'u'lláh concerning gossip and unseemly talk about others. Stories repeated about others are seldom good. A silent tongue is the safest. Even good may be harmful, if spoken at the wrong time, or to the wrong person." [72]

And here is guidance from the Universal House of Justice:

"You ask in your letter for guidance on the implications of the prohibitions on backbiting and more specifically whether, in moments of anger or depression, the believer is permitted to turn to his friends to unburden his soul and discuss his problem in human relations. Normally, it is possible to describe the situation surrounding a problem and seek help and advice in resolving it, without necessarily mentioning names. The individual believer should seek to do this, whether he is consulting a friend, Bahá'í or non-Bahá'í, or whether the friend is consulting him." [73]

We are told to focus on our own faults and imperfections.

"O EMIGRANTS!

The tongue I have designed for the mention of Me, defile it not with detraction. If the fire of self overcome you, remember your own faults and not the faults of My creatures, inasmuch as every one of you knoweth his own self better than he knoweth others." [74]

"It is my hope that you may consider this matter, that you may search out your own imperfections and not think of the imperfections of anybody else. Strive with all your power to be free from imperfections. Heedless souls are always seeking faults in others. What can the hypocrite know of others' faults when he is blind to his own?... As long as a man does not find his own faults, he can never become perfect. Nothing is more fruitful for man than the knowledge of his own shortcomings. The Blessed Perfection says, 'I wonder at the man who does not find his own imperfections.'" [75]

'Abdu'l-Bahá tells us to be silent about the faults of others:

"To be silent concerning the faults of others, to pray for them, and to help them, through kindness, to correct their faults. To look always at the good and not at the bad. If a man has ten good qualities and one bad one, to look at the ten and forget the one; and if a man has ten bad qualities and one good one, to look at the one and forget the ten. Never to allow ourselves to speak one unkind word about another, even though that other be our enemy." [76]

These are concrete examples that we can practice.

And Shoghi Effendi reiterates the importance of practice:

"He heartily agrees with you that unless we practise the Teachings we cannot possibly expect the Faith to grow, because the fundamental purpose of all religions -- including our own -- is to bring man nearer to God, and to change his character, which is of the utmost importance. Too much emphasis is often laid on the social and economic aspects of the Teachings; but the moral aspect cannot be over- emphasized." [77]

And to centre our energies on our beloved Faith:

"We must never dwell too much on the attitudes and feelings of our fellow believers towards us. What is most important is to foster love and harmony and ignore any rebuffs we may receive; in this way the

weakness of human nature and the peculiarity or attitude of any particular person is not magnified, but pales into insignificance in comparison with our joint service to the Faith we all love." [78]

The third wrong speech is harsh speech.

"A harsh word is like unto a sword, but gentle speech is like unto milk. The children of the world attain to knowledge and better themselves through this." [79]

Bahá'u'lláh tells us that if someone starts an argument with us, we should not use harsh words because we all know that it is generally the retort that starts a battle. We should talk quietly and approach the other in a gentle manner.

"Should anyone wax angry with you, respond to him with gentleness; and should anyone upbraid you, forbear to upbraid him in return, but leave him to himself and put your trust in God, the omnipotent Avenger, the Lord of might and justice." [80]

We must not be insolent, rude, angry or cruel. We also know that we are not to engage in conflict, in acts that hurt others, as Bahá'u'lláh points out:

"Ye have been forbidden in the Book of God to engage in contention and conflict, to strike another, or to commit similar acts whereby hearts and souls may be saddened." [81]

"This Wronged One hath forbidden the people of God to engage in contention or conflict and hath exhorted them to righteous deeds and praiseworthy character." [82]

"Contend not with your neighbor, and be ye of them that do good." [83]

'Abdu'l-Bahá adds:

"Be not a cause of grief, much less of strife and sedition." [84]

Sedition means rebellion, resistance to authority. Contention refers to quarrelling, arguments and disputes.

"Amity and rectitude of conduct, rather than dissension and mischief, are the marks of true faith." [85]

"Say: Sow not, O people, the seeds of dissension amongst men, and contend not with your neighbor. Be patient under all conditions, and place your

whole trust and confidence in God. Aid ye your Lord with the sword of wisdom and of utterance." [86]

So we are told to demonstrate friendliness and good conduct, to be patient and trust God and be wise in our speech.

And we are asked to obey the Golden Rule, the teaching given to us by all the Manifestations of God:

"O SON OF BEING!

Ascribe not to any soul that which thou wouldst not have ascribed to thee, and say not that which thou doest not. This is My command unto thee, do thou observe it." [87]

"Lay not on any soul a load which ye would not wish to be laid upon you, and desire not for any one the things ye would not desire for yourselves. This is My best counsel unto you, did ye but observe it." [88]

And if we have difficulties we refer to the Writings and His directions for us:

"Should differences arise amongst you over any matter, refer it to God while the Sun still shineth above the horizon of this Heaven and, when it hath set, refer ye to whatsoever hath been sent down by Him." [89]

It is difficult to discipline our selfish nature to turn away from anger and conflict. If we can be aware of our lower nature creeping in with its desire to respond negatively, perhaps we can quickly say a prayer and ask for God's help to handle the situation in a spiritual manner. And the following discussion will hopefully provide more answers for us.

Blame is a difficulty that results in contending with others. Buddha [90] said that we tend to blame others if they talk too much; we blame them if they talk in moderation; we blame them for being silent. No one is exempt from blame. So we need to accept blame. We need to be prepared to receive blame and accept it with resignation. Dhammananda says that the "ugliness" that we may see in people reflects our own nature. We need to be patient and not criticize, but put ourselves in the other person's shoes, to see their circumstances and what could have led to their actions. Through such a path, we adopt an attitude of forbearance, tolerance and acceptance.

Anger is conquered through loving kindness. 'Abdu'l-Bahá has told us not to become angry but to love others for the sake of God. Loving them for the sake of God helps us to be patient and tolerant, rather than expressing our anger. Bahá'u'lláh tells us *"not to lose one's temper"* [91] but *"should anyone wax angry with you, respond to him with gentleness..."* [92] And *"if he cometh upon wrath he shall manifest love."* [93]

But 'Abdu'l-Bahá makes a distinction between anger at injustice and anger for other reasons:

"If he exercises his anger and wrath against the bloodthirsty tyrants who are like ferocious beasts, it is very praiseworthy; but if he does not use these qualities in a right way, they are blameworthy." [94]

We are also given the remedy for many negative emotions:

"Verily the most necessary thing is contentment under all circumstances; by this one is preserved from morbid conditions and from lassitude. Yield not to grief and sorrow: they cause the greatest misery. Jealousy consumeth the body and anger doth burn the liver: avoid these two as you would a lion." [95]

In chapter 5, we discussed contentment as one of the secrets of detachment. Contentment also helps us to avoid negative emotions.

"Anybody can be happy in the state of comfort, ease, health, success, pleasure and joy; but if one will be happy and contented in the time of trouble, hardship and prevailing disease, it is the proof of nobility." [96]

We need to become peaceful, to learn to feel calm inside, to use peaceful language even when we're angry, to speak gently, courteously and respectfully. If we can learn to create inner peace through our daily prayer and meditation, we will learn contentment. Even if we are angry about an injustice, we cannot determine a course of action if we are in a distracted state of mind. We can try to observe it as a mental state and try not to direct it to the object of the anger. With more awareness, we gain confidence in controlling ourselves. The Buddha had suggestions for controlling anger. One was to recall the person's good qualities, just as 'Abdu'l-Bahá has advised us. Also, we may feel compassion for the person when we realize that he has to face the consequences of his actions.[97] We can also remember that we suffer more from the hatred or negativity we carry around in our minds than what others can do to us, so getting rid of our anger removes our real "enemy" from our lives. And we learn as much from those who treat us as enemies as we do from our friends and perhaps more, because our friends may not want to tell us about our weaknesses and we will certainly learn from our "enemies" how we can improve if we are only willing to pay attention. [98]

There are always going to be situations where we are put to the test and we have a choice to react with anger and negativity or with loving-kindness. Relying on God's help, we can learn to make the right choice, perhaps not the first time but as we keep practicing, it will get easier.

Bahá'u'lláh also warns us not to be envious:

"O SON OF EARTH!

Know, verily, the heart wherein the least remnant of envy yet lingers, shall never attain My everlasting dominion, nor inhale the sweet savors of holiness breathing from My kingdom of sanctity." [99]

Strong words! And again He says:

"Wherefore, O My servants, defile not your wings with the clay of waywardness and vain desires, and suffer them not to be stained with the dust of envy and hate, that ye may not be hindered from soaring in the heavens of My divine knowledge." [100]

We have already mentioned that *"jealousy consumeth the body"* and should therefore be avoided.

"That it is one's duty to be pitiful and harm no one, and to avoid jealousy and malice at all costs." [101]

'Abdu'l-Bahá tells us further:

"At the same time those who show forth envies, jealousies, etc. toward a servant, are depriving themselves of their own stations, and not another of his, for they prove by their own acts that they are not only unworthy of being called to any station waiting them, but also prove that they cannot withstand the very first test – that of rejoicing over the success of their neighbour, at which God rejoices ... Envy closes the door of Bounty, and jealousy prevents one from ever attaining to the Kingdom of Abha." [the next world] [102]

But it is difficult for us not be envious or jealous of others, particularly because in our materialistic society we are pitted against each other and are encouraged to be competitive in terms of our lifestyle and in the workforce. Hushidar Motlagh, a Bahá'í writer, tells us that envy *"is a deadly spiritual disease and a barrier to divine grace and assistance; moreover it spreads like a dark cloud, obscuring the radiance of unity and love among the believers."* [103] He discusses various levels of intensity in relation to envy:

1. "You are better than me. Perhaps you are more educated, perhaps you teach better, or write better or speak better. And you are in my way! I wish God would take you 'somewhere else' or something would happen to you, so I would be the best.

2. You surely stand out! I don't want anything to happen to you, but I wish you were out of my sight and out of my way. Whenever I see you I feel uneasy, insecure, perturbed.

3. You seem quite capable, and I respect you for that. But you are in my way! Frankly, I am surprised by your success and hope you will stay near where you are now. I know you have a right to be your best, but still I feel uneasy about all the respect and recognition you receive. I have somewhat mixed feelings about you. Perhaps I can only tolerate you, perhaps I feel indifferent toward you. I really don't know, and I would rather not think about it."

Let us now see envy subdued by love:

"You are great, and everyone should be proud of you. Seeing you growing gives me joy, for you have actualized my hopes and dreams. You have set an example for me to emulate. You have taught me what is possible. I know I can't be like you, but I will do my best to become my own true self- to become what I am potentially capable of becoming." [104]

I think that Motlagh's description really brings the problem of envy to light and gives us an example of doing the opposite: being proud of someone and cherishing the gifts they can bring to help others to meet their potential.

Gratitude can be a substitute for jealousy and envy:

"From amongst all mankind hath He chosen you, and your eyes have been opened to the light of guidance and your ears attuned to the music of the Company above; and blessed by abounding grace, your hearts and souls have been born into new life. Thank ye and praise ye God that the hand of infinite bestowals hath set upon your heads this gem-studded crown, this crown whose lustrous jewels will forever flash and sparkle down all the reaches of time.

To thank Him for this, make ye a mighty effort, and choose for yourselves a noble goal. Through the power of faith, obey ye the teachings of God,

and let all your actions conform to His laws. Read ye The Hidden Words, *ponder the inner meanings thereof, act in accord therewith. Read, with close attention, the Tablets of Tarazat (Ornaments), Kalimat (Words of Paradise), Tajalliyyat (Effulgences), Ishraqat (Splendours), and Bisharat (Glad Tidings),* [Writings of Bahá'u'lláh] *and rise up as ye are bidden in the heavenly teachings. Thus may each one of you be even as a candle casting its light, the centre of attraction wherever people come together; and from you, as from a bed of flowers, may sweet scents be shed . . ."* [105]

We can practice gratitude even when we're struggling because there is always something to be grateful for:

"If we should offer a hundred thousand thanksgivings every moment to the threshold of God for this love . . . we would fail to express our gratitude sufficiently." [106]

Another way to conquer negativity is by smiling and doing so sincerely. One of the essential conditions for Bahá'ís when they are consulting with one another is radiance of spirit. It is difficult to have radiance of spirit if we are not smiling and joyous. Bahá'u'lláh remarked on several qualities which He loved to see in people. One of them was enthusiasm and courage and another was *"a face wreathed in smiles and a radiant countenance"* [107]

And He said:

"Be worthy of the trust of thy neighbor, and look upon him with a bright and friendly face." [108]

Smiling and doing so sincerely helps us to conquer any negative emotions, even fear and anxiety, which are rampant in our society. We can help to conquer our fears by thinking of others, rather than dwelling on our own problems. *"I complained that I had no shoes until I met a man who had no feet."* (Persian proverb) [109] If your mind is occupied with a desire to help someone else, fear can't be present at the same time.

Serving others is a practical and loving way of demonstrating our gratitude and appreciation, according to the Bahá'í Writings:

"O SON OF MAN!

Deny not My servant should he ask anything from thee, for his face is My face; be then abashed before Me." [110]

"Forget your own selves, and turn your eyes towards your neighbor." [111]

"Blessed is he who preferreth his brother before himself." [112]

"The more we search for ourselves, the less likely we are to find ourselves; and the more we search for God, and to serve our fellow-men, the more profoundly will we become acquainted with ourselves, and the more inwardly assured. This is one of the great spiritual laws of life." [113]

And if we realize the Day in which we are living, we are more likely to live our lives in confidence.

"O ye beloved of the Lord! Beware, beware lest ye hesitate and waver. Let not fear fall upon you, neither be troubled nor dismayed. Take ye good heed lest this calamitous day slacken the flames of your ardour, and quench your tender hopes. Today is the day for steadfastness and constancy. Blessed are they that stand firm and immovable as the rock and brave the storm and stress of this tempestuous hour. They, verily, shall be the recipients of God's grace; they, verily, shall receive His divine assistance, and shall be truly victorious. They shall shine amidst mankind with a radiance which the dwellers of the Pavilion of Glory laud and magnify." [114]

"Wherefore are ye downcast and dejected? Why remain despondent when the Pure and Hidden One hath appeared unveiled amongst you? He Who is both the Beginning and the End, He Who is both Stillness and Motion, is now manifest before your eyes." [115]

The fourth wrong speech is idle babbling. Bahá'u'lláh exorts us about being careful in our speech in many Tablets:

"Say: Human utterance is an essence which aspireth to exert its influence and needeth moderation. As to its influence, this is conditional upon refinement which in turn is dependent upon hearts which are detached and pure. As to its moderation, this hath to be combined with tact and wisdom as prescribed in the Holy Scriptures and Tablets. Meditate upon that which hath streamed forth from the heaven of the Will of thy Lord, He Who is the Source of all grace, that thou mayest grasp the intended meaning which is enshrined in the sacred depths of the Holy Writings." [116]

"Not everything that a man knoweth can be disclosed, nor can everything that he can disclose be regarded as timely, nor can every timely utterance be considered as suited to the capacity of those who hear it." [117]

"Every word is endowed with a spirit, therefore the speaker or expounder should carefully deliver his words at the appropriate time and place, for the impression which each word maketh is clearly evident and perceptible. The Great Being saith: One word may be likened unto fire, another unto light, and the influence which both exert is manifest in the world. Therefore an enlightened man of wisdom should primarily speak with words as mild as milk, that the children of men may be nurtured and edified thereby and may attain the ultimate goal of human existence which is the station of true understanding and nobility. And likewise He saith: One word is like unto springtime causing the tender saplings of the rose-garden of knowledge to become verdant and flourishing, while another word is even as a deadly poison. It behoveth a prudent man of wisdom to speak with utmost leniency and forbearance so that the sweetness of his words may induce everyone to attain that which befitteth man's station." [118]

"O SON OF DUST! The wise are they that speak not unless they obtain a hearing, even as the cup- bearer, who proffereth not his cup till he findeth a seeker, and the lover who crieth not out from the depths of his heart until he gazeth upon the beauty of his beloved. Wherefore sow the seeds of wisdom and knowledge in the pure soil of the heart, and keep them hidden, till the hyacinths of divine wisdom spring from the heart and not from mire and clay." [119]

"He must never seek to exalt himself above any one, must wash away from the tablet of his heart every trace of pride and vainglory, must cling unto patience and resignation, observe silence, and refrain from idle talk. For the tongue is a smouldering fire, and excess of speech a deadly poison. Material fire consumeth the body, whereas the fire of the tongue devoureth both heart and soul. The force of the former lasteth but for a time, whilst the effects of the latter endure a century." [120]

And 'Abdu'l-Bahá who was our example, said:

"Follow thou the way of thy Lord, and say not that which the ears cannot bear to hear, for such speech is like luscious food given to small children. However palatable, rare and rich the food may be, it cannot be assimilated by the digestive organs of a suckling child. Therefore unto every one who hath a right, let his settled measure be given." [121]

Instead of idle talk, 'Abdu'l-Bahá listened, really listened. In the following passage, Bahá'u'lláh extolled 'Abdu'l-Bahá for his powers in listening:

"Consider the way in which the Master teaches the people. He listens very carefully to the most hollow and senseless talk. He listens so intently that

the speaker says to himself, 'He is trying to learn from me.' Then the Master gradually and very carefully, by means that the other person does not perceive, puts him on the right path and endows him with a fresh power of understanding." [122]

Motlagh explains, ". . . *The Master listened with enduring patience. He listened as though He were becoming aware of truths never known to Him. And no matter how irrational, biased, or unjust the ideas appeared to Him, He listened with deep interest and respect. He also demonstrated the mode and meaning of moderation in speech, never overpowering others with an excess of words."* [123]

Here is Howard Colby Ives' description of 'Abdu'l-Bahá's gift:

"How differently 'Abdu'l-Bahá met the questioner, the conversationalist, the occasion: To the questioner He responded first with silence-an outward silence. His encouragement always was that the other should speak and He listen. There was never that eager tenseness, that restlessness so often met showing most plainly that the listener has the pat answer ready the moment he should have a chance to utter it. I have heard certain people described as good listeners, but never had I imagined such a listener as Abdu'l-Bahá. It was more than a sympathetic absorption of what the ear received. It was as though the two individualities became one; as if He so closely identified Himself with the one speaking that a merging of spirits occurred which made a verbal response almost unnecessary, superfluous. As I write, the words of Bahá'u'lláh recur to me: When the sincere servant calls to Me in prayer I become the very ear with which He heareth My reply. That was just it! Abdu'l-Bahá seemed to listen with my ears . . . And when, under His encouraging sympathy, the interviewer became emptied of his words, there followed a brief interval of silence. There was no instant and complete outpouring of explanation and advice. He sometimes closed His eyes a moment as if He sought guidance from above himself; sometimes sat and searched the questioner's soul with a loving, comprehending smile that melted the heart. And when He finally spoke, and that modulated, resonant voice of music came, the words were so unexpected, often, so seemingly foreign to the subject, that the questioner was at first somewhat bewildered, but always, with me at least, this was followed by a calmness, an understanding which went much deeper than the mind." [124]

I'll mention a few more words about the issue of giving or taking offense which we discussed earlier in studying 'Abdu'l-Bahá's definition of a Bahá'í. It is important to be clear that Bahá'ís are asked not to give or take offense, both of which can lead to conflict and contention. They are told that they must not give or take offense when consulting in their Assemblies.

"The second principle is that of detachment in consultation. The members of an Assembly must learn to express their views frankly, calmly, without passion or rancour. They must also learn to listen to the opinions of their fellow members without taking offence or belittling the views of another. Bahá'í consultation is not an easy process. It requires love, kindliness, moral courage and humility. Thus no member should ever allow himself to be prevented from expressing frankly his view because it may offend a fellow member; and, realizing this, no member should take offence at another member's statements." [125]

Bahá'ís are advised to consult in all their affairs:

"Take ye counsel together in all matters, inasmuch as consultation is the lamp of guidance which leadeth the way, and is the bestower of understanding." [126]

"The question of consultation is of the utmost importance, and is one of the most potent instruments conducive to the tranquillity and felicity of the people. For example, when a believer is uncertain about his affairs, or when he seeketh to pursue a project or trade, the friends should gather together and devise a solution for him. He, in his turn, should act accordingly. Likewise in larger issues, when a problem ariseth, or a difficulty occurreth, the wise should gather, consult, and devise a solution. They should then rely upon the one true God, and surrender to His Providence, in whatever way it may be revealed, for divine confirmations will undoubtedly assist. Consultation, therefore, is one of the explicit ordinances of the Lord of mankind." [127]

More information about the requirements for Bahá'í consultation are given in the next chapter.

Taking offence is a response to someone's lower nature. If we can remember that the person is being held captive by their lower nature at that moment in time, we can more readily forgive them.

St. Rain[128] reprinted an editorial originally published in *Canadian Bahá'í News* August 1969 on taking offense. The author clearly indicates the fallacies we are operating under both by giving and taking offence. Perceiving our enemies as friends, as 'Abdu'l-Bahá asks us to do, is important and it becomes easier for us to do if we realize that we need to experience tests from people in our lives in order to grow spiritually and to learn how to love all of humanity. We need to love all people because of our love for God and not just love those who are "easy" to love. We need to love those who are difficult to love, who may push people away from them, who are filled with loneliness, fear, guilt and shame and need a tender, sincere love to *"thaw their frozen hearts"*.[129] We are not doing very well if we can love only those who love us. If this is the case, the author states that we need to immerse ourselves in the Bahá'í Writings, to pray to be able to love all people, *"to seek reconciliation"*,[130] to serve our fellow-believers regardless of how painful it may be and to teach the Bahá'í Faith. The author continues:

"Many people took offence at 'Abdu'l-Bahá Himself. Was the Perfect Exemplar responsible for their being offended? In such a case it is clear that offence can be taken when none is intended nor any cause given. 'Abdu'l-Bahá was the object of the most despicable behaviour which men are capable of, yet did He ever assume the role of a man offended? It is possible to exercise the spiritual muscles of forbearance, forgiveness, mercy and to refuse to take offence or be hurt . . .

Bahá'u'lláh says that He desires to see us as one soul in many bodies. The one who hurts us is simply stuck on a different hurdle in the spiritual race. And we, in being hurt, are stuck on another. If we truly believe in the oneness of mankind we must love wisely enough and well enough to pray that we will both learn to take our separate hurdles in our stride, and in the meantime, love, love and love again."

This is the ideal that we aim for. But there is something about the idea of taking offence that makes us jump up and declare that we're not going to take it; it's not just and has to be dealt with. If someone did me wrong, I felt that I needed to deal with it and instant forgiveness was not what came to mind. Even if I didn't deal with such a problem right away and gave myself time to think about what to do, I always came back to the idea of seeking justice. Erica Toussaint-Brock referred to the need to instantly forgive, as 'Abdu'l-Bahá tells us to do, in her 2010 talk at a Social and Economic Development Conference. Someone asked her the question: What if someone is taking advantage of you? There it is again – the idea of someone walking all over us and getting away with it. Someone has to teach that person a lesson. And of course in our society, that will be the perception. Erica stated that individuals are not to fight it out individually with each other; they are to overlook each other's faults. We must still treat that person kindly and with compassion, and instantly forgive him but we can take action when justice needs to be done, such as reporting an incident that has repercussions for other people or, if it is within the Bahá'í community and is a reflection on the Bahá'í Faith, consulting with the Assembly. Here I am reiterating 'Abdu'l-Bahá's explanation of Christ's meaning about forgiveness and pardon, cited previously. When we are dealing one-on-one with an individual, our instructions are clear. We have only to obey. When we are concerned about being taken advantage of, who is worried? We can ask ourselves – who is in charge here, my lower nature or my higher nature because if we are detached and dependent on God, our hearts will be happy and contented that we are in God's hands and He has promised us that He won't harm our souls. And, by the way, speaking of teaching someone a lesson, how did 'Abdu'l-Bahá teach a lesson? I'm not talking about the incidences where justice was violated and 'Abdu'l-Bahá became angry and dealt with the situation directly. I'm taking about his dealings with individuals. He encouraged, he overlooked faults and praised without distinction. Howard Colby Ives tells us this story about 'Abdu'l-Bahá:

"I was present at an interview sought by a Unitarian clergyman, who was preparing an article on the Bahá'í Cause . . . The minister was quite advanced in age . . . The Master sat quite silent throughout the interview, listening with unwearied attention to the long hypothetical questions of the reverend doctor. . . 'Abdu'l-Bahá answered mainly in monosyllables. He never flagged in interest but it seemed to be more an interest in the questioner than in his questions. He sat perfectly relaxed, His hands in His lap with palms upward, as was characteristic of Him. He looked at the interviewer with that indescribable expression of understanding love which never failed. His face was radiant with an inner flame.

The doctor talked on and on. I grew more and more impatient . . . Why did not 'Abdu'l-Bahá recognize the superficial nature underlying all these questions? Could He not see that their object was only to gain substantiation for a critically adverse magazine article for the writing of which a substantial check might be anticipated? Why was not the interview cut short and the talker dismissed? But if others in the group grew impatient 'Abdu'l-Bahá did not. He encouraged the doctor to express himself fully. If the speaker flagged for a moment 'Abdu'l-Bahá spoke briefly in reply to a question and then waited courteously for him to continue.

At last the reverend doctor paused. There was silence for a moment, and then that softly resonant voice [of 'Abdu'l-Bahá] *filled the room . . . He spoke of 'His Holiness Christ,' of His love for all men, strong even unto the Cross; of the high station of the Christian ministry 'to which you, my dear son, have been called'; of the need that men called to this station should 'characterize themselves with the characteristics of God' in order that their people should be attracted to the divine life . . . He spoke, too, of the coming Kingdom of God on earth for which Christ had told us to pray and which, in accordance with His promise, Bahá'u'lláh . . . had come to this world to establish.*

Within five minutes, His questioner had become humble, for the moment, at least, a disciple at His ['Abdu'l-Bahá's] feet. He seemed to have been transported to another world, as indeed we all were. His face shone faintly as though he had received an inner illumination. Then 'Abdu'l-Bahá rose . . . He lovingly embraced the doctor and led him towards the door. At the threshold He paused. His eyes had lighted upon a large bunch of American Beauty roses which one of the friends had brought to Him that morning. There were at least two dozen of them, perhaps three. There were so many and their stems so long that they had been placed in an earthenware umbrella stand . . .

No sooner had 'Abdu'l-Bahá's eyes lighted upon them than He laughed aloud; His boyish hearty laughter rang through the room. He stooped, gathered the whole bunch in His arms, straightened and placed them all in the arms of His visitor. Never shall I forget that round, bespectacled head above that immense bunch of lovely flowers. So surprised, so radiant, so humble, so transformed! Ah! 'Abdu'l-Bahá knew how to teach the Love of God!" [131]

We may take offence because we are sensitive beings but perhaps we have not yet learned that tenderness – that essence of vulnerability in exposing our hearts and being confident that all will be well. I will refer more to "tenderness" later in the chapter. It is our animal nature, our egos, that take offence, because they do not want to be exposed or demonstrate their fragility. It is only when our spiritual nature is in charge that our openness, our ability to be attuned to God and our fellow-man has the power to shrug off enmity and darts that are thrown our way. 'Abdu'l-Bahá asks us to do it for Him:

"Perhaps the greatest test Bahá'ís are ever subjected to is from each other; but for the sake of the Master [Abdu'l-Bahá] they should be ever ready to overlook each other's mistakes, apologize for harsh words they have uttered, forgive and forget." [132]

And Shoghi Effendi always reminds us of the right actions:

"You should not allow the remarks made by the Bahá'ís to hurt or depress you, but should forget the personalities, and arise to do all you can, yourself, to teach the Faith." [133]

"... *if you close your eyes to the failings of others, and fix your love and prayers upon Bahá'u'lláh, you will have the strength to weather this storm, and will be much better for it in the end, spiritually. Although you suffer, you will gain a maturity that will enable you to be of greater help to both your fellow-Bahá'ís and your children."* [134]

"We must never dwell too much on the attitudes and feelings of our fellow believers towards us. What is most important is to foster love and harmony and ignore any rebuffs we may receive; in this way the weakness of human nature and the peculiarity or attitude of any particular person is not magnified, but pales into insignificance in comparison with our joint service to the Faith we all love." [135]

And so we conclude our discussion about the four wrong speeches. It is easy to see how we can affect our relationships negatively with our words. It will always be a struggle for us to speak and behave lovingly towards one another. But it is clear from the Bahá'í Writings and our discussion in this chapter that it is our deeds, not our words that take precedence. We started this chapter with the words "act in accordance with the counsels of the Lord". It is our actions that distinguish us. And it is easy to speak about how we should behave but we need to prove it through our deeds, according to Bahá'u'lláh:

"O SON OF MY HANDMAID!

Guidance hath ever been given by words, and now it is given by deeds. Every one must show forth deeds that are pure and holy, for words are the property of all alike, whereas such deeds as these belong only to Our loved ones. Strive then with heart and soul to distinguish yourselves by your deeds. In this wise We counsel you in this holy and resplendent tablet." [136]

"Say: Beware, O people of Bahá, lest ye walk in the ways of them whose words differ from their deeds. Strive that ye may be enabled to manifest to the peoples of the earth the signs of God, and to mirror forth His commandments. Let your acts be a guide unto all mankind, for the professions of most men, be they high or low, differ from their conduct. It is through your deeds that ye can distinguish yourselves from others. Through them the brightness of your light can be shed upon the whole earth. Happy is the man that heedeth My counsel, and keepeth the precepts prescribed by Him Who is the All-Knowing, the All-Wise." [137]

Bahá'u'lláh is very clear about the importance of deeds:

"The essence of faith is fewness of words and abundance of deeds; he whose words exceed his deeds, know verily his death is better than his life." [138]

"Say, O brethren! Let deeds, not words, be your adorning." [139]

'Abdu'l-Bahá advised:

"Love ye all religions and all races with a love that is true and sincere and show that love through deeds and not through the tongue; for the latter hath no importance, as the majority of men are, in speech, well-wishers, while action is the best." [140]

And He said:

"What profit is there in agreeing that universal friendship is good, and talking of the solidarity of the human race as a grand ideal? Unless these thoughts are translated into the world of action, they are useless.

The wrong in the world continues to exist just because people talk only of their ideals, and do not strive to put them into practice. If actions took the place of words, the world's misery would very soon be changed into comfort.

A man who does great good, and talks not of it, is on the way to perfection.

The man who has accomplished a small good and magnifies it in his speech is worth very little.

If I love you, I need not continually speak of my love -- you will know without any words. On the other hand if I love you not, that also will you know -- and you would not believe me, were I to tell you in a thousand words, that I loved you.

People make much profession of goodness, multiplying fine words because they wish to be thought greater and better than their fellows, seeking fame in the eyes of the world. Those who do most good use fewest words concerning their actions.

The children of God do the works without boasting, obeying His laws." [141]

'Abdu'l-Bahá provides us with a clear mandate:

"Therefore strive that your actions day by day may be beautiful prayers. Turn towards God, and seek always to do that which is right and noble.

Enrich the poor, raise the fallen, comfort the sorrowful, bring healing to the sick, reassure the fearful, rescue the oppressed, bring hope to the hopeless, shelter the destitute!

This is the work of a true Bahá'í, and this is what is expected of him. If we strive to do all this, then are we true Bahá'ís, but if we neglect it, we are not followers of the Light, and we have no right to the name.

God, who sees all hearts, knows how far our lives are the fulfilment of our words." [142]

"*Think ye at all times of rendering some service to every member of the human race . . . Be ye sincerely kind, not in appearance only. Let each one of God's loved ones centre his attention on this: to be the Lord's mercy to man; to be the Lord's grace. Let him do some good to every person whose path he crosseth, and be of some benefit to him.*" [143]

Generosity is a virtue that can only be expressed through our deeds and it is highly praised by Bahá'u'lláh. "*To give and to be generous are attributes of Mine; well is it with him that adorneth himself with My virtues.*" [144]

When we provide service to our fellow-men, we are being generous. In any situation we can be observant and sensitive to the needs of others and extend a helping hand to all people, not just people who are easy to help or friends. Generosity awakens our appreciation and feelings of gratitude because we become aware of how we've been helped as we extend similar assistance to others. It also deepens our empathy and compassion for our fellow-man.

"'*Abdu'l-Bahá's generosity was natural to Him already in childhood. A story is recorded of the time when young Abbas Effendi ['Abdu'l-Bahá] went to the mountains to see the thousands of sheep which His Father then owned. The shepherds, wishing to honour their young Guest, gave Him a feast. Before Abbas was taken home at the close of the day, the head shepherd advised Him that it was customary under the circumstances to leave a present for the shepherds. Abbas told the man that He had nothing to give. Yet the shepherd persisted that He must give something. Whereupon the Master gave them all the sheep.*

We are told that when Bahá'u'lláh heard about this incident, He laughed and commented, 'We will have to protect 'Abdu'l-Bahá from Himself – some day he will give himself away.'" [145]

And of course He did!

"'Friday mornings at seven there is another picture. Near the tent in the garden one may see an assemblage of the abject poor – the lame, the halt and the blind – seldom less than a hundred. As 'Abdu'l-Bahá passes among them He will be seen to give to each a small coin, and to add a word of sympathy or cheer; often an inquiry about those at home; frequently He sends a share to an absent one. It is a sorry procession as they file slowly away, but they all look forward to this weekly visit, and indeed it is said that this is the chief means of sustenance for some of them. Almost any morning, early, He may be seen making the round of the city, calling upon the feeble and the sick; many dingy abodes are brightened by His presence." [146]

If you go back and read the first quotation in this chapter, you will notice the use of the word "tenderness". The word "tenderness" struck a cord for me and reminded me that I had encountered it elsewhere in the Writings. One of these was the prayer:

"O God, my God! Aid Thou Thy trusted servants to have loving and tender hearts. Help them to spread, amongst all the nations of the earth, the light of guidance that cometh from the Company on high. Verily Thou art the Strong, the Powerful, the Mighty, the All-Subduing, the Ever-Giving. Verily Thou art the Generous, the Gentle, the Tender, the Most Bountiful." [147]

This is a prayer which embodies 'Abdu'l-Bahá's instructions about how we should treat each other. How important is tenderness! Perhaps a focus on "tenderness" will help those of us who become discouraged by the daunting standards of virtue and behavior mentioned in the Bahá'í Writings and turn away, saying that these are standards of perfection and they can only do their best or they stay busy in all facets of their life to avoid thinking about it. In the Oxford dictionary and definitions in Google, "tender" is defined as *"soft, not tough or hard; frail and delicate; easily hurt and sensitive; susceptible to pain or grief (tender heart); characterized by or expressing gentleness, given to sympathy, tendency to express warm and affectionate feeling; compassionate, considerate and protective; demonstrating benevolence, kindness, mildness and mercy."* It seems to have a different component to it in comparison to love, a softness and gentleness, a vulnerability and openness of heart. It takes a great deal from us personally as we are touched, moved to pity and feel something deeply. Perhaps it is something that we do not want to experience. We want to run away because we feel our vulnerability and are afraid our hearts will be broken. But if we can feel tenderness we are truly in touch with our hearts, that deepest part of us that belongs to God. As Bahá'u'lláh explains:

"Thy heart is My home; sanctify it for My descent." [148]

"All that is in heaven and earth I have ordained for thee, except the human heart, which I have made the habitation of My beauty and glory . . ." [149]

I am reminded of Bahá'u'lláh's daughter and 'Abdu'l-Bahá's sister, Bahíyyih Khánum, when I think about living a life of tenderness, feeling it deeply, coping with fortitude through extremes of pain and grief. And if we can turn to others with tenderness, we can endure all difficulties from the people; we will have learned to accept it all graciously; we will have manifested tenderness, as The Greatest Holy Leaf did:

"You were sure that if one tried to hurt her she would wish to console him for his own cruelty. For her love was unconditioned, could penetrate disguise and see hunger behind the mask of fury, and she knew that the most brutal self is secretly hoping to find gentleness in another. She had that rarest heart- courage, - to uncover the very quick of tenderness to any need. And so deep was her understanding that she plumbed all the miseries of the human heart and read their significance, blessing both the victim and the valid pain itself.

So alive was she to the source of all bounty that she had no consciousness of her own bounty. When she made a gift she seemed to be thanking you for it. The prompting included gratitude. When she gave joy she blessed you for it. It was almost as if she did not distinguish giving from receiving . . . she took nothing for granted in the way of devoted service and even in her last hours she whispered or smiled her thanks for every littlest ministration . . .

And as she would not lock away her small treasures, neither would she store up her wisdom and her riches of experience. In her, experience left no bitter ash. Her flame transmuted all of life, even its crude and base particles, into gold. And this gold she spent. Her wisdom was of the heart. She never reduced it to formula or precept; we have no wise sayings of hers that we can hang motto-like on our walls, just by being what she was she gave us all she knew.

. . . Something greater than forgiveness she had shown in meeting the cruelties and strictures in her own life. To be hurt and to forgive is saintly but far beyond this is the power to comprehend and not be hurt. This power she had . . . She was never known to complain or lament. It was not that she made the best of things, but that she found

in everything, even in calamity itself, the germs of enduring wisdom. She did not resist the shocks and upheavals of life and she did not run counter to obstacles. She was never impatient. She was as incapable of impatience as she was of revolt. But this was not so much long-suffering as it was quiet awareness of the forces that operate in the hours of waiting and inactivity. Always she moved with the larger rhythm, the wider sweep, toward the ultimate goal. Surely, confidently, she followed the circle of her orbit around the Sun of her existence, in that complete acquiescence, that perfect accord, which underlies faith itself." [150]

And we have Shoghi Effendi's description of the bonds between The Báb and Bahá'u'lláh:

"Especially, we notice the feeling and life in the work; authentic everywhere, he is particularly sensitive when recording tenderness and love, which he understood so well that in the end he could not live with the knowledge of it, could not contain it. There is, for instance, that passage where he explains the bonds between the Báb and Bahá'u'lláh, and shows how they matched agony for agony; then he says: **'Such love no eye has ever beheld, nor has mortal heart conceived such mutual devotion. If the branches of every tree were turned into pens, and all the seas into ink, and earth and heaven rolled into one parchment, the immensity of that love would still remain unexplored, and the depths of that devotion unfathomed.'"** [151]

And this description of 'Abdu'l-Bahá:

"Tea was brought in -- in the little clear glasses always used in 'Akká -- and He served us with His own hands. Then, seating Himself again on the divan, He called the four children who were with us . . . and with a lavish tenderness, a super abundance of overflowing love, such as could only have come from the very Centre and Source of Love, He drew all four to His knees, clasped them in His arms, which enclosed them all, gathered and pressed and crushed them to His Heart of hearts . . . He sat on the floor in their midst, He put sugar into their tea, stirred it and fed it to them, all the while smiling celestially, an infinite tenderness playing on the great Immortal Face like white light. I cannot express it! In a corner sat an old Persian believer, in a state of complete effacement before his Lord, his head bowed, his eyelids lowered, his hands crossed on his breast. Tears were pouring down his cheeks." [152]

And Shoghi Effendi:

"These details are few and incomplete. They say nothing of Shoghi Effendi's tenderness toward the believers: cables when they were ill, tributes when

they died. All too often, every affliction from which they suffered made its way straight to him. They say nothing of the sums he disbursed for the poor, denying himself, traveling inexpensively when he was abroad for a brief rest, carrying little luggage along. They say nothing of how, when Howard Carpenter fell mortally ill in Tehran, the Guardian, unasked, sent me money through the Tehran Assembly; or how, in California one year later, on the day and at the very moment when I came home from Howard's burial to a life that had collapsed, I was handed a cable from Shoghi Effendi." [153]

And this is how we are asked to be with others:

"... I ask God to make thee a new creature so that the lights of human perfections may shine through thee and to make thee kind hearted unto all human beings so that thou mayest be a mercy unto souls, absolute goodness to all, a sign of kindness, a word of tenderness ..." [154]

"If thou wishest to guide the souls, it is incumbent on thee to be firm, to be good and to be imbued with praiseworthy attributes and divine qualities under all circumstances. Be a sign of love, a manifestation of mercy, a fountain of tenderness, kind-hearted, good to all and gentle to the servants of God, and especially to those who bear no relation to thee, both men and women. Bear every ordeal that befalleth thee from the people and confront them not save with kindness, with great love and good wishes." [155]

And we take the tenderness that comes from Heaven and bestow it upon all men:

"O ye my loved ones! The world is wrapped in the thick darkness of open revolt and swept by a whirlwind of hate. It is the fires of malevolence that have cast up their flames to the clouds of heaven, it is a blood-drenched flood that rolleth across the plains and down the hills, and no one on the face of the earth can find any peace. Therefore must the friends of God engender that tenderness which cometh from Heaven, and bestow love in the spirit upon all humankind. With every soul must they deal according to the Divine counsellings and admonitions; to all must they show forth kindness and good faith; to all must they wish well. They must sacrifice themselves for their friends, and wish good fortune to their foes. They must comfort the ill-natured, and treat their oppressors with loving-kindness. They must be as refreshing water to the thirsty, and to the sick, a swift remedy, a healing balm to those in pain and a solace to every burdened heart. They must be a guiding light to those who have gone astray, a sure leader for the lost. They must be seeing eyes to the blind, hearing ears to the deaf, and to the dead eternal life, and to the despondent joy forever." [156]

Here are some practical things to try to keep us on the path of loving kindness:

1. *"Every morning, establish the intention to be kind and loving that day."* [157] *"Throughout the day, deliberately and actively bring kindness into your actions, your speech and most of all, your thoughts."* [158]

2. Think of a world in which there is only love. Hold that thought for several minutes every day.

3. *"Walk into a room and silently bless everyone in it."* [159]

4. *"Every day, try to have compassion for five kinds of people: someone you're grateful to . . . a loved one or a friend, a neutral person, someone who is difficult for you – and yourself."* [160]

5. *"Each day make an attempt to serve others in some small way and do not tell anyone."* [161]

6. *"Defend the absent . . .You can wonder out loud how that person would explain the ways of being that are being criticized, and suggest that there may be more than what is seen on the surface. . . Always ask, 'Who here is defending the person who isn't here to defend himself?'"* [162]

7. Begin to keep track of judgement thoughts you allow yourself each day. Redirect your thoughts. Consider the fullness of God in the person.[163] This increases your awareness of a tendency to judge others. When you notice that you are judging someone, start to break this habit and replace it with thoughts of being connected with all you meet.

8. *"Set some time aside each day specifically to practice not making other people wrong. Instead of attacking when you find yourself in disagreement, try saying something like 'Tell me more – that's a point of view I've never considered before.' Your detachment from the need to be right will defuse suffering and antagonisms and help you to create a more peaceful inner life. You already know that most people are not going to have the same opinion. By detaching yourself from the need to disagree, you open up the lines of communication, end your frustration at the people who disagree with you, and find yourself more in balance. It can be done without much of a struggle. Simply open yourself up by offering others your comments and thoughts, rather than jumping down their throats with your opinions and your attachment to proving them wrong."* [164]

9. It is important to move slowly on the inside when things on the outside are moving fast, as Williamson points out in her book, *The Gift of Change*. We need to be slow, conscious and prayerful when things are happening, to take time to think, meditate and pray. We need to recognize that time is not that important and to take time for others, to give them all the time that they need and to really listen to them. It is not easy to do because our world seems to be moving so fast and we are all affected by the speed, but it is what we are called to do.

Chapter 8
Becoming a Channel

Chapter 8
Becoming a Channel

Now we have come full circle. We began by examining the insistent self, referring to our lower nature, the promptings that are part of our heritage as human beings and will always be present, requiring us to be ever-vigilant and to use our volition and effort in order to stay tuned to our noble selves and follow a spiritual path.This is particularly true in the western world as its rampant materialism continues unabated. A few days ago I saw a TV program with a count-down of the ten most commonly eaten foods. Numbers 1 and 2 were hamburgers and French fries and the list included chocolate, potato chips, fried chicken and ice-cream. And how did they get to be the most common? Through availability, through marketing and through our tendency to be gullible and to be lulled in our materialistic culture to follow the trends and take the easy way out without questioning our choices or lifestyle. And because they are fast foods well-suited to our pace of life that keeps us running faster and faster on the treadmill of this life and less conscious of our souls and the purpose of our being.

In the following chapters, we studied the requisites for our souls. We discussed prayer, meditation and fasting, to counteract the forces of our lower nature as well as materialism. We stressed the need for detachment from the things of the world, to turn away from selfish needs and surrender ourselves and make sacrifices for God and for mankind. We discussed the significance of tests. Having investigated thoroughly the work we need to do on ourselves, we then turned to the purpose of our being, our need to make a spiritual connection with others and to love all with pure, unselfish, tender care. What more do we need to include? Having a plan for our personal transformation and dedicating our lives to our fellow-man, what more is required of us? We learn to know and love God, we acquire virtues and we love all as we are commanded to do. So this chapter only serves to reinforce the others – to stress our obligation and responsibility to serve mankind and to impart the Teachings of Bahá'u'lláh to others, at the same time recognizing that our aims can not be realized without unity. And in following these guidelines, we become channels for God's grace to flow through us:

"Bahá'u'lláh (may my life, my soul, my spirit, be offered up as a sacrifice unto His lowly servants) hath, during His last days on earth, given the most emphatic promise that, through the outpourings of the grace of

God and the aid and assistance vouchsafed from His Kingdom on high, souls will arise and holy beings appear who, as stars, would adorn the firmament of divine Guidance; illumine the dayspring of loving kindness and bounty; manifest the signs of the unity of God; shine with the light of sanctity and purity; receive their full measure of divine inspiration; raise high the sacred torch of faith; stand firm as the rock and immovable as the mountain; and grow to become luminaries in the heavens of His Revelation, mighty channels of His grace, means for the bestowals of God's bountiful care, heralds calling forth the name of the one true God, and establishers of the world's supreme foundation." [1]

Our responsibility is service to mankind. Bahá'u'lláh has emphasized its importance:

"How great the blessedness that awaiteth him that hath attained the honor of serving the Almighty! By My life! No act, however great, can compare with it, except such deeds as have been ordained by God, the All-Powerful, the Most Mighty. Such a service is, indeed, the prince of all goodly deeds, and the ornament of every goodly act. Thus hath it been ordained by Him Who is the Sovereign Revealer, the Ancient of Days." [2]

"That one indeed is a man who, today, dedicateth himself to the service of the entire human race. The Great Being saith: Blessed and happy is he that ariseth to promote the best interests of the peoples and kindreds of the earth." [3]

"Spread abroad the sweet savors of thy Lord, and hesitate not, though it be for less than a moment, in the service of His Cause." [4]

And it is our purpose:

"This Wronged One testifieth that the purpose for which mortal men have, from utter nothingness, stepped into the realm of being, is that they may work for the betterment of the world and live together in concord and harmony." [5]

"Man's merit lieth in service and virtue and not in the pageantry of wealth and riches." [6]

"O MY SERVANT!

The basest of men are they that yield no fruit on earth. Such men are verily counted as among the dead, nay better are the dead in the sight of God than those idle and worthless souls." [7]

'Abdu'l-Bahá tells us that this service is a sign of nobility:

". . . is there any deed in the world that would be nobler than service to the common good?" [8]

"And the honor and distinction of the individual consist in this, that he among all the world's multitudes should become a source of social good. Is any larger bounty conceivable than this, that an individual, looking within himself, should find that by the confirming grace of God he has become the cause of peace and well-being, of happiness and advantage to his fellow men? No, by the one true God, there is no greater bliss, no more complete delight." [9]

"Man is he who forgets his own interests for the sake of others. His own comfort he forfeits for the well-being of all. Nay, rather, his own life must he be willing to forfeit for the life of mankind. Such a man is the honor of the world of humanity. Such a man is the glory of the world of mankind. Such a man is the one who wins eternal bliss. Such a man is near to the threshold of God. Such a man is the very manifestation of eternal happiness . . .

Consider how the greatest men in the world -- whether among prophets or philosophers -- all have forfeited their own comfort, have sacrificed their own pleasure for the well-being of humanity. They have sacrificed their own lives for the body politic. They have sacrificed their own wealth for that of the general welfare. They have forfeited their own honor for the honor of mankind. Therefore it becomes evident that this is the highest attainment for the world of humanity." [10]

And it is through his faith that he is able to accomplish this:

"Whoso hath recognized Me, will arise and serve Me with such determination that the powers of earth and heaven shall be unable to defeat his purpose." [11]

"Sincerity is the foundation-stone of faith. That is, a religious individual must disregard his personal desires and seek in whatever way he can wholeheartedly to serve the public interest; and it is impossible for a human being to turn aside from his own selfish advantages and sacrifice his own good for the good of the community except through true religious faith . . . That individual . . . will for the sake of God abandon his own peace and profit and will freely consecrate his heart and soul to the common good." [12]

'Abdu'l-Bahá tells us:

"Faith is the magnet which draws the confirmation of the Merciful One. Service is the magnet which attracts the heavenly strength. I hope thou wilt attain both." [13]

'Abdu'l-Bahá raises service to the rank of worship:

". . . all effort and exertion put forth by man from the fullness of his heart is worship, if it is prompted by the highest motives and the will to do service to humanity. This is worship: to serve mankind and to minister to the needs of the people. Service is prayer. A physician ministering to the sick, gently, tenderly, free from prejudice and believing in the solidarity of the human race, he is giving praise." [14]

By serving mankind, we are serving God, as 'Abdu'l-Bahá clearly points out:

"With hearts set aglow by the fire of the love of God and spirits refreshed by the food of the heavenly spirit you must go forth as the disciples nineteen hundred years ago, quickening the hearts of men by the call of glad tidings, the light of God in your faces, severed from everything save God. Therefore, order your lives in accordance with the first principle of the divine teaching, which is love. Service to humanity is service to God." [15]

"I have come to this country in the advanced years of my life, undergoing difficulties of health and climate because of excessive love for the friends of God. It is my wish that they may be assisted to become servants of the heavenly Kingdom, captives in the service of the will of God. This captivity is freedom; this sacrifice is glorification; this labor is reward; this need is bestowal. For service in love for mankind is unity with God. He who serves has already entered the Kingdom and is seated at the right hand of his Lord." [16]

"If thou seekest eternal glory, let thyself be humble and meek in the presence of the beloved of God; make thyself the servant of all, and serve all alike. The service of the friends belongs to God, not to them. Strive to become a source of harmony, spirituality and joyfulness to the hearts of the friends and the maid-servants of the Merciful. This is a cause of great satisfaction to 'Abdu'l-Bahá." [17]

"There is no greater result than bonds of service in the divine Kingdom and attainment to the good pleasure of the Lord." [18]

And there is a sense of urgency:

"On the outspread tablet of this world, ye are the verses of His singleness; and atop lofty palace towers, ye are the banners of the Lord. In His bowers are ye the blossoms and sweet-smelling herbs, in the rose garden of the spirit the nightingales that utter plaintive cries. Ye are the birds that soar upward into the firmament of knowledge, the royal falcons on the wrist of God.

Why then are ye quenched, why silent, why leaden and dull? Ye must shine forth like the lightning, and raise up a clamouring like unto the great sea. Like a candle must ye shed your light, and even as the soft breezes of God must ye blow across the world. Even as sweet breaths from heavenly bowers, as musk-laden winds from the gardens of the Lord, must ye perfume the air for the people of knowledge, and even as the splendours shed by the true Sun, must ye illumine the hearts of humankind. For ye are the life-laden winds, ye are the jessamine-scents from the gardens of the saved. Bring then life to the dead, and awaken those who slumber. In the darkness of the world be ye radiant flames; in the sands of perdition, be ye well-springs of the water of life, be ye guidance from the Lord God. Now is the time to serve, now is the time to be on fire. Know ye the value of this chance, this favourable juncture that is limitless grace, ere it slip from your hands.

Soon will our handful of days, our vanishing life, be gone, and we shall pass, empty-handed, into the hollow that is dug for those who speak no more; wherefore must we bind our hearts to the manifest Beauty, and cling to the lifeline that faileth never. We must gird ourselves for service, kindle love's flame, and burn away in its heat." [19]

'Abdu'l-Bahá tells us that we need to serve with extreme humility:

"The ones in real authority are known by their humility and self-sacrifice and show no attitude of superiority over the friends. Some time ago a tablet was written stating that none are appointed to any authority to do anything but to serve the Cause as true servants of the friends-and for this no tablet is necessary; such service when true and unselfish, required no announcement, nor following, nor written document. Let the servant be known by his deeds, by his life! To be approved of God alone should be one's aim." [20]

". . . In the religion of Bahá'u'lláh all are servants and maidservants, brothers and sisters. As soon as one feels a little better than, a little

superior to, the rest, he is in a dangerous position, and unless he casts away the seed of such an evil thought, he is not a fit instrument for the service of the Kingdom." [21]

Our service to mankind is crucial:

". . . we must never forget that our service is a spiritual one. Mankind is dying for lack of true religion and this is what we have to offer to humanity. It is the love of God, manifest in the appearance of Bahá'u'lláh, which will feed the hungry souls of the world and eventually lead the peoples out of the present morass into the orderly, uplifting, and soul-inspiring task of establishing God's Kingdom on earth." [22]

And so we consecrate our lives in service:

"O army of God! Make ye a mighty effort: perchance ye can flood this earth with light, that this mud hut, the world, may become the Abha Paradise. [the Kingdom of God] The dark hath taken over, and the brute traits prevail. This world of man is now an arena for wild beasts, a field where the ignorant, the heedless, seize their chance. The souls of men are ravening wolves and animals with blinded eyes, they are either deadly poison or useless weeds -- all except for a very few who indeed do nurture altruistic aims and plans for the well-being of their fellow men: but ye must in this matter -- that is, the serving of humankind -- lay down your very lives, and as ye yield yourselves, rejoice." [23]

Here is a story about Grace Robarts Ober and how she learned about service at the hands of the Master. Grace was a dedicated Bahá'í, described as a *"friend to all the world"* with the *"habit . . . of considering the welfare of everyone."* [24] *"So she went to 'Abdu'l-Bahá and begged that, when he returned to New York, she might help with that household . . . 'Abdu'l-Bahá looked at her very searchingly and said, 'Greece (His loving nickname for Grace) Greece, are you SURE you wish to serve ME?' Grace said, 'Oh, YES! More than anything else in the world!' 'Abdu'l-Bahá made no answer but walked away. The next morning this scene was repeated. On the third morning, Grace . . . went to Him a third time – and this time He became very stern. Are you VERY SURE you wish to SERVE ME? Grace was startled at the sternness but she didn't waver. 'YES I am VERY SURE!'*

So then he nodded. 'Very well go, settle up your affairs, and we will meet in New York.' Jubilant and radiant, Grace settled up her 'affairs'. Then with wings on her feet, she went to New York. Lua was already there and together they prepared for 'Abdu'l-Bahá's arrival. [Lua Getsinger was another devoted and well-known Bahá'í who travelled extensively for the Bahá'í Faith and spent some time with 'Abdu'l-Bahá in the Holy Land.] *The day came . . . He came in. He welcomed Lua warmly, glanced at Grace as at a complete stranger, and turned away. Grace was appalled, shocked. Hadn't He recognized her? Had He forgotten her? Had she misunderstood the permission to come to New York? Or had she displeased Him and was this punishment?*

Whatever it was, it continued with no let-up . . . She worked in that household until long after midnight – cleaning, cooking, scrubbing, and then she would rise at five in the morning to begin all over again. She worked as she had never worked before in all her life and 'Abdu'l-Bahá ignored her completely.

[One day, when 'Abdu'l-Bahá had gone out], she thought of the white roses that had been delivered that morning, as they were daily, for 'Abdu'l-Bahá's room. The one bright spot in these dreadful days for Grace had been that she was the one to arrange these roses each morning. So, with the long florists' box in her arms, she climbed up to 'Abdu'l-Bahá's room at the top of the house, where He had wished to be. She reached the top of the third flight – and found the door not only closed, but locked against her. And always before it had stood wide open! This, for Grace, was the last straw . . . she sank down on the floor and wept with the fallen roses scattered around her. At last, the sobs faded, her tears spent themselves, and, exhausted, she gathered up the roses and went back downstairs.

. . . Grace- it was now past noon – was hungry. So, she went down to the kitchen to get something to eat. And in that house that fed, each day, so many dozens of people, there was nothing to eat but one egg and a small piece of leftover bread in 'Abdu'l-Bahá's breadbox . . . So Grace boiled her one egg and put her small portion of bread on a plate. Putting the egg in an egg cup, she chipped the shell – and the egg, as bad as an egg can get, exploded in her face. She cleaned up the mess and returned to her bit of leftover bread. And, as she crumbled the bread, eating it crumb by crumb, she realized, suddenly, exactly what she was doing – she was, blessedly, eating the crumbs of the bread of life from 'Abdu'l-Bahá's table. She began to eat even more slowly as the spirit of prayer came to possess her.

Not long after this the household returned . . . and that evening Lua came to Grace and said, 'The Master has asked me to tell you that He knows you wept.' And this was the first time it had occurred to Grace that all this dreadful experience might have a reason, a pattern. And – if this were true she must find out what the reason could be. So she went up to her room to pray about it. To pray for illumination and wisdom and the selflessness to understand. And as she prayed she heard a small voice saying 'Are you as happy scrubbing the garbage pails as you are arranging the roses?' And she suddenly realized what the spirit of true service was. It was to rise to selfless joy in offering the service, no matter what form that service might take. And as this truth swept over her, suffusing her, illuminating her, the door opened, and 'Abdu'l-Bahá walked into the room. His arms were outstretched; His dear face was glorified. 'Welcome!' He cried to Grace, 'Welcome to the Kingdom!' And He held her close, embracing her deeply. And never did He withdraw Himself from her again." [25]

'Abdu'l-Bahá was truly a Servant. It was said that He would write up to ninety letters a day and *"pass many a night, from dusk to dawn, alone in His bed-chamber engaged in a correspondence which the pressure of His manifold responsibilities had prevented Him from attending to in the day-time."* [26] And we have the description of 'Abdu'l-Bahá's letter-writing service in this report from Ahmad Sohrab, a secretary who travelled with 'Abdu'l-Bahá:

"The many difficult problems of the Bahá'í world are solved by him. Now he writes to Persia on how to hold an election, then to far-off America on how to rent a hall. One Bahá'í desires to know whether she should cook food for her child; another person asks how to proceed to buy a piece of land. There are some misunderstandings in this assembly to be removed; the feelings of some person are ruffled, and must be smoothed down. One man's mother or father is dead, he requests a Tablet of visitation, another desires to have a wife. To one a child is born; she begs for a Bahá'í name; another has taught several souls, he asks for Bahá'í rings for them. This man has had business reverses, he must be encouraged, another has fallen from a ladder, he implores for a speedy recovery. One has quarrelled with his wife, and he wants advice on how to be reconciled; another supplicates for blessings upon his marriage. The Master goes over these one by one with infinite patience and with his words of advice, creates order out of chaos. The sorrows of the world troop along in review before him, and as they pass, lo, the transformation happens! The sorrowful becomes joyful, the ill-tempered good-natured, the lazy active, the sleepy one awakened. With magical words he transmutes iron into gold and darkness into light. At last he rises from his seat and for a while walks to and fro, still dictating Tablets to the philosopher and to the simple; soaring toward the empyrean of spirituality, giving us a vision of sanctity, and of the roses of Paradise, and for a while we roam, guided by him, in those delectable gardens of

Abha, intoxicated with the fragrance of God; and then we find ourselves in the streets, walking home upborne on the wings of light." [27]

Bahá'u'lláh emphasizes the importance of respecting and serving our parents:

"The fruits that best befit the tree of human life are trustworthiness and godliness, truthfulness and sincerity; but greater than all, after recognition of the unity of God, praised and glorified be He, is regard for the rights that are due to one's parents." [28]

"Verily, We have enjoined on every son to serve his father. Such is the decree which We have set forth in the Book." [29]

"Show honor to your parents and pay homage to them. This will cause blessings to descend upon you from the clouds of the bounty of your Lord, the Exalted, the Great." [30]

"Beware lest ye commit that which would sadden the hearts of your fathers and mothers. Follow ye the path of Truth which indeed is a straight path. Should anyone give you a choice between the opportunity to render a service to Me and a service to them, choose ye to serve them, and let such service be a path leading you to Me." [31]

And 'Abdu'l-Bahá advises:

"Assuredly engage in service to thy father, and as well, whenever thou findest time, diffuse the divine fragrances." [32]

But we must not allow service to our parents to deter us from our spiritual path:

"If thou wouldst show kindness and consideration to thy parents so that they may feel generally pleased, this would also please Me, for parents must be highly respected and it is essential that they feel content, provided they deter thee not from gaining access to the Threshold of the Almighty, nor keep thee back from walking in the way of the Kingdom. Indeed it behoveth them to encourage and spur thee on in this direction." [33]

We must look after the poor, according to the Bahá'í Writings:

"O YE RICH ONES ON EARTH!

The poor in your midst are My trust; guard ye My trust, and be not intent only on your own ease." [34]

"Service to the friends is service to the Kingdom of God, and consideration shown to the poor is one of the greatest teachings of God." [35]

"What could be better before God than thinking of the poor? For the poor are beloved by our heavenly Father. When His Holiness Christ came upon the earth those who believed in him and followed him were the poor and lowly, showing the poor were near to God. When a rich man believes and follows the Manifestation of God it is a proof that his wealth is not an obstacle and does not prevent him from attaining the pathway of salvation. After he has been tested and tried it will be seen whether his possessions are a hindrance in his religious life. But the poor are especially beloved of God. Their lives are full of difficulties, their trials continual, their hopes are in God alone. Therefore you must assist the poor as much as possible, even by sacrifice of yourself. No deed of man is greater before God than helping the poor. Spiritual conditions are not dependent upon the possession of worldly treasures or the absence of them. When physically destitute, spiritual thoughts are more likely. Poverty is stimulus toward God. Each one of you must have great consideration for the poor and render them assistance. Organize in an effort to help them and prevent increase of poverty." [36]

And Bahá'u'lláh tells us to receive God's blessings:

"If ye meet the abased or the down-trodden, turn not away disdainfully from them, for the King of Glory ever watcheth over them and surroundeth them with such tenderness as none can fathom except them that have suffered their wishes and desires to be merged in the Will of your Lord, the Gracious, the All-Wise. O ye rich ones of the earth! Flee not from the face of the poor that lieth in the dust, nay rather befriend him and suffer him to recount the tale of the woes with which God's inscrutable Decree hath caused him to be afflicted. By the righteousness of God! Whilst ye consort with him, the Concourse on high will be looking upon you, will be interceding for you, will be extolling your names and glorifying your action. Blessed are the learned that pride not themselves on their attainments; and well is it with the righteous that mock not the sinful, but rather conceal their misdeeds, so that their own shortcomings may remain veiled to men's eyes." [37]

And it is our duty to teach the Cause of God:

"Say: Teach ye the Cause of God, O people of Bahá, for God hath prescribed unto every one the duty of proclaiming His Message, and regardeth it as the most meritorious of all deeds." [38]

Teaching is regarded as the most meritorious deed because in doing so we are bringing a soul to its God. What could be more precious in life?

"O SON OF BEING!

Make mention of Me on My earth, that in My heaven I may remember thee, thus shall Mine eyes and thine be solaced." [39]

"Of all the gifts of God the greatest is the gift of Teaching. It draweth unto us the Grace of God and is our first obligation." [40]

But as Taherzadeh explains, there are prerequisites for teaching this beloved Cause. He summarizes them as *"living one's life in accordance with Bahá'í teachings"*.[41] 'Abdu'l-Bahá tells us that *"the intention of the teacher must be pure"*. [42]

And so we approach our duty with extreme humility and deep love in our hearts for others:

"Show forbearance and benevolence and love to one another. Should any one among you be incapable of grasping a certain truth, or be striving to comprehend it, show forth, when conversing with him, a spirit of extreme kindliness and good-will. Help him to see and recognize the truth, without esteeming yourself to be, in the least, superior to him, or to be possessed of greater endowments." [43]

"A kindly approach and loving behavior toward the people are the first requirements for teaching the Cause. The teacher must carefully listen to whatever a person has to say – even though his talk may consist only of vain imaginings and blind repetitions of the opinions of others. . . . The teacher must avoid disputes which will end in stubborn refusal or hostility, because the other person will feel overpowered and defeated. Therefore, he will be more inclined to reject the Cause. One should rather say, 'Maybe you are right, but kindly consider the question from this point of view.' Consideration, respect and love encourage people to listen and do not force them to respond with hostility. They are convinced because they see that your purpose is not to defeat them, but to convey truth, to manifest courtesy, and to show forth heavenly attributes. This will encourage the people to be fair. Their spiritual natures will respond and, by the bounty of God, they will find themselves re-created." [44]

"Consort with all men, O people of Bahá, in a spirit of friendliness and fellowship. If ye be aware of a certain truth, if ye possess a jewel, of

which others are deprived, share it with them in a language of utmost kindliness and goodwill. If it be accepted, if it fulfill its purpose, your object is attained. If anyone should refuse it, leave him unto himself, and beseech God to guide him. Beware lest ye deal unkindly with him. A kindly tongue is the lodestone of the hearts of men. It is the bread of the spirit, it clotheth the words with meaning, it is the fountain of the light of wisdom and understanding." [45]

'Abdu'l-Bahá admired Juliet Thompson and Lua Getsinger, both Bahá'ís who were strong in their faith, because they taught with their hearts and souls. 'Abdu'l-Bahá said:

"I have met many people who have been affected by you, Juliet. You are not eloquent, you are not fluent, but your heart teaches. You speak with a feeling, an emotion which makes people ask: 'What is this she has?' Then they inquire; they seek and find. It is so too with Lua. You never find Lua speaking with dry eyes!" [46] *And He also said to Juliet, "You teach with ecstasy. You ignite the souls. A great bounty will descend upon you. I have perfect confidence in you as a teacher. Your heart is pure, absolutely pure."* [47]

'Abdu'l-Bahá wrote a letter to a woman indicating how she should live her life and, therefore demonstrate Bahá'u'lláh's Teachings to others:

"To live the Life you must be the very kindest woman, you must be the most pure, you must be absolutely truthful, and live a perfectly moral life.

Visit your neighbors when they are sick or in trouble, offer your services to them, try to show them that you are longing to serve them.

Feed the poor, divide what you have. Be contented to remain where God has placed you; be faithful in your care of those to whom He has trusted you, never waver in this – show by your life you have something different, so that all will see and will say, 'What has this person that I have not?'

Show the world that in spite of the utmost suffering, poverty, sickness, you have something which gives you comfort, strength and peace – that you are happy – serene- satisfied with all that is in your life.

Then they, too, will want what you possess and will need no further teaching after you tell them what it is." [48]

'Abdu'l-Bahá gives us the method of bringing the Message to others and explains that we are teaching for the sake of God:

"The teacher should teach as though offering a gift to a king, humbly and submissively, not with force of insistence . . . but with gentleness and sweetness: submitting the argument and truth to the heart and intellect of the hearer as the servant of God, and therefore His servant- taking care at all times to adapt the offered food to the condition and station of the listener, giving milk for babes and meat for those grown stronger. This food is to be offered for the sake of God only, not for the hearer's sake, not for the benefit of yourself, but simply because God wishes His Manifestations to become known and to become loved by those who come to know Him.

If one teaches one whom he loves because of his love for him, then he will not teach one whom he loves not; and that is not of God. If one teaches in order to derive the promised benefits to himself, this too is not of God. If he teaches because of God's will that God may be known- and for that reason only, he will receive knowledge and wisdom and his words will have effect- being made powerful by the Holy Spirit, and will take root in the soul of those who are in the right condition to receive them. In such a case the benefit to the teacher in growth is as ninety per cent compared to the ten per cent of gain to the hearer, because he becomes like a tree bearing fruit through the power of God.

We are urgently instructed that the only real way to attain growth in the knowledge of the Truth of God, is not be hearing, but by doing; by being alive with the on fire of the love of God and imparting as best we can to others the Tidings of the coming of the Kingdom. This is the day of teaching. We are all commanded to teach, but only in the way and for the purpose above named.

It is plain that this means entire self-abnegation, cutting the self from the world, abandoning all else save God and His Will, and in all humbleness doing His service for His sake only." [49]

When we teach this Beloved Faith, we are promised assistance and confirmation from the Heavenly Kingdom:

"Arise in the name of Him Who is the Object of all knowledge, and, with absolute detachment from the learning of men, lift up your voices and proclaim His Cause. I swear by the Day Star of Divine Revelation! The very moment ye arise, ye will witness how a flood of Divine knowledge will gush out of your hearts, and will behold the wonders of His heavenly wisdom manifested in all their glory before you." [50]

"It is better to guide one soul than to possess all that is on earth, for as long as that guided soul is under the shadow of the Tree of Divine Unity, he and the one who hath guided him will both be recipients of God's tender mercy, whereas possession of earthly things will cease at the time of death." [51]

"By the righteousness of God! Whoso openeth his lips in this Day and maketh mention of the name of his Lord, the hosts of Divine inspiration shall descend upon him from the heaven of My name, the All-Knowing, the All-Wise. On him shall also descend the Concourse on high, each bearing aloft a chalice of pure light. Thus hath it been foreordained in the realm of God's Revelation, by the behest of Him Who is the All-Glorious, the Most Powerful." [52]

But we may not feel confident that we can teach the Cause and that we will receive confirmations. Shoghi Effendi explains:

"Perhaps the reason why you have not accomplished so much in the field of teaching is the extent you have looked upon your own weaknesses and inabilities to spread the Message. Bahá'u'lláh and the Master have both urged us repeatedly to disregard our own handicaps and lay our whole reliance upon God. He will come to our aid if we only arise and become an active channel for God's Grace.

Do you think it is the teachers who make converts and change human hearts? No, surely not. They are only pure souls who take the first steps and then let the spirit of Bahá'u'lláh move and make use of them. If any one of them should even for a second think or consider his achievements as due to his own capacities, his work is ended and his fall starts. This is the fact why so many competent souls have, after wonderful services, suddenly found themselves utterly impotent and perhaps thrown aside by the spirit of the Cause as useless souls. The criterion is the extent to which we are ready to have the will of God work through us." [53]

It seems to me that often Bahá'ís do not consider their obligation to teach the Faith in a balanced manner. They are called to love all of God's creatures and to be ready to serve them. If someone is interested, a Bahá'í can then tell that person about Bahá'u'lláh's Teachings. But it is necessary to have the utmost consideration for every soul who is encountered and to serve each one according to his or her needs and wants. If a dear soul wants to hear about the Bahá'í Faith, having come to know a Bahá'í and to appreciate his way of life, spiritual qualities and spirit of service, and subsequently asks him for the source of his inspiration, then it is incumbent upon that Bahá'í to tell his friend about Bahá'u'lláh and His Message. And only if someone is interested are they to give this Message. I feel that often Bahá'ís may be in a hurry to convey the Teachings of the Bahá'í Faith because they know it is their obligation. And in that process, they lose sight of the person sitting beside them. They know that proselytization (or trying to persuade someone to change their beliefs or way of life) is forbidden in the Bahá'í Faith. But if someone asks them something about the Bahá'í Teachings, and they bombard him with everything they can remember to share, perhaps it is indeed proselytization and they are then not following the commandment of God. And it is so much against Bahá'u'lláh's teachings to hurt a precious soul who may wish to know something about the Bahá'í Faith but needs to be respected and loved first, then given the pure essence of the Teachings to which he or she may aspire. And of course every individual must investigate for himself. Let us not lose sight of the purpose of teaching, that of guiding a soul to Bahá'u'lláh, Whose Teachings assist us in living our individual lives as spiritual beings and help us to build a new world.

Bahá'u'lláh tells us that it is impossible for us to serve and to teach the Cause of God without unity among the believers of God.

"O friends! Be not careless of the virtues with which ye have been endowed, neither be neglectful of your high destiny. Suffer not your labors to be wasted through the vain imaginations which certain hearts have devised. Ye are the stars of the heaven of understanding, the breeze that stirreth at the break of day, the soft-flowing waters upon which must depend the very life of all men, the letters inscribed upon His sacred scroll. With the utmost unity, and in a spirit of perfect fellowship, exert yourselves, that ye may be enabled to achieve that which beseemeth this Day of God. Verily I say, strife and dissension, and whatsoever the mind of man abhorreth are entirely unworthy of his station. Center your energies in the propagation of the Faith of God. Whoso is worthy of so high a calling, let him arise and promote it." [54]

When Bahá'u'lláh proclaimed His Message He made it clear that the first step for mankind is its unity.

"O ye children of men", He writes, *"the fundamental purpose animating the Faith of God and His Religion is to safeguard the interests and promote the unity of the human race..."* [55]

"The well-being of mankind, its peace and security, are unattainable unless and until its unity is firmly established." [56]

"So powerful is the light of unity that it can illuminate the whole earth . . . Exert yourselves that ye may attain this transcendent and most sublime station, the station that can insure the protection and security of all mankind. This goal excelleth every other goal, and this aspiration is the monarch of all aspirations." [57]

Most people in our society who are working to help the less fortunate, to remedy the ills of mankind, perceive unity as the ultimate goal. But Bahá'ís have been taught that we must have unity first, which is a great challenge in a stressful world where people are pitted against each other in causes and revenge and retribution are common actions. It is acceptable and often the norm to formalize a grievance against a co-worker or even a friend. In the midst of this chaos, Bahá'ís must have unity among themselves to be able to assist mankind to achieve unity.

'Abdu'l-Bahá spoke to the friends in France about unity in response to a problem between two believers:

"In this Cause, hundreds of families have sacrificed themselves. There have been more than twenty thousand martyrs. The breast of His Highness the Báb was riddled by dozens of bullets; Bahá'u'lláh suffered years and years in prison; and We have had all these difficulties and borne all these trials that the canopy of Oneness might be uplifted in the world of humanity, that Love and Unity might be established amongst mankind, until all countries become as one country, all religions be merged into one religion, all the continents be connected and between all hearts a perfect understanding and love may appear.

The people of Bahá must be the cause of uniting all the nations. They must dispel inharmony and dispute. So now we must consider deeply how the Bahá'ís must really be, what characteristics they must have and what actions they must perform. And if there is not this love and harmony among Bahá'ís how can they cause it to appear among the inhabitants of the earth? How can an ill man nurse others? . . . the first thing the Bahá'ís must do is to feel love and unity in their hearts before they can spread it among others.

Is it possible to conceive that all the troubles, all the trials of Bahá'u'lláh and the martyrs have been without result? Surely you will not have it so! If you would all act entirely in accordance with the Teachings of

Bahá'u'lláh no discord would ever appear. Then all disagreements will vanish, and be certain that the pavilion of Unity will be hoisted in the world of man . . .

I know you would not have all these trials and difficulties produce nothing. Therefore I am waiting and expecting to hear that love and harmony have blossomed in the hearts of all the Bahá'ís in America.

Now the Bahá'ís must be occupied in spreading the Cause of God and furthering the instructions of Bahá'u'lláh, and not spend their time in disputing with one another. If they do the first, all will be happy; they will be assisted by the Breath of the Holy Spirit and become the beloved of His Heart." [58]

It is also a test for Bahá'ís to allow their compassion and concern for their fellow-man to divert their energies into channels which are ultimately doomed to failure because they do not arise out of unity. The Báb was the first to alert us to the need for unity:

"Become as true brethren in the one and indivisible religion of God, free from distinction, for verily God desireth that your hearts should become mirrors unto your brethren in the Faith, so that ye find yourselves reflected in them, and they in you. This is the true Path of God, the Almighty, and He is indeed watchful over your actions." [59]

'Abdu'l-Bahá refers to a spiritual unity which is more than the unity of mankind. This is the highest ideal of unity:

"The unity which is productive of unlimited results is first a unity of mankind which recognizes that all are sheltered beneath the overshadowing glory of the All-Glorious; that all are servants of one God; for all breathe the same atmosphere, live upon the same earth, move beneath the same heavens, receive effulgence from the same sun and are under the protection of one God. This is the most great unity, and its results are lasting if humanity adheres to it; but mankind has hitherto violated it, adhering to sectarian or other limited unities such as racial, patriotic or unity of self-interests; therefore no great results have been forthcoming. Nevertheless it is certain that the radiance and favors of God are encompassing, minds have developed, perceptions have become acute, sciences and arts are widespread and capacity exists for the proclamation and promulgation of the real and ultimate unity of mankind which will bring forth marvelous results. It will reconcile all religions, make warring nations loving, cause hostile kings to become

friendly and bring peace and happiness to the human world. It will cement together the Orient and Occident, remove forever the foundations of war and upraise the ensign of the 'Most Great Peace'. These limited unities are therefore signs of that great unity which will make all the human family one by being productive of the attractions of conscience in mankind.

Another unity is the spiritual unity which emanates from the breaths of the Holy Spirit. This is greater than the unity of mankind. Human unity or solidarity may be likened to the body whereas unity from the breaths of the Holy Spirit is the spirit animating the body. This is a perfect unity. It creates such a condition in mankind that each one will make sacrifices for the other and the utmost desire will be to forfeit life and all that pertains to it in behalf of another's good. This is the unity which existed among the disciples of His Holiness Jesus Christ and bound together the prophets and holy souls of the past. It is the unity which through the influence of the divine spirit is permeating the Bahá'ís so that each offers his life for the other and strives with all sincerity to attain his good-pleasure. This is the unity which caused twenty thousand people in Persia to give their lives in love and devotion to it. It made the Báb the target of a thousand arrows and caused Bahá'u'lláh to suffer exile and imprisonment forty years. This unity is the very spirit of the body of the world. It is impossible for the body of the world to become quickened with life without its vivification. His Holiness Jesus Christ -- may my life be a sacrifice to him! -- promulgated this unity among mankind. Every soul who believed in Jesus Christ became revivified and resuscitated through this spirit, attained to the zenith of eternal glory, realized the life everlasting, experienced the second birth and rose to the acme of good fortune." [60]

'Abdu'l-Bahá tells us that there are three conditions that must be met before we can attain that exalted state of *"incarnate light and personified spirit"*, [61] of becoming an *"Apostle of Bahá'u'lláh"*.[62] One of these is fellowship and love among the believers of God:

"The second condition: Fellowship and love amongst the believers. The divine friends must be attracted to and enamored of each other and ever be ready and willing to sacrifice their own lives for each other. Should one soul from amongst the believers meet another, it must be as though a thirsty one with parched lips has reached to the fountain of the water of life, or a lover has met his true beloved. For one of the greatest divine wisdoms regarding the appearance of the holy Manifestations is this:

The souls may come to know each other and become intimate with each other; the power of the love of God may make all of them the waves of one sea, the flowers of one rose garden, and the stars of one heaven. This is the wisdom for the appearance of the holy Manifestations! When the most great bestowal reveals itself in the hearts of the believers, the world of nature will be transformed, the darkness of the contingent being will vanish, and heavenly illumination will be obtained. Then the whole world will become the Paradise of Abhá, every one of the believers of God will become a blessed tree, producing wonderful fruits.

O ye friends! Fellowship, fellowship! Love, love! Unity, unity! -- so that the power of the Bahá'í Cause may appear and become manifest in the world of existence. My thoughts are turned towards you, and my heart leaps within me at your mention. Could ye know how my soul glows with your love, so great a happiness would flood your hearts as to cause you to become enamored with each other." [63]

'Abdu'l-Bahá refers to the importance of unity among the believers many times. He states that if we become true believers, we will demonstrate a tenderness that is otherworldly:

"In the same way, when any souls grow to be true believers, they will attain a spiritual relationship with one another, and show forth a tenderness which is not of this world. They will, all of them, become elated from a draught of divine love, and that union of theirs, that connection, will also abide forever. Souls, that is, who will consign their own selves to oblivion, strip from themselves the defects of humankind, and unchain themselves from human bondage, will beyond any doubt be illumined with the heavenly splendours of oneness, and will all attain unto real union in the world that dieth not." [64]

And with such unity we do everything to make the other believers happy:

"O ye beloved of God! As long as ye can strive to set aglow the hearts with love, be attracted to one another and be members of each other. Every soul of the beloved ones must adore the other and withhold not his possession and life from them, and by all means he must endeavor to make that other joyous and happy. But that other (the recipient of such love) must also be disinterested and life-sacrificing. Thus may this Sunrise flood the horizons, this melody gladden and make happy all the people, this divine remedy become the panacea for every disease, this Spirit of Reality become the cause of life for every soul." [65]

Through our unity we will attract others to the Cause:

"... for the foundation of Bahá'u'lláh is love ... you must have infinite love for each other, each preferring the other before himself. The people must be so attracted to you that they will exclaim, What happiness exists among you! and will see in your faces the lights of the Kingdom; then in wonderment they will turn to you and seek the cause of your happiness." 66

Shoghi Effendi wrote many letters to the believers to assist them to strive towards unity among themselves and with all mankind:

"He was very pleased to hear that the Convention was so well attended, and the believers enthusiastic and united. One of the most paramount needs of the Cause in ... is that the friends should unite, should become really keenly conscious of the fact that they are one spiritual family, held together by bonds more sacred and eternal than those physical ties which make people of the same family. If the friends will forget all personal differences and open their hearts to a great love for each other for the sake of Bahá'u'lláh, they will find that their powers are vastly increased; they will attract the heart of the public, and will witness a rapid growth of the Holy Faith." 67

Shoghi Effendi explains that this unity is more important than selflessness, detachment, the exercise of prudence and caution, carrying out God's will and constant awareness of Bahá'u'lláh's Presence and the example He gave us of how to live our lives. But please read it for yourselves:

"Unity amongst the friends, selflessness in our labors in His Path, detachment from all worldly things, the greatest prudence and caution in every step we take, earnest endeavor to carry out only what is His Holy Will and Pleasure, the constant awareness of His Presence and of the example of His Life, the absolute shunning of whomsoever we feel to be an enemy of the Cause ... these, and foremost among them is the need for unity, appear to me as our most vital duties, should we dedicate our lives for His service." 68

Bahíyyih Khánum, Bahá'u'lláh's daughter wrote:

"May the Light of Union radiate with greater clearness and brilliancy day by day among the people in your great country -- for to this country God has given much and much is expected from it. But without harmony and love existing among those who call themselves Bahá'ís, nothing will be seen from it whatsoever; for verily the Believers are the pivots upon which the fate of nations hang; and a difference among two believers is

quite sufficient to consume and destroy a whole country. The one who works for harmony and union among the hearts of the people in these days will receive the greatest blessings and the most abundant bounties. There is no greater work for one to do upon this earth than to try and unite the hearts of the people -- and especially those who are calling upon the Holy Name of God." [69]

Doris McKay, another Bahá'í, in her book, *Fires in Many Hearts*, referred to unity as *"a light-giving essence"*.[70] She stated that *"unity must change the believers before the believers could change the world."* Howard Colby Ives, a Bahá'í mentioned in the last chapter, wrote in a letter to Doris, *"Unity is the great key to spiritual progress. The unity of believers must be of such a character that never, NEVER must one single thought of anything but love and sympathy and kindness and severance enter into such a heart. 'Abdu'l-Bahá says that when we see even the slightest traces of love for Bahá'u'lláh in any soul, we must reverence that soul. How great then must the reverence we have for those souls who are fully confirmed in the Cause of God and have arisen for service. But our great task, as individual believers, is to see that, in the group in which God has called us to serve, never does the slightest breath of anything but love arise. And that constantly, at every moment of our spiritual journey, every selfish desire, every human attachment [must be banished and we must] find our greatest joy in becoming 'as dust beneath the feet of the friends'. This is the station of unity in this Day to which the believers of God are called . . ."* [71]

A prayer of 'Abdu'l-Bahá's demonstrates this love explicitly:

"O God, my God! Have mercy then upon my helpless state, my poverty, my misery, my abasement! Give me to drink from the generous cup of Thy grace and forgiveness, stir me with the sweet scents of Thy love, gladden my bosom with the light of Thy knowledge, purify my soul with the mysteries of Thy oneness, raise me to life with the gentle breeze that cometh from the gardens of Thy mercy -- till I sever myself from all else but Thee, and lay hold of the hem of Thy garment of grandeur, and consign to oblivion all that is not Thee, and be companioned by the sweet breathings that waft during these Thy days, and attain unto faithfulness at Thy Threshold of Holiness, and arise to serve Thy Cause, and to be humble before Thy loved ones, and, in the presence of Thy favoured ones, to be nothingness itself.

Verily art Thou the Helper, the Sustainer, the Exalted, the Most Generous." [72]

If we are unsuccessful in trying to reconcile our differences and become estranged from each other, we are doomed and must do all we can to overcome this problem, as Bahá'u'lláh reminds us:

"Nothing whatsoever can, in this Day, inflict a greater harm upon this Cause than dissension and strife, contention, estrangement and apathy, among the loved ones of God." [73] *". . . should the least trace of estrangement prevail the result shall be darkness upon darkness . . ."* [74]

Thoughts of enmity and intolerance can arise in us because we're caught in our lower natures. Our society is submerged in negativity, blame and proving that "I am right; you are wrong". Because we may have been taught this or at least are exposed to it daily and we may blindly imitate what we see around us, it is easy for individuals to become alienated and estranged. Bahá'ís know that it is important to strive for unity but without role models they may cling to such emotions as anger and bitterness and vent them freely to others. They need to immerse themselves in the Writings and pray for guidance to see things in a new way and from their higher nature. And they can find fellow-believers in the Bahá'í community and other spiritual communities to become their new role models for unity. Shoghi Effendi wrote many letters to believers about dealing with estrangement and lack of unity.

"They must endeavor to promote amity and concord amongst the friends, efface every lingering trace of distrust, coolness and estrangement from every heart, and secure in its stead an active and whole-hearted cooperation for the service of the Cause." [75]

"The thing the friends need -- everywhere -- is a greater love for each other, and this can be acquired by greater love for Bahá'u'lláh; for if we love Him deeply enough, we will never allow personal feelings and opinions to hold His Cause back; we will be willing to sacrifice ourselves to each other for the sake of the Faith, and be, as the Master said, one soul in many bodies." [76]

"A greater degree of love will produce a greater unity, because it enables people to bear with each other, to be patient and forgiving." [77]

If Bahá'ís sometimes feel discouraged about a lack of unity in their communities, The Guardian promises that they can still have an effect:

"One soul can be the cause of the spiritual illumination of a continent. Now that you have seen, and remedied, a great fault in your own life, now that you see more clearly what is lacking in your own community, there is nothing to prevent you from arising and showing such an example, such a love

and spirit of service, as to enkindle the hearts of your fellow Bahá'ís." [78] If Bahá'ís are to be living examples of the Bahá'í teachings, they must have unity and remove all traces of estrangement:

"Most important of all is that love and unity should prevail in the Bahá'í Community, as this is what people are most longing for in the present dark state of the world. Words without the living example will never be sufficient to breathe hope into the hearts of a disillusioned and often cynical generation." [79]

"All should be ready and willing to set aside every personal sense of grievance -- justified or unjustified -- for the good of the Cause, because the people will never embrace it until they see in its Community life mirrored what is so conspicuously lacking in the world: love and unity." [80]

". . . The people of the world are carefully watching the Bahá'ís today, and minutely observing them. The believers must make every effort, and take the utmost care to ward off and remove any feelings of estrangement . . ." [81]

The practice of Bahá'í consultation provides opportunities for unity and 'Abdu'l-Bahá outlines the method:

"The first condition is absolute love and harmony amongst the members of the assembly. They must be wholly free from estrangement and must manifest in themselves the Unity of God, for they are the waves of one sea, the drops of one river, the stars of one heaven, the rays of one sun, the trees of one orchard, the flowers of one garden." [82]

"The prime requisites for them that take counsel together are purity of motive, radiance of spirit, detachment from all else save God, attraction to His Divine Fragrances, humility and lowliness amongst His loved ones, patience and long-suffering in difficulties and servitude to His exalted Threshold." [83]

"The purpose is to emphasize the statement that consultation must have for its object the investigation of truth. He who expresses an opinion should not voice it as correct and right but set it forth as a contribution to the consensus of opinion, for the light of reality becomes apparent when two opinions coincide. A spark is produced when flint and steel come together. Man should weigh his opinions with the utmost serenity, calmness and composure. Before expressing his own views he should carefully consider the views already advanced by others. If he finds that a previously expressed opinion is more true and worthy, he should accept

it immediately and not willfully hold to an opinion of his own. By this excellent method he endeavors to arrive at unity and truth. Opposition and division are deplorable . . . Therefore, true consultation is spiritual conference in the attitude and atmosphere of love. Members must love each other in the spirit of fellowship in order that good results may be forthcoming. Love and fellowship are the foundation." [84]

We should expect to have difficulties and conflict in our relationships with others because we are all unique and have different views based on our personalities and our life experiences. But difficulties in a relationship are opportunities for us to practice our virtues – patience, tolerance, acceptance, empathy, understanding, sincerity, tenderness, wisdom and generosity. Our relationships help us to grow. We are forced to face our issues, family history, personality dynamics and methods of communicating. Through relationships we can become more fully alive as they bring forth the goodness and the strength already in us, enhanced by our relationship with God and our daily practices of prayer and meditation. We are given the opportunity to practice awareness, gentleness and courage with ourselves and the willingness to tolerate and accommodate different views. We need to forget every insult and remember every kindness. We will never be able to fully understand another human being, but we can learn to accept the person as he is.

Mirza Abu'l-Fadl, whom I have mentioned previously in this book because of his extreme humility, once gave a talk in which he analyzed the ideal of love for humanity. He said it was easy to sit in the comfort of our homes and say we love humanity. But he stated that love can only become real when tested. He stated that we need to have fought many battles and been wounded for love to be able to claim that we love with any authority or assurance.[85]

I believe as a fitting ending for this enterprise I would like to refer to the early teachers of the Faith who had learned to *"walk above the world by the power of the Greatest Name"*. [86]

"In His presence and through His Teachings, they had found a new range of spirit- an altitude of station beyond the human kingdom . . . a higher plane of existence." Doris McKay referred to it as *"the plus level"*. 'Abdu'l-Bahá called it *"the Spirit of Faith . . . The rising and falling between the higher and lower levels of Nearness is part of the process by which maturity is won. It was their firmness of intention that never wavered. Even while swept by emotional tests, they remained firm as a rock."* [87]

Related to our theme is this excerpt from a talk by Mr. Ali Nakhjavani, former member of the Universal House of Justice:

"I thought I could tell you about a tablet, a very short tablet, revealed by 'Abdu'l-Bahá. The contents of this Tablet are as follows: the Master says the relationships of the believers to the Cause of God are of two kinds. One kind is like the relationship of the flower to the garden. The other relationship is that of the ray of the sun to the sun. 'I hope,' the Master says, 'that your relationship will be of the second kind.' And that is the end of the Tablet.

Now, I have been thinking about this Tablet, and I have been wondering why 'Abdu'l-Bahá says that he prefers the second kind to the first kind. There is nothing wrong in being a flower in the garden of Bahá'u'lláh. In fact, we have prayers, 'O God, make me a flower in Thy garden'. Why is it that 'Abdu'l-Bahá prefers the other type, which is the ray of the sun? The sun is the Cause of God, and the ray emanates from it. So I am offering my views, my humble views, about this beautiful, simple Tablet of 'Abdu'l-Bahá. I thought like this, I said, OK, we have a flower in a garden, the flower says, 'I like this garden', in other words, we say, we like the Cause. 'I like this garden, I grow in this garden, I am proud of my garden, I am named after this garden'. (I am a Bahá'í) OK, this is all good. We take the ray of the sun. The ray says exactly all these things, he says, 'I am from the sun, I am proud of the sun, I depend everything, all my life on the sun,' etc, etc, exactly the same thing. But, if you bring one ray and you bring the second ray, what happens? The two rays become one. But if you bring one flower and you bring another flower, they remain two flowers.

If on an Assembly or a Bahá'í committee, you bring nine rays and bring them together, they become one strong united ray. But if you bring nine flowers and bring them together, they are a beautiful bouquet, a beautiful flower arrangement, but they are nine different flowers, and, if we credit the flower with some thinking, some intelligence and some ego, the flower will say, 'Really, I don't want to say, but I think I'm better than the others. I think I'm more beautiful, I think I have a more beautiful scent. I don't want to talk about it, but . . . never mind . . . ' This is what the flower will do. Why, because of the ego. The ego is inside. And believe me, this animal ego is in all of us. If we have 20 people in this room, there are 20 egos, no exception. And this ego will be with us till the very last breath. When we go to the next world, we separate, we say goodbye. But until that day, it is with us, it suggests things to us, it deviates us from the right path, because that is the animal in us, it wants everything for itself.

OK, let's go to the ray now. The ray says, 'I have no name, it doesn't matter. I don't have colour, it doesn't matter. I am from the sun. My job is to be faithful and to carry the light of the sun, the heat of the sun. That is my *duty. And I am doing it.' It is so pure that if you take a chair, and you go outside where there is the sun, you say, 'I am sitting in the sun.' Ha! You are not sitting in the sun. The sun is up there! But the ray is so faithful, so pure, that it carries all the qualities of the sun, in a pure way, so much so that you say I am sitting in the sun.*

Now, another difference is that the flower is on the receiving end. 'Soil, give me good soil, water, give me good water, light and sun, I want more light.' It's all the time receiving. 'Give me.' What does the ray do? It doesn't want anything, the ray gives, it helps the flowers to grow. Big difference between the two!

So, that is why I think 'Abdu'l-Bahá says, 'It's good to be a flower in the garden, but better still is to be the ray of the sun. This is my first choice for you, this is what I prefer you to be. To be a ray from the sun, so that you give to others, you are a way of helping others. You are not thinking of yourself. You are thinking of others, to assist others all the time, to give the light, to give the heat, the warmth.'" [88]

And now, parting words from 'Abdu'l-Bahá:

"If you are sincere in your love for me, then love and serve the believers of God; then love and serve your fellow-men.

These days, I do not feel very well. My remedy is to hear that the believers love each other. Any other news makes me sick and unhappy. Let everyone speak to me about love and I will love him more. The friends must be the real peacemakers; not stirrers up of strife nor sowers of seeds of discord, nor acting with superiority one over another.

I am now growing old. O, very old! All through my life I have carried on my back, gladly, the burdens of the believers; but now I ever anticipate hearing the good news of service actually accomplished by them. Save this, I have no other joy in the world.

Will they not make me happy?

Will they not answer my call, when the shadow of the last night of my earthly life is falling slowly across my path?

Will they not arise with superhuman energy and united effort to spread the Cause and impart to me new vigor?

Will they not listen to me?

How my heart leaps with joy when I hear the friends love each other, always overlooking one another's small mistakes; and that they are forgiving their enemies!" [89]

REFERENCES

1 'Abdu'l-Bahá, *Selections from the Writings of 'Abdu'l-Bahá*, 16, p. 34
2 'Abdu'l-Bahá, *The Promulgation of Universal Peace*, 15 June 1912, [4], p. 190
3 Shoghi Effendi, *The Compilation of Compilations* Vol. II, 1268, 30 October 1924, p. 2
4 'Abdu'l-Bahá, *Divine Philosophy*, p. 112
5 'Abdu'l-Bahá, *The Promulgation of Universal Peace*, 2 December 1912, [2-3], p. 453
6 Ibid., 17 August 1912, [8], p. 267
7 Ibid., 12 May 1912, [8], p. 120
8 Bahá'u'lláh, *The Hidden Words*, Arabic no. 68, p. 20
9 'Abdu'l-Bahá, *Bahá'í World Faith*, p. 445
10 'Abdu'l-Bahá, *Selections from the Writings of 'Abdu'l-Bahá*, 7, p. 20-21
11 'Abdu'l-Bahá, *The Promulgation of Universal Peace*, 27 August 1912, [7], p. 286-287
12 'Abdu'l-Bahá, *Selections from the Writings of 'Abdu'l-Bahá*, 8, p.24
13 'Abdu'l-Bahá, *Bahá'í World Faith*, p. 445
14 The Báb, *Selections from the Writings of The Báb*, p. 79
15 'Abdu'l-Bahá, *Some Answered Questions*, p. 269
16 'Abdu'l-Bahá, *Pilgrim Notes of Ali Kuli Khan*, p. 47-48
17 'Abdu'l-Bahá, *Some Answered Questions*, p. 270-271
18 The Universal House of Justice to an individual believer (1992, January 5), Gammage, Susan   http://susangammage.com
19 'Abdu'l-Bahá, *'Abdu'l-Bahá in London*, p. 91
20 Blomfield Lady, *The Chosen Highway* (Wilmette, IL: Bahá'í Publishing Trust, 1967), p. 171
21 Bahá'u'lláh, *Tablets of Bahá'u'lláh*, p. 173
22 'Abdu'l-Bahá, *The Promulgation of Universal Peace*, 5 May 1912, [4], p. 93
23 Shoghi Effendi, *The Compilation of Compilations* Vol. II, 1327, 4 October 1950, p. 22
24 Ibid.
25 'Abdu'l-Bahá, *Tablets of 'Abdu'l-Bahá 'Abbás* Vol. II, p. 436
26 'Abdu'l-Bahá, *Divine Philosophy*, p. 112
27 Gilstrap, Dorothy Freeman, *From Copper to Gold, The Life of Dorothy Baker*, p. 492
28 Bahá'u'lláh, *Bahá'í Scriptures*, 26, p. 38
29 Bahá'u'lláh, *Gleanings from the Writings of Bahá'u'lláh*, CXXXI, p. 287
30 Moorjani, Anita, *Dying to Be Me: My Journey from Cancer to Near Death, to True Healing* (Hay House, 2012)
31 Dhammandanda, K. Sri, How to Live Without Fear

and Worry (www.the bestfriend.org/wp- content/uploads/ThawkaDorThaAtTaBawaAhkhetAhkair.pdf)
32 Williamson, Marianne, *The Gift of Change*, p. 219
33 Ibid.
34 Ibid., p. 165
35 Ibid., p. 169
36 Ibid., p. 157
37 Ibid., p. 161
38 Ibid., p. 183
39 'Abdu'l-Bahá, *Paris Talks*, The Perfect Human Sentiments and Virtues, [6; 9], p. 113
40 Shoghi Effendi, *The Compilation of Compilations* Vol. II, 1267, 19 December 1923, p. 1-2
41 Bahá'u'lláh, *Gleanings from the Writings of Bahá'u'lláh*, CXXXIV, p. 290
42 Bahá'u'lláh, *The Hidden Words*, Arabic no. 1, p. 3
43 'Abdu'l-Bahá, *Selections from the Writings of 'Abdu'l-Bahá*, 129, p. 146
44 'Abdu'l-Bahá, *Tablets of 'Abdu'l-Bahá 'Abbás* Vol. III, p. 704
45 Bahá'u'lláh, *Tablets of Bahá'u'lláh*, p. 138
46 Shoghi Effendi, *The Advent of Divine Justice*, Spiritual Prerequisites, p. 25
47 Ibid.
48 'Abdu'l-Bahá, *Paris Talks*, Good Ideas must be Carried into Action, [1], p. 79
49 'Abdu'l-Bahá, *Bahá'í World Faith*, p. 384
50 Shoghi Effendi, *The Compilation of Compilations* Vol. II, 1273, 21 December 1927, p. 4
51 'Abdu'l-Bahá, *Some Answered Questions*, p. 215-216
52 Thompson, Juliet, *The Diary of Juliet Thompson* (Los Angeles: Kalimat Press, 1983, p. 332-333
53 Taherzadeh, Adib, *The Revelation of Bahá'u'lláh*, Vol. 4, p. 17
54 Bahá'u'lláh, *The Compilation of Compilations* Vol. II, 2046, p. 335-336
55 Ibid., 2024, p. 329-330
56 Bahá'u'lláh, *Tablets of Bahá'u'lláh*, p. 37
57 'Abdu'l-Bahá, *The Compilation of Compilations* Vol. II, 2058, p. 339-340
58 Ibid., 2059, p. 340
59 Ives, Howard Colby, *Portals to Freedom* (Oxford: George Ronald, 1983, p. 46
60 Ibid., p. 45
61 Dhammananda, K.Sri, How to Live Without Fear and Worry http://www.thebestfriend.org/wp-%20content/uploads/ThawkaDorThaAtTaBawaAhkhetAhkair.pdf
62 Bahá'u'lláh, *The Hidden Words*, Arabic no. 27, p. 10
63 'Abdu'l-Bahá, in *Lights of Guidance*, 305, p. 88
64 Ibid., 312, p. 91

65 Shoghi Effendi, Ibid., 305, p. 88
66 Bahá'u'lláh, *The Hidden Words*, Arabic no. 26, p. 10
67 Ibid., Persian no. 44, p. 37
68 Shoghi Effendi, *The Compilation of Compilations* Vol. II, 1272, 12 May 1925, p. 3-4
69 Bahá'u'lláh, *Gleanings from the Writings of Bahá'u'lláh*, CXLVI, p. 315
70 'Abdu'l-Bahá, *Selections from the Writings of 'Abdu'l-Bahá*, 193, p. 230-231
71 Ma'ani, Bahárieh Rouhani, *Leaves of the Twin Divine Trees* (Oxford: George Ronald, 2011), p. 331
72 'Abdu'l-Bahá, *'Abdu'l-Bahá in London*, p. 125
73 The Universal House of Justice, *Lights of Guidance*, 311, p. 90
74 Bahá'u'lláh, *The Hidden Words*, Persian no. 66, p. 45
75 'Abdu'l-Bahá, *The Promulgation of Universal Peace*, 25 July 1912, [4], p. 244
76 Esslemont, Dr. J.E., *Bahá'u'lláh and the New Era*, p. 83
77 Shoghi Effendi, *The Compilation of Compilations* Vol. II, 1311, 6 September 1946, p. 16
78 Shoghi Effendi, Ibid., 1320, 19 September 1948, p. 19
79 Bahá'u'lláh, *Bahá'í Scriptures*, 50, p. 132
80 Bahá'u'lláh, The *Kitab-i-Aqdas*, [153], p. 75
81 Ibid., [148], p. 72-73
82 Bahá'u'lláh, *Tablets of Bahá'u'lláh*, p. 88
83 Bahá'u'lláh, *Gleanings from the Writings of Bahá'u'lláh*, CXXVIII, p. 277
84 'Abdu'l-Bahá, *A Traveller's Narrative* (Wilmette, IL: Bahá'í Publishing Trust, 1980), p. 84
85 Bahá'u'lláh, *Gleanings from the Writings of Bahá'u'lláh*, C, p. 205
86 Ibid., CXXXVI, p. 296
87 Bahá'u'lláh, *The Hidden Words*, Arabic no. 29, p. 10
88 Bahá'u'lláh, *Gleanings from the Writings of Bahá'u'lláh*, LXVI, p. 128
89 Bahá'u'lláh, The *Kitab-i-Aqdas*, [53], p. 38
90 Dhammananda, K.Sri, *How to Live Without Fear and Worry*, p. 178
91 Bahá'u'lláh, The *Kitab-i-Aqdas*, p. 161
92 Ibid., [153], p. 75
93 Bahá'u'lláh, *The Seven Valleys and the Four Valleys*, p. 13
94 'Abdu'l-Bahá, *Bahá'í World Faith*, p. 320
95 Bahá'u'lláh, *The Compilation of Compilations* Vol. I, 1020, p. 460
96 'Abdu'l-Bahá, *Bahá'í World Faith*, p. 363
97 Dhammananda, K.Sri, *How to Live Without Fear and Worry*, p. 153-154
98 Ibid., p. 187
99 Bahá'u'lláh, *The Hidden Words*, Persian no. 6, p. 24
100 Bahá'u'lláh, *Gleanings from the Writings of Bahá'u'lláh*, CLIII, p. 327
101 'Abdu'l-Bahá, *Paris Talks*, Good Ideas must be Carried into Action, [1], p. 79
102 'Abdu'l-Bahá, *Star of the West*, Vol. 6, no. 6, p. 44

103 Motlagh, Hushidar, *Teaching, The Crown of Immortal Glory* (Mt. Pleasant, Michigan: Global Perspective, 1993, p. 370
104 Ibid., p. 370-371
105 'Abdu'l-Bahá, *Selections from the Writings of 'Abdu'l-Bahá*, 17, p. 35-36
106 'Abdu'l-Bahá, *The Promulgation of Universal Peace*, 21 April 1912, [1], p. 37
107 Furutan, Ali-Akbar, *Stories of Bahá'u'lláh* (Oxford: George Ronald, 1986, p. 51
108 Bahá'u'lláh, *Epistle to the Son of the Wolf*, p. 93
109 http://www.educationworld.com/a_lesson/TM/WS_back_to_school_quotes.shtml
110 Bahá'u'lláh, *The Hidden Words*, Arabic no. 30, p. 11
111 Bahá'u'lláh, *Gleanings from the Writings of Bahá'u'lláh*, V, p. 9
112 Bahá'u'lláh, *Tablets of Bahá'u'lláh*, p. 71
113 Shoghi Effendi, *Lights of Guidance*, 391, p. 114-115
114 'Abdu'l-Bahá, *Selections from the Writings of 'Abdu'l-Bahá*, 5, p. 17-18
115 Bahá'u'lláh, *Gleanings from the Writings of Bahá'u'lláh*, LXXXV, p. 168
116 Bahá'u'lláh, *Tablets of Bahá'u'lláh*, p. 143
117 Bahá'u'lláh, *Gleanings from the Writings of Bahá'u'lláh*, LXXXIX, p. 176
118 Bahá'u'lláh, *Tablets of Bahá'u'lláh*, p. 172-173 119 Bahá'u'lláh, *The Hidden Words*, Persian no. 36, p. 34-35
120 Bahá'u'lláh, *Gleanings from the Writings of Bahá'u'lláh*, CXXV, p. 264-265
121 'Abdu'l-Bahá, *Selections from the Writings of 'Abdu'l-Bahá*, 214, p. 268-269
122 Motlagh, Hushidar, *Teaching, The Crown of Immortal Glory*, p. 124
123 Ibid,, p. 124-125
124 Ives, Howard Colby, *Portals to Freedom*, p. 194-196
125 The Universal House of Justice, *Lights of Guidance*, 590, p. 179-180
126 Bahá'u'lláh, *Tablets of Bahá'u'lláh*, p. 168
127 'Abdu'l-Bahá, *The Compilation of Compilations* Vol. I, 179, 96-97
128 St. Rain, Justice, *Falling into Grace*, p. 63
129 Ibid.
130 Ibid., p. 64
131 Ives, Howard Colby, *Portals to Freedom*, p. 47-49
132 Shoghi Effendi, *The Compilation of Compilations* Vol. II, 1308, 18 December 1945, p. 15
133 Shoghi Effendi, *The Unfolding Destiny of the British Bahá'í Community*, 15 August 1957, p. 462
134 Shoghi Effendi, *Lights of Guidance*, 2047, p. 603
135 Ibid., 397, p. 116
136 Bahá'u'lláh, *The Hidden Words*, Persian no. 76, p. 48-49
137 Bahá'u'lláh, *Gleanings from the Writings of Bahá'u'lláh*, CXXXIX, p. 305
138 Bahá'u'lláh, *Tablets of Bahá'u'lláh*, p. 156

139 Bahá'u'lláh, *The Hidden Words*, Persian no. 5, p. 24
140 'Abdu'l-Bahá, *Selections from the Writings of 'Abdu'l-Bahá*, 34, p. 69
141 'Abdu'l-Bahá, *Paris Talks*, The Duty of Kindness and Sympathy towards Strangers and Foreigners, [9-15], p. 16-17
142 Ibid., Good Ideas must be Carried into Action, [7-9], p. 81
143 'Abdu'l-Bahá, *Selections from the Writings of 'Abdu'l-Bahá*, 1, p. 3
144 Bahá'u'lláh, *The Hidden Words*, Persian no. 49, 39
145 Honnold, Annamarie, *Vignettes from the Life of 'Abdu'l-Bahá*, 32, p. 58
146 Ibid., 46, p. 70
147 'Abdu'l-Bahá, *Selections from the Writings of 'Abdu'l-Bahá*, 7, p. 22
148 Bahá'u'lláh, *The Hidden Words*, Arabic no. 59, 17
149 Ibid., Persian no. 27, p. 31
150 Ma'ani, Bahárieh Rouhani, *Leaves of the Twin Divine Trees*, p. 222-223
151 Gail, Marzieh, *Dawn over Mount Hira* (Oxford: George Ronald, 1976), p. 101
152 Thompson, Juliet, *The Diary of Juliet Thompson*, p. 40-41
153 Gail, Marzieh, *Arches of the Years* (Oxford: George Ronald, 1991), p. 316
154 'Abdu'l-Bahá, *Tablets of 'Abdu'l-Bahá 'Abbás* Vol. I, p. 50
155 'Abdu'l-Bahá, *Tablets of 'Abdu'l-Bahá 'Abbás* Vol. III, p. 619-620
156 'Abdu'l-Bahá, *Selections from the Writings of 'Abdu'l-Bahá*, 236, p. 318-319
157 Hanson, Rick, *Buddha's Brain*, p. 158
158 Ibid., p. 160
159 Williamson, Marianne, *The Gift of Change*, p. 213
160 Hanson, Rick, *Buddha's Brain*, p. 145
161 Dyer, Dr. Wayne W. *Your Sacred Self*, p. 25
162 Ibid., p. 270-271
163 Ibid., p. 312
164 Dyer, Dr. Wayne W. in Motlagh, Hushidar, *Teaching, The Crown of Immortal Glory*, p. 140

www.ingramcontent.com/pod-product-compliance
Lightning Source LLC
Chambersburg PA
CBHW070047100426
42734CB00040B/2558